TRADING MENTORS

TRADING MENTORS
LEARN TIMELESS STRATEGIES AND BEST PRACTICES FROM SUCCESSFUL TRADERS

BY PHILIP TEO

Copyright © 2019 by Traderwave Pte Ltd.
Print Edition

All Right Reserved. No part of this publication may be reproduced, distributed, or transmitted in any form or by any means, including photo-copying, recording, or other electronic or mechanical methods, or by any information storage and retrieval system without the prior written permission of the publisher, except in the case of very brief quotations embodied in critical reviews and certain other non-commercial uses permitted by copyright law.

For permission requests, write to the publisher, addressed "Attention: Permissions Coordinator," at the address below.

Traderwave Pte Ltd
www.traderwave.com

The author and publisher of this publication and the accompanying materials have used their best efforts in preparing for this publication. The author and publisher make no representation or warranties with respect to the accuracy, applicability or completeness of the contents of this publication. The information contained within this publication is strictly for educational purposes. Therefore, if you wish to apply ideas contained in this publication, you are taking full responsibility for your actions.

Thank you for supporting our work.

PRAISES FOR THE BOOK

PETER L. BRANDT, CEO of Factor Trading, Author of *Diary of a Professional Commodity Trader*

"In *Trading Mentors*, Philip Teo, a long-time associate, interviews a number of highly successful traders—not searching for the magic bullet, but for insight, wisdom and practical guidance. The result is a book that challenges novice traders to seek out the really important components of a trading program—developing a thoughtful process, understanding risk, and recognizing the emotional hurdles that can negatively impact performance."

RAY BARROS, Founder of BarroMetrics Trading School, Ex-Hedge Fund Manager, Author of *The Nature of Trends* and *The Ray Wave*

"*Trading Mentors* is full of practical advice. For me, trading success is a product of three key elements: a method that has a positive expectancy, an optimal risk management process, and a winning mental mind-set. The book covers methods that range from the discretionary, to the systematic, to the algorithmic trading approach. There was also a wealth of information on how to manage your trading risks and acquire a winning mind-set. In summary, this is the book that deserves a place on your bookshelf. Thanks, Philip, for making it available."

EDWARD K. LEE, Founder and Chairman of COL Financial Group

"Trading the stock market is a difficult challenge and a career that offers no guarantees. But when we deepen our understanding of how the market works and take our experiences as lessons to learn from, this industry can reap great rewards. *Trading Mentors* is a book that can significantly increase your odds of success in the market by viewing it from different perspectives and using it as a guide to developing your own approach. It's an in-depth collection of interviews that fully summarizes common mistakes others successful traders have made so that you can avoid them and the process behind their most successful executions. As Philip mentions, preparation is necessary before entering into any trade and this is as valuable a source as any to navigate you through your journey."

NITHIN KAMATH, Founder and CEO of Zerodha, Trader, Venture Capitalist

"*Trading Mentors* by Philip is now one of the books I would recommend to anyone who wants to learn to trade. The best way to learn is from someone who's done it, so read this book and learn from the mentors who have spent years perfecting their trade. The light-hearted conversational style of the book will keep the pages turning. A delightful read!"

JAMES CHEN, CMT, CFTe, Director of Trading & Investing at Investopedia, Former Head of Research at Forex.com (GAIN Capital)

"I found *Trading Mentors* to be an excellent read and exceptionally helpful for the novice or struggling traders. The author, Philip Teo, is a top-notch trader and market analyst in his own right. But he goes a few steps further with this book by featuring trading strategies and words of wisdom from several seasoned trading instructors. The advice and strategies given are sound. But best of all, the book provides specific and actionable ideas that may be put to use immediately by beginning traders. In addition, *Trading Mentors* appropriately stresses risk management, which is the most important aspect of prudent and successful trading. Overall, I highly recommend this book."

ATUL SURI, Founder and CEO of Marathon Trends Advisory

"I have benefited greatly from reading books on successful investors and traders, especially the *Market Wizards* series by Jack Schwager that created a monumental shift in my life.

Trading Mentors by Philip Teo was another engrossing read in a similar genre, which captured the journey of a number of successful traders. What was special about this book is that Philip has profiled numerous Asian traders. This is a welcome trend as Asian economies, markets and traders are expected to take center stage within the global financial markets in the years ahead."

J KISHORE KUMAR, Founder and CEO of Tradejini

"I am delighted to share my review of *Trading Mentors*, written by my friend Philip. This book is a solid attempt to help retail traders learn from the journey of other fellow independent traders who successfully made a fortune for themselves. Readers are offered practical scenarios that they will most likely face in the pursuit of their financial freedom through trading. Life is too short to learn from our own mistakes, so why not learn from these trading mentors who have booked their fair share of failures and successes in the past."

MARIO SINGH, Founder and CEO of Fullerton Markets, Author of *Secret Conversations with Trading Tycoons*

"Mentorship is the secret sauce to rapid success! Well done to Philip for assembling a stellar line-up of mentors to share their secrets. *Trading Mentors* will add massive value to the entire global trading community!"

EZONE CONSTANTINE, MSTA, CFTe, Founder of Borneo Stock Trader, Certified Trainer at F1 Academy

"Brilliant! I got to be honest with you, the moment I had the opportunity to read *Trading Mentors*, I got addicted to reading the next page. I had so many "AHA" moments. You can find good principles, trading ideas, money management, and trading wisdom all in one book. Philip interviewed a wide range of traders with excellent track records of profitability and honest trading strategies. Some of the ideas here are worth a fortune if you implement the strategies and take the necessary actions. Whether you are a newbie, advanced or pro trader, this book is a must-read."

NICHOLAS TAN, CMT, CFTe, Ex-Forex Trader for Numerous Global Banks, Author of *Handbook on Forex Trading*

"*Trading Mentors* is a book written by Phillip Teo, based on interviews with well-known trading mentors from around the globe, where these mentors shared their valuable, successful and proven trading strategies. Whether you are looking for a systematic or a discretionary approach to trading, you will be able to get insights from these mentors' experiences. The book may contain a few hundred pages, but the interview format makes it a light and interesting read."

TABLE OF CONTENTS

INTRODUCTION xv
 The Problems That Most Part-Time Independent Traders Face xv
 The Potential Solutions to Your Trading Issues xvi
 Why I Wrote This Book xviii
 Why You Should Read This Book xx
 How You Should Read This Book xxii

PART 1 (DISCRETIONARY TRADERS)

ADAM KHOO: The Award-Winning Trading Mentor from Singapore with More Than 8.7 Million Views On YouTube 3
 Formulating A Trading System with A Statistical Edge 6
 The Stock "Bounce" Trend-Following System 7
 The Forex "Trend Continuation Entry" Day Trading System 10
 The Stocks "Gap Up News Scalp" Scalping System 12
 Knowing How Much to Risk in Each of Your Trades 16
 Managing Your Psychology and Emotion to Become a Successful Trader 20

NISHANT ARORA: The Highly Respected Trading Mentor Who Started India's Most Engaged Facebook Trading Group 23
 The Difference Between Technical Trading and Value Investing 27
 The Right Way to Manage Your Trading Risks 34
 How to Become Your Own Trading Guru 36
 Why Beginners Should Stay Away from Day Trading 40
 What You Need to Do to Become a Good Trader 45
 The Main Reasons Why Most Traders Fail 50

EDMUND LEE: The Leading Trading Mentor of Philippines' Premier Financial Education Institute 55
 Using The FTSR Framework to Find That One Good Trade 58
 The Five Stock-Screening Criteria to Identify Potential Trading Ideas 64
 The Top Three Trading Mistakes Made by Traders 66
 Managing Your Losses Using The Value-At-Risk Methodology 68
 How to Use Profit Target and Trailing Stop to Exit Profitable Trades 70
 How to Prepare for The Inevitable Bearish Market Downturn 71

BRAMESH BHANDARI: The Prolific Trading Mentor Who Runs India's Top Trading Blog 75
  Building The Mental Strength to Take in Whatever the Market Throws at You . 78
  Seven Typical Psychological Issues That Traders Face 81
  Using a Systematic Process to Set Your Trading Goals 84
  How to Develop a Conscious Mind to Drive Your Trading Actions 85
  The Difference Between Discretionary Trading and Systematic Trading 88
  The Impact of Trading Psychology On Intraday Traders and Swing Traders 90

PART 2 (SYSTEMATIC TRADERS)

LOUISE BEDFORD: The Most Compelling Trading Mentor from Australia with a Passion for Candlestick Charting 97
  Why You Need to Understand the Nature of Volatile Markets 101
  How to Know When to Seek Risk and When to Avoid Risk 103
  The Main Concepts Behind Candlestick Chart Trading 108
  The Discovery of 3 New Candlestick Patterns 115
  Finding Your Personal Bliss Zone Through Passion, Skill, and Money 118
  Knowing When to Cut Your Losses and Take Your Profits 121

RAYNER TEO: The Generous Trading Mentor Who Created Singapore's Top Free Forex Trading Blog 129
  Transitioning from Day Trading into Swing and Position Trading 132
  The Most Suitable Trading Strategy for Retail Traders 134
  How to Implement a Systematic Trend-Following Trading Strategy 138
  Incorporating A Shorter Term Swing Trading Strategy 143
  The Proper Way to Building a Trading Workflow 145
  The Two Most Common Issues That Retail Traders Have to Deal With 149

ADAM GRIMES: The Practical Trading Mentor from the United States Who Is Out to Fight Trading Scams 155
  The Motivation Behind Providing Free Trading Education 160
  What A Trading Edge Is and Its Importance 161
  How to Build Trading Consistency 166
  The Role of Trading Psychology in The Evolution of a Trader 169
  How A Beginner Can Find His Trading Edge 171
  The Synergies Between Visual Discretionary Trading and Algorithmic System Trading 173

JET MOJICA: The Systematic Trading Mentor from The Philippines Who Embraces Quantitative and Visual Analysis 179
  How to Identify Market Leaders and Laggards 182
  Ranking Securities by Price Momentum 183
  Ranking Trades by Year-To-Date Returns 184
  Ranking Trades by Multiple Duration Returns 189
  Simplifying Momentum Trade Selection Using Data Visualization 190
  Simplifying The Asset Allocation Strategy and Balancing the Portfolio 200

Table of Contents

PART 3 (ALGORITHMIC TRADERS)

ANDREA UNGER: The Renowned Trading Mentor from Italy Who Won the World Cup Trading Championship Three Times in A Row 207
  Building a Trading System with The A.T.T.E.M.P.T Process..........................213
  Analyzing The Characteristics and Behavior of your Target Market...............215
  Verifying Your Trading Edge by Testing and Tuning Your Trading Strategy ...220
  The Importance of Evaluating Your Trading System and Firming Up Your Money Management Rules...223
  Build Your Portfolio of Strategies and Establish Your Trade Execution Rules.225
  Knowing When to Overhaul Your Trading Strategy.......................................229

GARY YANG: The Humble Trading Mentor from Singapore Who Trades for A Living as A Home-Based Independent Trader 235
  Why Beginner's Luck Is Detrimental to A New Trader's Journey....................238
  Find A Risk-Averse Person to Be Your Accountability Partner.......................242
  Build Confidence in Your Trading Strategy Through BackTesting..................243
  Three Things to Think About Before You Dive into Full-time Trading.............247
  Managing Your Trading Workflow and Risks Using Algorithmic Trading.........252
  How You Can Use Algorithmic Trading to Manage a Portfolio of Trading Strategies 255

CLOSING THOUGHTS 267

WE NEED YOUR HELP! 272

DON'T FORGET YOUR FREE BOOK BONUSES 273

ABOUT THE AUTHOR..274

GET IN TOUCH WITH THE MENTORS 275

BOOK BONUSES (FOR FREE!)

Claim Your FREE Book Bonuses Here!
www.tradingmentorsbook.com/bonus

INTRODUCTION

The Problems That Most Part-Time Independent Traders Face

"Hey Philip, thanks for your clear explanation of those basic trading principles, strategies and best practices," said Sam as he shook my hand right after the free three-hour introductory trading seminar that I just delivered to a big group of part-time retail traders in the SGX Auditorium.

"It's my pleasure, Sam. Hope I didn't overwhelm you with too much trading knowledge in just a short three hours," I replied. "I see too many new traders out there throwing thousands of dollars away learning all the wrong things about trading from the wrong people and then losing even more money in the market by applying all the wrong trading methods and strategies. So I wanted to impart as much foundational trading knowledge to you as I could in the shortest time possible so that you can avoid making these costly mistakes after you step out of this auditorium."

"I can relate to what you mentioned totally because I've already made all those mistakes," Sam replied with a rather sad tone. "I've wasted thousands of dollars learning from the so-called trading 'gurus' because I was attracted by their marketing gimmicks. I jumped from strategies to strategies because I was hoping to find that 'holy grail' trading strategy. I had wanted to try out swing trading but dived into day trading instead because someone told me day trading is more profitable. Now that I've attended your seminar, I truly want to find a good trading mentor, but I'm not sure who I can trust. I don't want to give up yet, but I'm at a loss what I should do next. Do you have any advice for me, Philip?"

Sam Lee has been working for the past 15 years as a senior computer engineer. Increasingly, he was getting frustrated with his job that requires him to work long hours doing mundane and repetitive work, but he couldn't bear to quit because of his good paycheck.

Through the years, he has accumulated a substantial amount of savings and is very concerned about inflation steadily eroding the value of his cash that was generating near zero interests in the bank.

By chance, a friend introduced Sam to the world of stock trading. Sam figured that if he's mildly successful, he'll be able to generate enough returns to beat the inflation effects on his savings. If he's lucky enough to become highly profitable, he might even be able to quit his job and just live off his trading profits.

Sadly, like most part-time retail traders out there, things didn't turn out to be as rosy as what Sam envisioned. Despite trading for more than a year, he was still losing money consistently and getting very discouraged with how things were heading.

Still, Sam was not about to throw in the towel yet, and that's how he ended up at my seminar.

The Potential Solutions to Your Trading Issues

"Before you make the jump and attempt to learn any specific trading strategy from any trading mentor, you need to widen

Introduction

your perspectives and understand trading first." I proceeded to answer Sam's question.

"There are many kinds of profitable trading methodologies out there, but not every methodology is a right fit for you. If a trading strategy is not a good fit with your belief system, you'll never be able to implement that strategy with confidence."

I went on. "I suggest that you explore as many different trading methodologies as you can get your hands on from the many successful traders out there before you drill down to the one trading methodology that is the best fit for your personality and lifestyle. After you have gone through this process, you will be equipped with the right foundational knowledge to search for that ideal trading mentor who can help shorten your path toward becoming a profitable trader."

That was all that I needed to say because I saw a glimmer of hope in Sam's eyes. Maybe my reply to him had provided that subtle enlightenment on what he needed to do next.

The frustrations faced by Sam prompted me to reflect on my trading journey over the years. I could still vividly remember how I was lucky enough to land a job many years back as a technical analyst of a sell-side investment research firm despite me knowing nothing about technical analysis or trading at all.

The HR manager told me that I was given the job because I displayed strong market analysis skills and excellent presentation skills (and probably also because my salary was low enough for the budget that the company had allocated for this role).

Nevertheless, I embraced the opportunity and embarked on my trading journey while earning a decent living at the same time. I was given a few months' grace by my boss to teach myself or "self-learn" everything that I need to know about technical analysis and stock trading before I start publishing my stock trading ideas to our clients.

Every day, I was looking at hundreds of technical charts and honing my ability to discover chart patterns and trading opportunities. Being an avid reader, I also read more than 50 books in those few months on all kinds of trading subjects like technical analysis, trading psychology, trading strategies, risk management, portfolio management, etc.

I believe that my consumption of such a wide range of trading books from many different trading experts was the main reason why I was able to avoid many of those mistakes made by the typical aspiring traders out there.

Since then, I went on to become the Chief Technical Analyst in that same investment research firm for the next eight years. Through those years, I've conducted many free educational trading seminars to thousands of retail traders in Singapore.

Even after leaving the research firm to launch Traderwave, my own trading software company, I've continued to partner with SGX Academy to provide free trading education seminars to the mass public.

Why I Wrote This Book

If you've picked up *Trading Mentors*, it's likely because you're still struggling in your journey as an independent part-time retail trader—just like Sam. You're eager to learn the proper approach toward trading but unsure who you can trust as you learn to trade.

One of the defining moments during my earlier days of self-learning was when I came across the *Market Wizards* series of books by Jack Schwager. His books were written from the transcripts of interviews done with many of the proven and successful proprietary traders and hedge fund managers.

From that series of books, I learned about the mistakes that these expert traders made before they became successful. I learned about all the trading principles they believed in that helped them become such prolific market experts.

Most importantly, I was able to look at trading from the perspectives of many different experts. That allowed me ample opportunities to ponder on what kind of trading style, strategy, and timeframe was the ideal fit for me.

Unlike my experiences as a professional in this industry, very few part-time and non-professional traders out there can relate to those "Market Wizards" who were managing millions or billions of dollars of their clients' money, with substantial financial and technological resources at their disposal, and possibly trading hundreds of instruments at the same time.

The motivation, circumstances, and constraints that you face as an independent trader are different from what those trading titans had to deal with.

Trading Mentors was written to fill this gap. I decided to publish this book because I want to curate the stories from the best trading mentors that I know out there.

The ten people that I've selected to be profiled in this book clearly articulate their personal, timeless strategies and best practices that helped them become successful independent traders, and I believe that you'll be able to get valuable insights from their sharing.

Why You Should Read This Book

With the vast and varied experience from these ten trading mentors, this book is a wealth of resources for any independent trader out there, regardless of whether you're new, struggling, or already proficient and profitable.

The financial market is dynamic and the world is constantly changing. The only way to maintain your competitive edge as a trader is to keep learning from other fellow traders or trading mentors who are at the forefront of the trading evolution.

This trading book is one of the few out there that offers you vast perspectives and insights into the world of trading, as told by these successful traders and trading mentors.

To put it simply, you have no more excuse to say that you didn't know any better after you finish reading this book. For the small price that you are paying to own, read, and re-read this book that contains more than a century worth of combined trading wisdom, I say you have nothing to lose in this trade.

That's a fantastic trade to take, don't you think so?

The publication of *Trading Mentors* was laid upon the foundation of the Online Trading Summit, which I organized and hosted in September 2018. The summit was possibly Asia's first virtual trading conference where more than 30 world-class trading experts from around the world accepted my invitation to present and be interviewed by me in the summit.

The summit turned out to be a huge success, as more than 25,000 participants signed up and participated in the event.

Following the summit, I contemplated how I could continue to use the best contents contributed by the speakers to reach out to more independent traders around the world. Selecting the top 10 speakers to be profiled in *Trading Mentors* seemed like the ideal way to go.

Over the years I've come to realize that a highly successful and profitable trader is not necessarily a great trading mentor, and the best mentor is not necessarily the most profitable trader. A good trading mentor might not even be a famous trading personality but just another regular retail trader who is consistently generating returns on his capital on his own terms.

More importantly, a trading mentor needs to be someone who has gone through the rites of passage and can articulate his mistakes, experiences, and knowledge in a simple-to-understand layman manner that can help enlighten anyone who is new to trading.

The best trading mentor is usually a humble and down-to-earth person. He (or she) does not proclaim to know everything about trading or expect you to blindly follow his strategy and instructions every step of the way.

Ultimately, a true trading mentor aims to equip you with the timeless trading strategies, principles, and best practices of trading so that you can think for yourself and find your own path in trading.

I might not be the most profitable trader around, and I'm definitely not an expert in every trading strategy and methodologies out there.

But over the years I've learned and experienced enough to know which trading gurus are pure marketing gimmicks and which trading mentors truly know their stuff—that's if I got the opportunity to ask them thought-provoking questions on trading.

All of the intriguing questions that I posted to the speakers during the Online Trading Summit were not provided to them in advance. As such, none of the speakers would have been able to prepare for any of my questions ahead of the interview. I believe that a competent trading mentor should be able to answer my questions and explain his thoughts coherently in an instant.

This was one of the main criteria I used to select the ten trading mentors out of the 32 speakers to be profiled in this book. The voting by the summit participants on the best speakers also had a part to play in deciding which speakers I chose to feature in this book.

How You Should Read This Book

The trading mentors that I've profiled in this book come from various backgrounds and have different trading styles in multiple timeframes. This book is divided into three parts based on the trading mentors' preferred trading style.

The first section focuses on trading mentors who are predominantly discretionary traders. This means that they tend to make trading decisions based on market conditions at any point in time, rather than follow a strict set of quantifiable rules. Trading mentors like Adam Khoo (Singapore), Nishant Arora (India), Edmund Lee (the Philippines), Bramesh Bhandari (India), are classified as traders under this particular trading style.

The second section focuses on trading mentors who are mainly systematic traders. Typically, these mentors adopt a very systematic approach toward their trade-selection process before executing those trades manually. This group includes trading mentors like Louise Bedford (Australia), Rayner Teo (Singapore), Adam Grimes (United States), and Jet Mojica (the Philippines).

Introduction

The final section consists of sharing by trading mentors who are algorithmic traders. This implies that their entire trading workflow is usually automated using rules and formulas, all the way from scanning for trade setups to trade executions. Trading mentors from this section include traders like Andrea Unger (Italy) and Gary Yang (Singapore).

Besides coming from different nations and focusing on different trading styles, most of these trading experts trade across different timeframes (e.g., day trading, swing trading, position trading, etc.) and different asset classes and instruments (e.g., stocks, Forex, futures indices, etc.) as well.

If you're a new trader still trying to build your foundational knowledge in trading, I suggest that you read the book slowly through to the end. Generally, a new trader needs to be familiar with discretionary trading concepts (Part 1 of this book) before progressing to systematic trading workflow (Part 2) and then moving on to algorithmic trading systems (Part 3).

This is not to say that algorithmic trading is the highest form of trading or that it's the best trading style to adopt. The reason why I recommend you read in the sequence described is that an excellent algorithmic trader usually needs to first have a strong foundational understanding of discretionary strategies and systematic trading workflow.

Ultimately, each of these trading styles has their pros and cons, and you will have to identify your personal inclination on which method to dive deep into in time to come.

If you're an experienced trader who's been trading for a while but is still struggling to become profitable, you might be facing similar issues as Sam. As such, I suggest that you empty your cup about what you think you know about trading and read this book from start to finish—just as a brand new trader would.

Having years of trading experiences means nothing if you started on the wrong foot and built up bad trading habits along the way. Sometimes the need to put aside your ego and return to the drawing board to relearn the right knowledge humbly might be a better option.

If you're already a consistently profitable trader, you obviously know what you're doing! This book might not be needed to help you dive deep into any specific trading methodology that you are already excelling in or are interested in pursuing.

That said, the useful ideas shared by the trading mentors in this book provide some insight into other trading styles, strategies, and workflow. In other words, you might be able to pick up some information from them that you deem useful for yourself and apply them.

In this case, feel free to jump around the book and read up on any of the trading mentors whose trading experiences are of interest to you.

That's it. I hope you enjoy the read and can apply the knowledge learned to turn yourself into a proficient and profitable trader.

PART 1
DISCRETIONARY TRADERS

ADAM KHOO: The Award-Winning Trading Mentor from Singapore with More Than 8.7 Million Views On YouTube

> *Do not expect to find a perfect trading system because every system has its pros and cons. More importantly, find and stick to a trading system that fits your personality and lifestyle.*

Adam is a professional stock and Forex trader, award-winning entrepreneur, best-selling author, and peak performance specialist.

As a fellow Singaporean, I learned of him a long time ago although we didn't have an opportunity to cross paths. Hosting the Online Trading Summit offered me an opportunity to get in touch with him, and I'm glad he agreed to come on board as one of our keynote speakers.

A self-made millionaire by the age of 26, Adam is the founder of the Piranha Profits online trading school. He is also the co-founder of one of Singapore's largest training and education companies, with business operations in Malaysia, Indonesia, Vietnam, and the Philippines.

As one of the most-watched trading mentors on YouTube, Adam's trading tutorial videos have clocked more than eight million views in just two years. In 2018, his channel ranked 12 on Feedspot's "Top 100 Trading YouTube Channels for Traders" and is one of the fastest-growing trading channels, with more than 200,000 subscribers as of this writing (late 2018).

Since 2002, Adam has touched the lives of more than 1.2 million people in more than 60 countries through his live programs, seminars, books, and online training. He has helped students, educators, professionals, investors, and business owners to achieve excellence by imparting his highly actionable success strategies.

Adam has written more than 16 best-selling books spanning the topics of academic mastery, personal development, parenting, finance, and entrepreneurship. These include *Winning the Game of Stocks, Secrets of Self-Made Millionaires*, and *Profit from the Panic*. His titles have sold more than 500,000 copies worldwide and have been translated into 12 languages.

Due to Adam's hectic traveling schedule, I was not able to conduct a one-on-one interview with him personally. However, he offered to record a video presentation especially for the participants of the Online Trading Summit, which I've transcribed and compiled into the following content for your reading pleasure.

In his presentation, Adam shared details about his three favorite trading systems: a stock swing-trading strategy, a Forex day-trading strategy, and a stock-scalping strategy. He also discussed extensively how a trader should size his trading positions and manage his trading psychology to become a winning trader.

Part 1 – Discretionary Traders / Adam Khoo

Adam: Hi everyone. It's an honor to be invited as the keynote speaker to this Online Trading Summit. I'm going to deliver what I think is a really important topic for you: "What it takes to be a winning trader".

Whether you're a beginner struggling to become profitable or an experienced trader wanting to up your game, I believe that my sharing will provide you the insights and the tools to help you reach your objectives a lot faster.

I've been trading for the last 26 years, since the age of 18. I've traded in the Singapore markets, the Hong Kong markets, the Malaysian markets, but my primary focus is on the US markets and Forex.

Generally, I trade throughout the entire day. I'm a swing trader where I open and hold trades over several days. I also do Forex day trading in which I get in and out of the market within 24 hours.

On top of that, I have a scalping strategy where I scout for news on specific stocks. Depending on the news, I typically get in and out of a scalping trade within a couple of minutes during the market opening. Finally, I have a long-term investment portfolio.

As you can see, I approach the markets in many different ways. Regardless if you're a short-term trader or long-term investor, I hope my experience will add tremendous value to you.

Besides my personal trading, I've also spent the past 12 years coaching people to become better investors and traders through the in-person Wealth Academy program that I conduct across Asia. My vision has always been to empower retail investors to profit alongside the professionals.

Piranha Profits is where I run an Online Training School where we reach out to students from all around the world who aspire to become semi-professional and professional traders.

Now that you know something about my background, I hope you'll be better able to relate to my trading experiences. Let's now talk about how you can become the winning trader that you deserve to be.

Formulating A Trading System with A Statistical Edge

What makes a winning trader? I believe that there are three qualities that you need to have.

First, you need to have a trading system with a positive expectancy, or what we call a statistical edge in the markets. What does that mean? If your system has a statistical edge, you will make money as you keep trading over time.

This doesn't mean that every trade will be a winning trade. Some trades will be winning trades, and some trades will be losing trades. And you will not know when you will get either one. In the short term, every trade outcome can be random.

But as long as you have a trading system that gives you an edge, you will win more than you lose over the long run. Your average winners will be bigger than your average losers, and that is what leads to consistent profits over time.

Let's now explore what a trading system is. A trading system is a specific set of entry rules and exit rules that you follow consistently without deviation, without emotions interfering and without intervention. And they must be based on a sound methodology that works in the markets, like fundamental or technical methodologies.

This might sound like common sense to you. But the reality is that most traders don't have a trading system. Even if they do, they usually don't follow it because they get distracted. They buy and sell based on their attempt to predict the future.

For example, they might think, "Oh, I think that the stock market is going to go up, so I'm going to buy now." Or they listen to opinions from "market experts" on CNBC or in the news.

That's not the right way to make trading decisions. These experts look at markets differently from you. They may use different strategies, and they may have different timeframes. Are you trading in the same timeframe as them? You need to stick to the approach that works for you and your timeframe.

So, what makes a good trading strategy? I'm going to share with you some of the swing-trading and day-trading strategies that I use. You will then have an idea of what constitutes a good trading system.

The Stock "Bounce" Trend-Following System

One of the systems I use to trade stocks is a trend-following, swing-trading system. It is based on daily candles, and I call this my Bounce strategy (see Figure 1.1).

Why does this system work? It is based on a sound methodology that prices tend to trend and that a stock on an uptrend is more likely to move up. A stock in a downtrend is more likely to move down. It is statistically proven, and that's why we base our system on this probability.

Figure 1.1 Stocks Trend-Following System (Bounce) Using Daily Candles

When a stock moves on a major uptrend, it doesn't go up in a straight line.

It moves in a series of impulsive and corrective wave patterns. Usually, after a bullish impulsive wave, we will see a bearish corrective wave due to profit taking by the traders. After that, another impulsive wave will form, followed by the appearance of a corrective wave and so on, until the major trend reverses.

With this trend-following swing-trading strategy, our objective is to enter right at the end of the corrective wave, which is also the start of a new bullish impulsive wave. If the trade works according to our view, the price will start to move higher, and we will then attempt to take profit towards the end of that impulsive move before the next corrective wave starts.

We call this a swing trade where we get in and get out in a matter of days. Now the question is, how would you know that the price is at the end of a corrective wave or the beginning of a new impulsive wave?

You can't predict or be sure about this, but based on probability we know that at the end of a corrective wave, we will usually see a bullish candlestick reversal pattern appearing around some kind of support.

I like to use the 50-day moving average as the support for this system. I will find an opportunity to enter when the price hits the 50-day moving average support and forms a bullish reversal candlestick pattern towards the end of the corrective wave.

To increase my probability of being right, I will also check the full stochastic oscillator indicator to see if the stock is oversold or overbought. When the stochastics oscillator shows an oversold signal, that is the best time to take the trade. Now that you understand the methodology, let's put our criteria into a trading system of rules.

Firstly, let's firm up the specific entry rules. Do bear in mind that I don't simply use this trading system on any kind of stocks. This strategy is used only on high-momentum stocks that are surging up on a high volume. They should display strong relative strength compared to the S&P 500 and have clear major uptrend patterns with the price making higher highs and higher lows.

I want to see the price retracing and testing the 50-day moving average support. Ideally, the price should have bounced off this same moving average at least once before to prove that this moving average is a reliable support.

Next, I want to see the stochastics oscillator having a value of less than 30. This tells me that this stock is oversold and is due for a bounce. With all of the above criterions satisfied, I can now place my buy order. Typically, I will place a buy order a few pips above the high of the first bullish candle that appears at the 50-day moving average support. These are my entry rules.

Let's now talk about my exit rules. I either exit at a loss or exit at a profit. I will pre-determine how much losses I'm willing to accept and how much profits I'm willing to take. I typically place my stop-loss level just below the lowest point of the retracement or what I call the swing low.

For example, I'm buying at $36.50, and my stop-loss is at $35.30. What is my initial risk per share? It's $1.20. I call this my 1R distance. If I'm risking $1.20 per share or 1R, I want to generate a profit of at least 2R to make it worth my while.

You must always have a risk to return ratio of at least 1 is to 1. You can use a 1 is to 2 ratio, 1 is to 3 ratio or whatever that works for you. Personally, I prefer to use a 1 is to 2 risk-return ratio for my system.

In this case, if I am risking $1.20, I want to make at least a $2.40 or 2R profit. This means that I have to set my profit target at $38.90. That is the level I will exit with a 2R profit if my trade works out. These are basically my exit rules.

As you can see, this is a very specific trading system, and I follow this system of entry-exit rules exactly as planned every single day. I don't have a winning trade all the time, but at the end of the month or the year, I'm always profitable.

The Forex "Trend Continuation Entry" Day Trading System

Now let me show you another trading system that I use to trade Forex intraday. I day trade this system using the 15-minute candles and my basic methodology is based on a trend-following system as well. And this strategy is called the trend continuation entry strategy or TC strategy in short (see Figure 1.2)

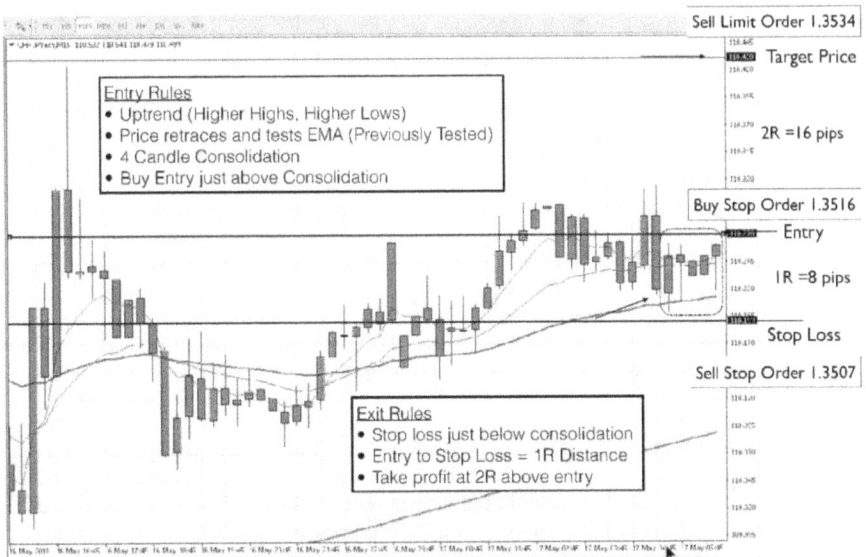

Figure 1.2 Forex Day Trading System (Trend Continuation Entry) Using 15-Minute Candles

So what are my entry rules for this strategy? First, I look for a currency pair on a very clear uptrend making higher highs and higher lows. I use a screener on all major currency pairs to find such trade setups every single day.

Next, I want to see the price retracing and testing the 50-period moving average that has been successfully tested previously. After the price touches the moving average, I look out for the candles to move sideways to form some kind of consolidation pattern. Typically, I look for at least a four candles consolidation.

Once I see a four candles consolidation pattern, I will place an order just above the consolidation pattern, so that when the price breaks out of the consolidation pattern, my buy order will be triggered. Meanwhile, I'll place my stop-loss level just below the consolidation pattern. And I will set my profit target at a level that offers me a one-to-two risk-to-return ratio, or a 2R return.

In this example, my buy order is at 110.27 while my stop-loss level is 8 pips away at 110.19. As I'm looking to make a profit of at least 16 pips (2R), I pegged my profit target level to 110.43.

Every single day I look for trades that have this pattern. I usually take up to three trades a day using this strategy. I keep following these rules consistently without fail. Again, not every trade is going to a winner, but at the end of every month I always end up positive for the strategy.

This is because I have a large sample of about 20 to 30 trades a month where the winners cover the losers and more to give me a profit. And this is how I trade currencies.

The Stocks "Gap Up News Scalp" Scalping System

Let me now share with you another strategy that I trade on the US stock market. This is my favorite strategy because it is one of the most profitable systems that I have. It's called the Gap Up News Scalp strategy or GUNS strategy in short.

This strategy is a scalping system, meaning I get in and out within a few minutes (see Figure 1.3). I trade this system using the 1-minute candlestick chart.

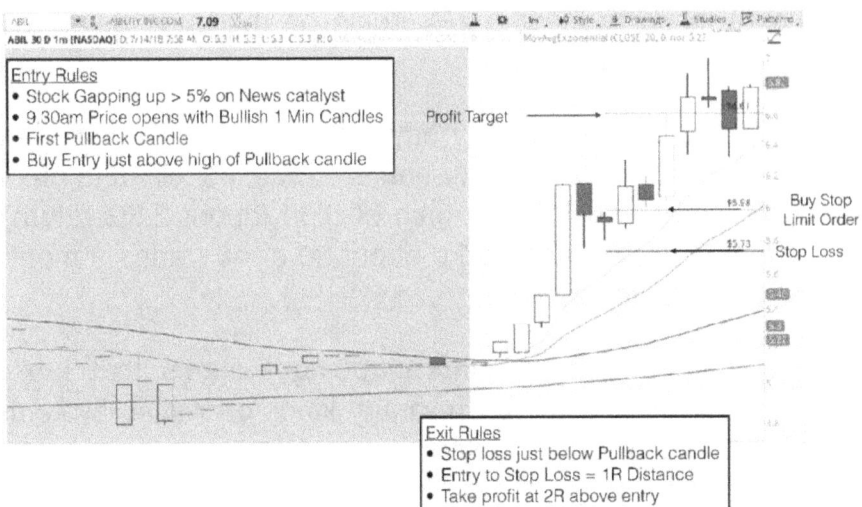

Figure 1.3 Stocks Scalping System (Gap Up News Scalp) Using 1-Minute Candles

About 30 minutes before the US market opens at 9:30 AM Eastern time (9:30 PM Singapore time), I will be building up my watch list of stocks that are gapping up on high volume.

Generally, I look for stocks that are gapping up more than 5% with news as the catalyst, which can be something like an earnings release or a patent approval, for example. Basically, I want to see any kind of news that can attract everyone to rush in to buy the stock.

Once the market opens at 9:30 PM SGT, I observe the price movements carefully. If the market opens and the stock turns bearish immediately, the trading idea will be invalidated. But if the market opens and a series of bullish one-minute candles start to emerge, I will prepare to get into the trade.

I will wait for the first bearish pullback candle to emerge before placing my buy order. I will put my buy stop order just above the high of this pullback candle. Meanwhile, my stop-loss order will be right below the low of this pullback candle. Again, I'm looking to make at least a 2R profits on my trade using this strategy.

In this particular example, my buy order was at 5.98 while my stop-loss is at 5.73. My risk per share is 0.25. I decided to place my profit target at 6.61 for a gain of 0.63 (about 2.5R return). This strategy allows me to take about 30 or 40 trades a month and be profitable every month.

I've just shared with you three trading systems that I use personally. In reality, there are many kinds of trading systems out there that can be profitable.

There are trading systems that can be used on different instruments like stocks, Forex, options, or futures. There are also systems that are based on different timeframes like scalping, day trading, swing trading, or position trading. In addition, there are trading systems that focus on trend-following or counter-trend methodologies (see Figure 1.4)

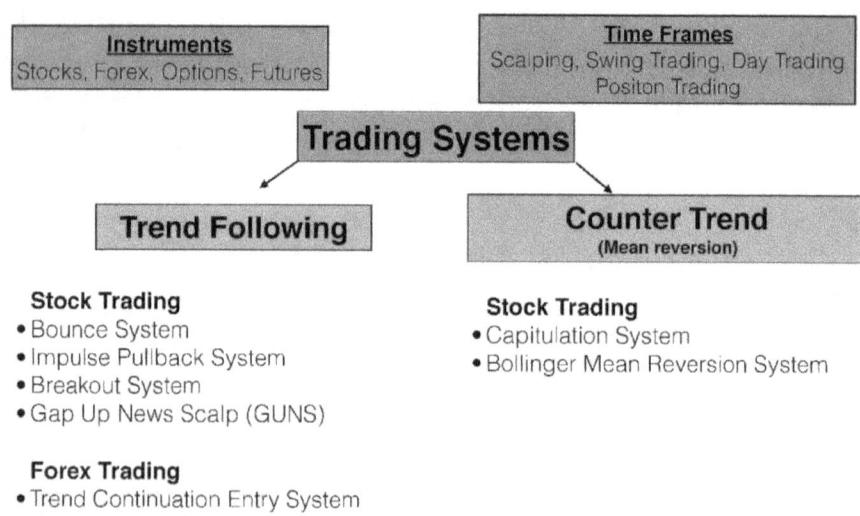

Figure 1.4 Different Types of Trading Systems

Ultimately, there is a trading system for everyone. Don't expect to find a perfect trading system because every system has its pros and cons. What's important is that you identify and stick to a trading system that fits your personality and lifestyle.

For example, if you don't have the time to look at the markets throughout the day, then it is going to be hard for you to trade Forex on 15-minute candles. But if you're a full-time professional trader like me, a day trading system could work for you.

If you've got a day job and can only look at the markets for only 30 minutes a day, then you might want to focus on a swing trading system using daily candles. If you are free at 9:00 PM SGT every evening, you can trade my GUNS system where you get in and out within just a few minutes and be done by 10 PM SGT.

I teach my students all of these different types of trading systems, but I always tell them that they don't have to use all of them.

If you're a part-time trader, you can just follow one trading system and apply it consistently. With that, you can be very profitable and make good extra income for yourself. Some of my students who trade full time professionally might use multiple systems at the same time. At the end of the day, it is really up to you.

Despite me spending so much time sharing with you about the different types of trading systems, I believe that a good trading system contributes just 10% to a trader's success. There are two other qualities that I think are more important than a good trading strategy because it takes practice and experience to internalize those qualities.

Knowing How Much to Risk in Each of Your Trades

Position sizing or money management is what makes up another 30% of your trading success. You can have the best trading system, but if you have a poor money management method or if you don't know how to size your positions the right way, you can also end up losing money.

Position sizing is about knowing exactly how many shares to buy, how many shares to sell, or how many contracts to trade. You should never decide the number of shares to trade based on your emotions. You should not buy more shares just because you feel more confident about this trade or buy fewer shares just because you feel uncertain about that trade.

The number of shares you buy should be based on a mathematical formula. You must only risk a small percentage of your capital on any single trade, ranging from 1% to a maximum of 3% of your capital.

There is a reason for this. No matter how good a trading system you have, you will go through losing streaks. You need to be prepared to lose 5 or 10 consecutive trades in a row because this happens to everyone, even the best traders in the world.

If you risk too much on each trade (e.g., 10%) and encounter a losing streak of 10 losses in a row, you can blow up your account, causing you to give up. Therefore, only risk a maximum of 3% on each trade so that you can preserve your capital in the event of an inevitable losing streak.

Let me show you a table on the statistical probability of a losing/winning streak (see Figure 1.5).

Generally, a typical trader's win rate hovers somewhere between 50% to 60%. That is a reasonable win rate for any trading system.

You might encounter a winning streak with a 70% to 80% win rate, but that doesn't happen every month. There will also be certain months where you will be unlucky, and your win rate might drop to 45 or 40%.

This is why, on average, you should have a win rate of between 50 to 60%. That is a healthy win rate.

Win %	Probable streak
40%	21
45%	18
50%	16
60%	12
70%	9
80%	7
90%	5

Figure 1.5 Statistical Probability of a Losing or Winning Streak

Even with a 50% to 60% win rate, there is still a probability that you will encounter 12 to 16 consecutive winning or losing trades in a row. Just like coin tossing, although the probability for either side is 50%, it is still possible for you to get consecutive heads or tails over a limited number of tosses.

This is why we need to calculate our position sizes very conservatively by risking just a small percentage of our capital in each trade. So how do we calculate our position sizing or the number of shares to buy in each trade?

Here are the rules. Please follow them diligently (see Figure 1.6).

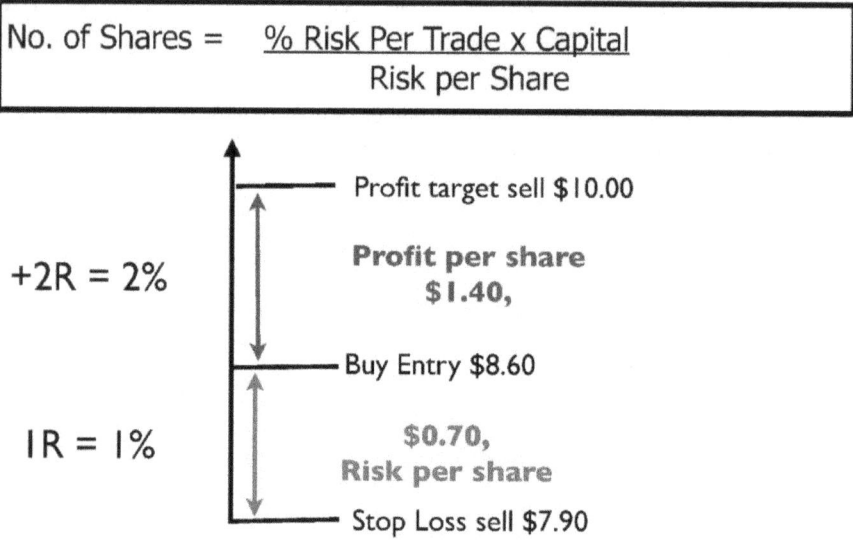

Figure 1.6 How to Calculate Position Sizing

Let's assume that you decided to risk just 1% on every single trade. With a hypothetical starting capital of $10,000, this means that you can afford to risk up to $100 on each trade.

Let's say your entry level is $8.60 and your stop-loss level is $7.90. Your risk per share in this trade will be $0.70. You take your total risk ($100 in this case) and divide that by your risk per share ($0.70 in this case) to get 143 shares—the maximum number of shares that you can buy.

At the entry price of $8.60 per share, you will need to fork out $1229.80 in total to purchase those shares. That is your total position size in monetary terms.

Please remember that your risk for this trade is $100 and not $1229.80. If you hit your stop-loss at $7.90 and get out, you will lose only $100 in total for this trade.

Let's now take a closer look at the mathematics behind a trading system with a positive expectancy. Expectancy is your expected profit per trade calculated based on a large sample of trades done in the past.

We want to calculate expectancy to know your system's historical performance so that you can trade your system with confidence. Here's an example (see Figure 1.7).

- 1R = Percentage % Risk per trade
- Where 1R = 1%-3%

Expected Profit Per Trade (Expectancy)
= (% Win x Average Win) - (% Loss x Average Loss)

Example:
Starting Capital $10,000
Average loss = -1R
Average Win = +2R

Expected Profit = (% Win x Average Win) - (% Loss x Average Loss)
= (50% x 2R) - (50% x 1R)
= 1R - 0.5R = 0.50R per trade

120 trades in a year
= 120 x 0.5R = 60R per Year
= 60% a Year

Figure 1.7 How to Calculate Your Trading System's Expectancy

Let's imagine you have a starting capital of $10,000 and is using a trading strategy that gives you an average loss of 1R with an average win of 2R.

Let's also assume that your system has a conservative win rate of 50%. Based on the provided expectancy formula, your expected profit per trade will be a positive 0.5R.

This means that on average, you will generate 0.5R per trade by trading this system over a large number of trades. As long as your trading system has a positive expectancy, it is a good trading system.

Let's say you execute about 120 trades per year. That is equivalent to about 10 trades per month. With an expectancy of 0.5R, you should expect to get 60R of profits in a year. Since R stands for the initial risk that we mentioned earlier on, if you decide to risk 1% on each trade, this means that you will expect to generate 60% of returns on your capital per year using this trading system.

Before I move on, let's recap the two qualities that I shared earlier on. The first quality that you need to have is a trading system that has a statistical edge in the markets. The second quality is that you have to manage your money well by following a position sizing system where you will only risk a small percentage of your capital in each trade.

Managing Your Psychology and Emotion to Become a Successful Trader

Now, I'm going to share with you the final piece of the puzzle that will constitute 60% of your success as a trader (see Figure 1.8): your trading psychology. I'm sure you have heard about this before, and I can't emphasize it enough.

Trading psychology is the main reason why so many people are unable to succeed as a trader despite learning and acquiring a sound trading system from the experienced gurus.

Why is that the case? It is because they don't have the right trading psychology, emotional management, and discipline.

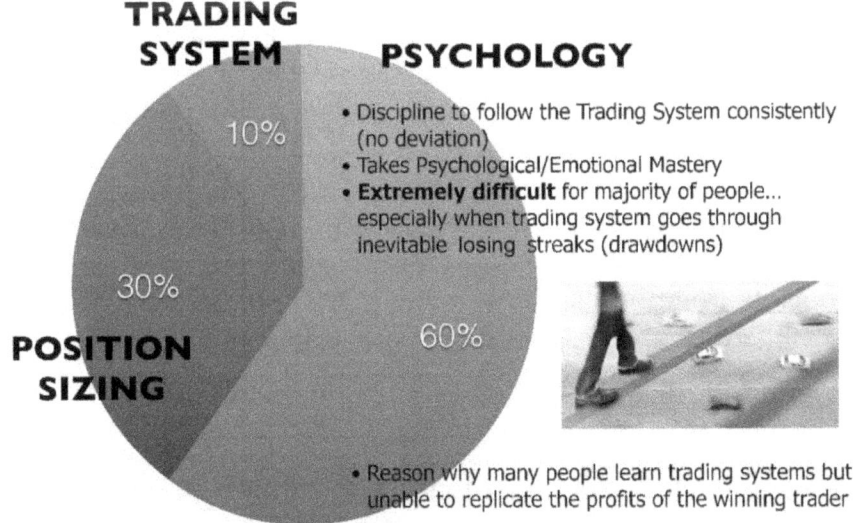

Figure 1.8 What Makes a Successful Trader

In my trading courses, I put a lot of emphasis on trading psychology. Most traders are not able to learn trading psychology from just a lecture because what goes in one ear will often go out the other.

Trading psychology can only be learned through experience. I help my students cope with their trading psychology by putting them through games that simulate the real environment, where their emotions of greed and fear are being triggered so that they can observe how those emotions affect them.

You will make a lot of money from trading only if you're able to trade in a Zen mode with no emotions and can execute your trading plan without deviation.

To have the discipline to follow your trading system consistently with no deviation, you need to achieve psychological and emotional mastery. That's extremely difficult for most people who don't know how to manage their emotions.

That's why I find learning neurolinguistic programming (NLP) so useful because with NLP, I'm able to control my emotions really well. I can eliminate fear and build confidence within seconds, especially during periods when my trading system goes through those inevitable losing streaks.

Traders who have not developed strong trading psychology often freak out when they are hit with losing streaks. They start to deviate from their system, revenge trade or become afraid to take the next trade. They might break their trading rules and fiddle around with their trading strategy until everything starts falling apart.

I want to remind you again that losing streaks happen all the time. When this occurs, many traders break their rules, change their system or give up. On the other hand, you might also encounter winning streaks. That doesn't mean that you're a genius trader or you have found a holy grail trading system.

This is why I keep telling traders "When you have a losing streak, don't be upset. If you have a winning streak, don't be happy." In the short run, each outcome is insignificant. If you keep following your system that has a positive expectancy, you know that you will always make money in the end.

It's just like in the casino where the house always wins in the end because they've got a system that gives them an edge over the players. It is okay not to win all the time as long as you have a net gain at the end of the month, quarter and year.

I hope that from my presentation, you are now able to understand what it truly takes to become a winning trader. I wish you the very best in your trading journey!

NISHANT ARORA: The Highly Respected Trading Mentor Who Started India's Most Engaged Facebook Trading Group

" *In the financial market, there is no beginning and there is no ending. It begins when you put on a trade, it ends when you exit that trade. So everything starts and stops at you.*

Nishant is an up-and-coming top trading educator in India.

I got to know about him through a Facebook group named TFS – Train For Success. Unlike many other trading Facebook Groups that had 50,000 to 100,000 members, TFS had only 10,000 members when I came across their group.

But despite having only 10,000 members, what stood out in TFS for me was its highly engaged and participative community.

Instead of the regular posts in other groups where people just kept asking for trading ideas or sharing "free" stock tips, the members in TFS were regularly sharing and discussing materials and books that dealt with trading best practices, trading knowledge, trading psychology and more.

It was refreshing to come by a trading Facebook group that focuses on imparting and exchanging information that is crucial to the growth of a trader, rather than giving the illusion that anyone can simply become rich just by asking for stock tips from other people.

I knew I had to find out more about the key people running and moderating this group, and that was how I first got to know Nishant, the leading man behind this interesting trading Facebook group.

Nishant's community loved and adored him because he was authentic in his approach toward sharing his trading knowledge and upheld strong values within the group that trading is about hard work, self-responsibility, and personal growth.

Many trading gurus like to showcase their trading results to the public to "prove" to potential students that they are the best traders. But putting aside the authenticity of those trading results, an ability to trade does not naturally translate into the ability to teach and inspire.

A world-class trading educator needs to be authentic in his approach toward helping his disciples find their individual motivation to become better at trading. He needs to be able to dissect difficult and complicated trading concepts into simple layman analogies that average people can understand.

He needs to be inspirational enough so that his students are willing to follow his cues and put in all the necessary hard work to become the very best trader they can possibly become.

Nishant is one such trading "guru" in India, and under his philosophical approach toward becoming a better trader, I believe his community members have secured the right foundation to become better traders.

When I decided to host the Online Trading Summit, I knew I had to invite him to participate. Unsurprisingly, Nishant's summit video was one of the most watched and highly commented video by the summit participants.

In my interview with Nishant, we discussed some of the fundamental principles behind trading best practices and the issues that hinder most traders from becoming successful. He also shares some ideas on how traders can overcome their problems to become more profitable and proficient traders.

Philip: Hi, Nishant. Welcome to the Online Trading Summit. How's everything going for you?

Nishant: Hi. Philip. It's wonderful. For a start, let me congratulate you on conceptualizing and, more than that, executing such a wonderful online event.

It's great that this virtual conference brings together so many wonderful traders across the globe and allows beginners to learn so many things without leaving the comforts of their home. It's a one-of-kind opportunity, and I wished that I had access to such events when I started trading 11 years ago.

Philip: Yeah, I think it's partly because of technology advancements that allow us to organize and host such event for a global audience. And again, thank you so much for agreeing to come on board this summit as one of the speakers to share your trading experiences with the participants.

I understand that you have a very engaged group of Faccbook trading followers. I hope that this interview can offer them more insights about your personal life as a trader as well as to provide more inspiration for them and other beginners in India.

Before we go more in-depth about your trading philosophy, would you mind telling us more about how you got started in the financial markets? How long ago was that and what was the experience like for you?

Nishant: I grew up in a middle-class family. My father was an accountant in a private company, and my mother ran a small school with about four to five hundred students. Because of my mother's profession, she always encouraged me to read books on all kinds of topics. That's how the seed of reading was planted in my life.

When I went to college, I studied Computer Engineering, although I don't use that knowledge anymore. Post that, I did my MBA in Marketing and I was recruited to become a sales executive in a multinational company.

I always knew I had a Type A personality and I wanted to achieve bigger things in life. But in most big companies like the MNCs, you don't have much to do. You're given certain basic things to do, and you have to work within those limitations.

So I left the MNC in six months and joined a small company that dealt in HP, IBM, and other brands of computers. I took a pay cut off of more than 50% to take this job.

I was very eager to learn more about business, and this small company gave me a lot of opportunities to do that. So I started my career as a ground salesman, possibly the lowest-ranked guy in the company. I was given a territory within which I had to keep moving around to find customers. I didn't have any existing customers to start with, so I had to find all of them from scratch.

And that was when reality punched me in my face. Despite having an MBA in Marketing, I'm a nobody in the eyes of my potential corporate customers. I still remember a visit to a potential customer, in which the security guard looked down on me and tried to shoo me away by saying, "Go away! You don't have an appointment."

So that's how my career started. You know, it was full of struggle; it was full of sweat and tears. And from there on, I gradually climbed up the ranks. I got to a position where I was heading the entire sales department in that company.

It was around that time that I started to discover the entrepreneurial spirit in me. It got to a point where I felt I couldn't contain it anymore. I knew I had to leave my role as an employee and do something else.

And again I left my job, but this time around I started a small venture in event management. Through this small event business, I had the opportunity to learn about exporting products. That kind of business intrigued me, and being a voracious reader, I read everything that I could to know more about the export industry.

I traveled extensively across the globe for my export business. One of my primary markets was South East Asia, and so there was a period of time when I was spending between 15 to 20 days in my target market every month. I acquired a lot of customers while exporting Fast Moving Consumer Goods and IT products and my business was growing significantly.

The Difference Between Technical Trading and Value Investing

Throughout that journey, I never stopped reading. I was reading business biographies, and I was reading management books. I was reading everything related to the world of money and business. And there was this one occasion when I got hold of a book called *Snowball*.

That book happened to be Warren Buffett's biography. Little did I know that my life was going to change forever when I got hold of that book. You see, throughout my life, knowledge is something that I live for. And here is a guy and a profession who has made such great fortunes by just reading and making investing decisions.

I thought to myself then that investing was probably a profession that I wouldn't mind working on for the rest of my life. That was my first encounter with the financial markets, and Warren Buffett was the trigger that got me into investing big-time.

Philip: And how long ago was that? How old were you then actually?

Nishant: I think I was about 24 years old then.

Philip: I see. It seems like you're one of those people who started off looking at the markets from a fundamental analysis or value-investing perspective before moving on to technical trading. So how long did it take you before you started to look at the financial market from a trading perspective?

Nishant: As I shared with you earlier on, I was already managing a couple of businesses by then and was pretty settled in my life. And because of my knowledge in running businesses, investing through fundamental analysis made the most sense to me.

I did a lot of fundamental investing and was pretty successful in that. But at some stage of my investing journey, I started to feel a big contrast between Warren Buffett and me.

And that contrast was that by the time Buffett was famous for his investing capabilities, he was already managing a lot of money and was taking controlling stakes in companies.

As you know, fundamental investing is about understanding a company through its financials, assets, earnings, debts, growth prospects and coming up with an intrinsic value to measure that company's worth.

I was buying companies that were trading at a big margin of safety from the intrinsic value, but I had no say on how to run the company. There were many companies that I felt were undervalued by a significant margin and I knew what to do precisely to unlock value, but I couldn't do anything to make that happen.

Buffett, on the other hand, is usually the biggest stakeholder in that company. He could sit with the promoter, he could sit with the board, and he could dictate how the company should be run. I couldn't do that. So when there's such a big contrast between what he can do versus what I can do, I thought that the methods should also be different, considering that our situations and circumstances are different.

That was the starting point of how I got started in trading. As you know, I was still reading actively. And there was this occasion that I managed to get a copy of the book *Market Wizards*. When I got hold of that book, I didn't know that it was a legendary trading book. It was merely another book to me.

However, that book provided me with answers to the many questions that I had in my mind about the contrast between Buffett and me.

From reading that book, I learned about what to do when you're not in control of the markets or the companies that you're invested in. It opened a whole new world for me, and by the time I finished that book, I realized that my soul is that of a trader. Investing is something that I understand intellectually, as I can value any asset and I can value any company. However, trading is something that appeals to my heart.

Philip: So do you consider your reading of *Market Wizards*, as the "aha" moment for you in terms of the way you look at trading? Or was it something that slowly set the stage for you to want to learn more about trading?

Nishant: It was a spontaneous and instant realization. By the time I finished the segment on Michael Marcus and Bruce Kovner, I was already very sure that trading was what I wanted to do.

Philip: What was it that you read in the book that gave you that kind of enlightenment moment?

Nishant: Being in control of your trading activities, being in control of your losses and your profits; that's completely lacking in investing because in investing, I'm not in control.

Philip: All right, so what happens after that? What did you do after reading that book? What kind of actions did you take after that?

Nishant: I had built up a pretty good capital base from my business and my investing. I took a part of it and opened a separate trading account. I think that's one of the best decisions that I've ever made in my life. I kept my investing account and trading account completely separate. I continued to learn more about trading after that.

After I was done with the *Market Wizards* book, I naturally wanted to learn more about technical analysis and that was the path I took. I started to read technical analysis books by Edwards and Magee, John Murphy and Richard Wyckoff, and more. Yet, the more I read about technical analysis, the more I found a disconnection between technical analysis and trading.

Those technical analysts were portraying the market as a scientific laboratory as if the market obeys some kind of law and science in terms of the way it moves. Somehow my gut feeling tells me something is not right. When I read about Michael Marcus and Bruce Kovner, I always had an intuition that they were more artistic than scientific about the market.

Finally, a guy came along one day and filled that gap of disconnection in my mind about technical analysis and trading. That guy was Mark Douglas. He gave me answers to everything that I wanted to know about technical analysis and trading. And that was the second "aha" moment for me. It put me on the path that I am on right now.

And thanks to Mark Douglas, I was able to connect the dots. Most beginners think that trading is all about technical analysis and fail to realize that technical analysis is just a small part of trading. I wanted to destroy that cloud of confusion, and so I started Techno-Funda Society to help new traders.

Philip: I see. So could you elaborate more on that second "aha" moment that you had? What was it that helped you clear up that disconnection between technical analysis and trading?

Nishant: As you know, when a beginner starts to trade, he learns about trend lines, moving averages, Fibonacci retracements, and all of that. He takes a view and assumes that markets are predictable with the use of technical analysis.

He thinks that the use of technical analysis can help him predict where the market is going tomorrow. But that doesn't work, and it sets a wrong expectation for the trader. Mark Douglas has said that a good trader doesn't need to predict anything to make money in the market.

You don't have to predict because you just can't predict. There are countless variables in the market, and you can't possibly know all of them. A chart is just showing you a collection of people, a group of bulls and bears and undecided participants who all contributed to the movement of the price.

Let me explain this in some more detail. Trading is one of the very few areas in which you can have the illusion of succeeding without knowing anything. If you have zero knowledge about archery or shooting, what is the chance that you can hit a bull's eye? Almost zero.

If you have zero knowledge about brain surgery, what is the chance that you can perform a successful operation? Zero. If you have zero knowledge about law, how much is the chance that you can try a case in the court and win? Zero.

But if you have zero knowledge about trading, what is the chance that you can put on a trade and win? 50%. You see, that's a big illusion. Every beginner who comes into the market is bound to suffer from this illusion. The most challenging thing about trading is that it looks easy on the surface because it is possible to win without knowing anything.

I always tell my students that the worst thing that can happen to you is that your first trade is a winning trade because it took you nothing to be a winner. When that happens, you become overconfident and start to bet bigger.

If you have a winning streak of profitable trades, which is pretty much possible for any beginner, you start to think that you're a good analyst and a good trader. When the first losing trade comes, you blame your loss on the market. Instead of taking self-responsibility, you blame the market for taking away your capital or profits. Usually, this results in two kinds of consequences.

The first consequence is that you develop an adverse relationship with the market. You start to think of the market as some sort of an enemy who is trying to take your money away from you.

That's a terrible mindset to start with because it puts you at a disadvantage. The market is like an ocean. The market doesn't love you, and the market doesn't hate you. In fact, the market doesn't even know that you exist.

In the financial market, there's no beginning, and there's no end. It begins when you put on a trade, it ends when you exit that trade. So everything starts and stops at you. However, beginners don't see the market that way. They think the market has done the damage, so therefore the market is an enemy. But when you think of someone as an enemy, you can never be in sync with it.

Now, this is the essential truth about trading: the only way that you can become a successful trader is that you get in sync with the flow of the markets. You have no prejudice, and you have no preconceived notions about how the market should behave.

The second consequence is that you start to believe that the solution to your trading problem lies in how good you are with technical analysis. This leads me into your question about the disconnection between trading and technical analysis.

When a beginner gets into an analysis mode, he usually never comes out of it. You know, I tell every student of mine, "When you start learning analysis, it's fine; you must learn something to start with." But down the road, a trader more often than not forgets the main reason why he's learning technical analysis.

He forgets that he's learning technical analysis only as a starting point to becoming a proficient trader. He gets too much into the academic side of technical analysis, and he starts counting degrees, percentages, centimeters, and inches of price movement. Now he starts behaving more like an analyst rather than as a trader.

The world is full of great analysts, but not all of them are good traders. Now comes the next stage for new traders. Once you learn something about technical analysis, you start to think that you know the market.

You put on a trade and the market moves in the opposite direction. The market punches you in your face, and then you hate the market more. You think you need to learn more and do more to know more about the market.

You start adding indicators. First, it's RSI; then it's MACD. Soon, you begin to add Stochastics, and then it's Bollinger Bands. As time goes by, you start getting into that state of mind that you want to look for that "Holy Grail" technical analysis trading strategy.

I headed down this path before. But after I read the books by Mark Douglas and Van Tharp, I realized that technical analysis is not the answer. I started to understand that the answer to all the questions is that you have to accept the risk.

The Right Way to Manage Your Trading Risks

Most traders think they're risk takers. If you ask any trader, "Are you a risk taker?" He'll probably answer you, "Yes, I am a risk taker." But he is usually not telling the truth because whenever a trade is in a losing position, he starts feeling fearful. He starts feeling bad about it. This shows that he never accepted risk in the first place.

In trading, you have to learn to accept the risk. Without risk, trading will not exist. More importantly, you have to learn to risk just enough so that any losses will not derail you and affect your state of mind. If you start getting fearful and feeling pain from your losses, you're probably risking money that you can't afford to lose.

If I were to take this opportunity to provide a message to everybody out there, this is what I would say: the outcome of every single individual trade is random. However, the result of a block of trades over a period of time is not random. That is where a trader's skills and edge play out.

Trading is about trade management, mind management, money management, and risk management. Even if only 30% of your trades are profitable, you'll be okay if the profits that you made in these trades are more than enough to offset the losses you incurred in the other 70% of your trades.

Philip: So when you first started to learn technical analysis, it's pretty much the same journey as how a new trader starts off. He thinks that when a trade is not profitable, maybe there's something wrong with his analysis. What he doesn't realize is that technical analysis improves one's edge over a large number of trades and it's not meant to ensure a win in an individual trade.

As a result, they keep diving into and swimming around technical analysis strategies, trying to find that Holy Grail, so much so that they totally overlook what's more critical in trading as a whole. Now, after you've had that "aha" moment about technical analysis and trading, how did you evolve? Did you change something drastically, or did you just continue to refine your trading methodology?

How to Become Your Own Trading Guru

Nishant: It took me about two years to get to this "aha" moment. For two good years, I was behaving like a technical analyst and not like a trader. I was doing Elliott Wave analysis, Gann circles, and so on.

Let me take you through the journey of technical analysis gurus. People love gurus, and everybody wants gurus. Alexander Elder said that beginners walk with their umbilical cords in their hands so that they can plug those cords into those gurus.

In the early '70s, there was a guy called Edson Gould. He developed an analysis methodology called speed lines. So they were basically trend lines, which took into consideration the angles, the velocity of trend lines. It worked for three to four years, but then it stopped working. But Gould didn't stop pushing the method in the market.

Alexander Elder mentioned in his path-breaking book, *Trading for a Living*, that R.N. Elliott, the founder of Elliott Wave Theory, died a relatively poor man.

Alexander Elder also met with W.D. Gann's son, who said that his father had been unable to support his family by trading. Instead, Gann earned his living by writing and selling instructional courses. When Gann died in the 1950s, his estate, including his house, was valued at slightly over $100,000.

You know something? Analysis is not the way. If you go too deep into analysis, you become a seller. Too much analysis works only for one person, the seller, the salesman who's selling you that analysis, and it will not help you as a trader. An analyst becomes rigid about his thesis whereas the most significant attribute of a trader is flexibility.

Fortunately, I think people have grown more intelligent that they no longer blindly accept a guru. Most of the people these days like the Millennials are very intelligent; they don't take anything at face value. And I think that's what TFS is trying to do. If you go through the posts that we do on TFS, we tell everybody to stop looking for any guru.

I want to teach people to be self-dependent by reading books and thinking more. I always tell people that just as R&D (research and development), is the key for any company to grow, R&T (reading and thinking) is the key for any individual to develop. So R&T is the only way that you go through life.

Going back to your question, after I read the book by Mark Douglas, the most significant shift in my mindset was understanding that losses are bound to happen. It's a distribution curve of wins and losses. You can do nothing about it. The only thing you have control over is how you contain your losses.

You can't control your outcome on a trade-to-trade basis. If you look at the tendencies of many novice traders out there, they don't cut their losses as quickly as they should, and they book their profits too soon. People attach too much importance to every trade, causing them to be apprehensive.

Many people have a "jackpot" mentality. They think that the next trade is going to change their lives. The next trade will enable them to leave their jobs and become their own boss. When you think like that, you're bound to have too many biases in your head. What I learned from Mark Douglas was that my next trade owes me nothing.

In fact, when you put on a trade, expect it to be a losing trade. You have done some analysis, and you supposedly have a trading edge, but you have to expect your edge to play out over a period of time and over a large number of trades. Before you read Douglas, you think like a gambler, after you read Douglas, you think like a casino.

Douglas teaches you to think like a casino. When you study the game of blackjack, you'll realize that the casino has an edge of 4.5% over the players. To a beginner or novice trader, he will think it's a small edge. But that is not a small edge at all.

If 100 million dollars of bets are placed, the casino will make 4.5 million dollars. So they know that for a big sample size, they will make money. As such, they don't try to control the betting or the gambling outcomes on a bet-to-bet basis.

Similarly, I have stopped thinking from a trade-to-trade perspective. In terms of analysis, I used to count waves but I don't do that anymore. I see a chart as a battleground of buyers and sellers.

I don't need to make it too decorative by using too many lines and too many things. I use very classical technical analysis principles like areas of demand and supply. When I look at those areas, I get my answers. Since I'm not concerned about the trade-to-trade outcome, I don't tend to over analyze any chart or trading idea.

People often ask me about my favorite trade setup. In fact, this is a question that I get asked the most often on Twitter, Facebook, and everywhere. And I often disappoint them with my answer. They expect me to tell them something like "I enter a trade when the 10-day moving average crosses above 50" and so on. But I don't do that.

So usually, I'll just tell them that my favorite trading setup is when I notice an opportunity in which the risk of me being wrong is losing at most 2% of my capital. This is how I look at it. If the distance between my entry and distance between the point of being wrong is within 2% of my capital, that is a beautiful trade setup.

People then start asking me what is the target that I set. And I tell them that I don't know where the price will go. People begin to think that I know nothing and I think it can cost me a lot of followers.

But the fact is, I really don't know what the price will do next. The only thing that I have control over is my loss, and I make sure that I execute full control over that controllable variable. And if the market moves in my favor, I just keep going with it, that's it.

So I think the biggest lesson for every beginner out there is; please stop looking at trading from a trade-to-trade basis because trading is not done in that fashion. Trading is about having an edge over many trades. It is okay to use a moving average, Fibonacci, or RSI to understand the different dynamics of the price movement, but there really isn't any Holy Grail out there.

Analysis gives you an edge, and that edge plays out over a large number of trades. So you have to have money management in place so that you can survive through those large numbers of trades to have your edge play out into profitability for you.

Philip: What kind of trader are you? Are you an intraday trader, are you a swing trader, or are you a longer-term position trader? What kind of timeframe do you think is suitable for a novice trader?

Why Beginners Should Stay Away from Day Trading

Nishant: I started my trading journey in the equity cash segment. I studied the behavior of the shares that I was trading and then I started doing positional trading and swing trading. I find that day trading is not something that a beginner should start with.

Day trading is something that you evolve into. You don't become a day trader from the start until you understand trading. I don't think that a novice trader should start with day trading. Ideally, you should be profitable in swing trading first before you can get into day trading. I began with swing trading and positional trading before I evolved into a day trader.

Right now, I still do value investing because it works! But a part of my portfolio is also into trading. Within trading, I am more of a swing trader.

My favorite timeframe and duration of a trade is somewhere between two to three days to a couple of weeks. So that's the main trading horizon that I play in, and there is a reason for that which I'll explain later. Finally, there is a small part of my capital that I use for day trading.

Personally, I believe that the time duration of a trade or the timeframe of a chart is inversely proportional to the randomness of price movements. What I mean is that the higher the timeframe, the lower the randomness, the lower the timeframe, the higher the randomness.

Randomness on a daily or weekly chart is generally lower compared to a 5- or 10-minute chart. If you see a price pattern like head and shoulders or a double bottom on a daily chart or weekly chart, it usually plays out much better compared to when it appears on a 5- or 10-minute chart.

Generally, the time horizon of a chart is inversely proportional to the randomness of the price movement, meaning the longer the timeframe, the less random the price movement is. At the same time, when the price shows lesser random movement, this will also improve a trader's profitability. Essentially, this means that the higher the timeframe you trade, the greater the probability of your success as a trader.

Philip: You mentioned that you were already doing pretty well in value investing. What is the primary motivation for you to spend additional time and effort to go into position trading, swing trading, and subsequently into intraday trading?

Nishant: It gives me the capital to invest.

Philip: So what do you mean by "it gives me the capital to invest"? Is it because shorter-term trading helps you to generate returns more quickly so that you will have more cash flow to invest on a fundamental perspective?

Nishant: When you invest, you're mainly investing in the growth of the company. But you're not running the company, so you have no control over the time period in which the returns can be generated. I have some investments that worked out over a period of five to seven years, but how will I get my cash flow? How will I be able to sustain for those five to seven years?

Trading, on the other hand, depends on the kind of timeframe you choose to trade in and so in a way you can control the timeframe of your returns. That gives you more control over your cash flows. Over the last two years, I have not increased the size of my trading portfolio; it is like a linear portfolio. I have come to a point where I am not reinvesting my trading profits back into my trading account.

Philip: What percentage of your total capital do you set aside for your value-investing portfolio? What percentage for position trading, swing trading, and intraday trading? Your answer will provide a better perspective for everyone to think about how to manage their trading and investing from a portfolio perspective.

Nishant: I think my answer is going to disappoint a lot of beginners. To start with, I wish to emphasize again that a beginner should not start with day trading. A trading beginner should not day trade at all.

Day trading is full of noise. I am not saying that day trading doesn't work. I'm making money from day trading, so it is working for me, but I believe that day trading doesn't work for a beginner. A beginner should start with swing trading and should not use derivatives.

Personally, I'm a futures trader, and I do both swing trading and intraday trading. But if I have to tell any beginner on what to do, I will suggest that he does not start with intraday trade or derivatives.

After you've gathered some experience in swing trading, you'll start to feel markets in a better way. You'll begin to accumulate knowledge about trading, and you'll have more control over your emotions. You'll no longer suffer from fear, greed, revenge, or recovery.

That's when it is the right time for you to start looking at day trading. You don't have much time to think in intraday trading; you have to use your instinct to act most of the time. A better way is to build up your market instinct in swing trading before you move into the fast-paced world of intraday trading.

On the topic of capital allocation, the ratio between trading and investing capital allocation changes from time to time, depending upon the opportunities. But most of the time it stays linear: 50–50. Within the trading universe, around 70% of my trading portfolio is in swing trading; that's where the returns are.

Many people might not agree with me, but the main reason I think people promote day trading is that they have something to sell. If you see the statistics, most of the billionaires come from investing. There are even many who achieved their billionaire status from swing and positional trading. But how many billionaires can you count who made their fortune from day trading? Nearly none at all.

So day trading is not a full business in itself. Day trading is something that can be part of your trading business, but it can't be your entire business. This is what I have learned, and I really don't care if people criticize me for my views because they have been hypnotized by the industry.

Your broker wants you to day trade because that's how he makes most of the commissions from you. So many gurus want you to day trade because that's how they sell their courses. But a beginner should think for himself. I have given you a proven statistic.

Just tell me the names of 10 billionaires who made their fortune purely from day trading; you cannot do that because there aren't any. Even if you talk about traders like Bruce Kovner, Michael Marcus, Paul Tudor Jones or Marty Schwartz, are they pure intraday traders? No, they're not. They're mainly swing traders who happen to day trade as well.

So my advice to a new trader is this. You have to know how to drive a car first. You can't start your driving lesson with a sports car. If you do that, you might have some adrenaline rush, but you will be set for a big car accident.

The first step is to drive a regular car for a couple of years without having any dent on your car. Once you can do that, then gradually you can shift to a sports car, but even then you cannot drive your sports car on every terrain and in every situation.

Philip: So how do you know at what point that you can start looking into intraday trading? Is there a particular stage where you know that you can do it and you should try it?

Nishant: I think it's more of a qualitative and intangible feeling. Let's go back to the example of the car. When you learn to drive a car, you look at the gear whenever you need to shift it. You look at the clutch to check if your foot is stepping correctly on it.

You cannot possibly start driving a fast car when you have to check all your steps manually. You have to build all of these steps into your instinct so that when you drive a fast car, you don't need to think because you don't have the time to think.

It is the same thing in trading. In swing trading and position trading, you can take your time to analyze and check everything before taking a trade. However, day trading is not a game of analysis. Day trading is a game of reflexes. You have to have very strong reflexes about the market. You need to build your intuitions about the market before you can do day trading effectively.

So what are intuitions? Intuitions are nothing but pop-ups of the knowledge database that you have collected over a period of years. When you have a database of knowledge, and when you have been trading for a few years, you have an understanding of how markets behave. That is when you can start to lower your timeframe.

Imagine this. You see something like a Head and Shoulders pattern on a minute chart, and you still have to stop to think about what to do when you see such a pattern. If you still need to spend significant time to think about all these things, you're not ready for day trading. Day trading is something that you have to make a decision and act on the subconscious level.

There are generally four different stages of competencies.

The first stage is unconscious incompetence; you don't know what you don't know. The second stage is conscious incompetence; you know what you don't know. The third stage is conscious competence; you know what you know, but you are continuously thinking about it. The fourth stage is unconscious competence. You know what you know and how to behave without actively thinking about it.

It's like a concert pianist who is already very familiar with his art. He can play a piece beautifully without needing to think which note comes next and which key should he be pressing. That's day trading for you.

Philip: Let's go back a bit to talk more about swing trading since you think that's the ideal strategy or timeframe for most people to start with. So what do you think is a better process to start swing trading on the right foundation?

What You Need to Do to Become a Good Trader

Nishant: Let's start with the sequence of how a trader should look at the chart. Most people start off their analysis by trying to find patterns. When they see a head and shoulders pattern, they go short. When they see a cup and handle pattern, they go long.

You have to shed that mentality if you really want to become a proficient trader.

The first thing that I personally look at is price structure. The second thing I look at is price pattern. The third thing I find is the particular candle pattern. The fourth thing is the indicator, if any.

The biggest irony is that most traders begin from the fourth and they never reach the first. They focus on a tree and miss the entire forest. They keep trying to find the price patterns and end up missing the big picture.

So the first thing that I'll encourage everybody to learn is that, if anybody wants to become a swing trader, is to try to understand the character of the price first. To do this, you don't need any indicator, and you don't need any oscillator.

You just need a price—accompanied by some good questions: "Is this stock more prone to be caught in ranges? Does it trend most of the time? When it rises, does it rise steeply? When it falls, does it fall steeply? What has happened over the history? When it falls steeply, does it form a range there or does it form a V bottom?"

The reason I'm saying all this is because the big boys and the big hands in a stock rarely change. When stock prices move significantly, it is usually due to decisions made by the same set of people who are managing the stock for an extended period of time.

There are certain stocks that tend to create big candles; there are individual stocks that tend to make smaller candles. This is about getting into the skin of the stock and into the soul of that instrument.

Once you're able to do that, then you start looking at the patterns. Patterns don't exist in a vacuum; they exist as part of a structure. So that's why I said to focus more on the structure first.

If this isn't complex enough, wait till you consider the interplay of timeframes as well. You see, most beginners miss this picture. Everybody's timeframe is different, everybody's personality is different, and everybody's capital size is different.

Trading opportunities and markets exist in every timeframe; there's a market in the minute chart, there are trading opportunities in the hourly chart, and there are also trading activities going on in the weekly chart.

A stock that is in a beautiful uptrend on a weekly chart can be in a pathetic downtrend on the 5-minute chart. So there is really no point asking anybody what you should do because nobody knows what kind of timeframe you're trading in.

If you ask me what kind of trader I am, my trading style consists of an interplay of timeframes. If I have to name a trader whom I feel the closest in terms of how we see price, it has to be Brian Shannon.

Brian Shannon is also an advocate of the philosophy of using the interplay of multiple timeframes. Most people think that if they're day trading, they should just focus on 10-minute, 20-minute or 30-minute charts and ignore daily and weekly charts.

That is not the way. You have to see the daily and weekly charts, even if you're day trading. The reason is that you know where the critical levels are when you look at the more significant timeframe.

For example, if I see a strong resistance at a certain level on the weekly chart, I need to be aware of it when day trading. If you don't do this, you'll be wondering why a bullish-looking five-minute chart crashed when it reached that key resistance level that appeared on the weekly chart.

Trading can't be one-dimensional. The market exists in so many timeframes, so you have to look across all of them.

Philip: So you advocate that a short-term trader should look at a bigger timeframe to get a big picture before narrowing down to the smaller timeframe to find the exact signal and precise entry levels?

Nishant: Yes, I always trade in the direction of the longer timeframe. That's the filter I use.

Philip: What are some of the principles that help you decide whether to get into a specific trade?

Nishant: I'm more of a manual scavenger. A lot of people ask me what screeners I use, but I really don't use any screeners. I'm a futures trader, and there are just a little more than 200 single stock futures in India. It's actually very easy to visually see 200 charts every day if you have your fixed chart patterns, charts setups, and know what you're looking for.

This is what I do every day when the market closes. I go through more than a hundred charts every single day. As I visually scan through, there are specific charts that I feel have no trading opportunities because the chart structure is not looking good, the chart pattern is not clear, prices are moving randomly, and there is no entry structure for me to base a trade on.

I typically have three watch lists.

Watchlist 1 is what I use to keep charts that are in a No Trading Zone (NTZ) because they are not showing any trading opportunities at all.

Watchlist 2 is where I keep charts that are showing good structure, good pattern but does not offer a good entry yet. I call that a Tentative Trading Zone (TTZ).

Watchlist 3 is what I use to hold charts that are in an Immediate Trading Zone (ITZ). These are the charts that are looking good in terms of structure and patterns, and where the price is also at a point where it seems like a great entry point in which risk is not more than 2% to 3% of my trading capital.

My stop-loss exits are all technical stops. If I'm going long in a trade, my stop-loss exit has to be a point where the chart tells that the long side thesis is wrong on that specific timeframe that I am trading in.

To me, swing trading is more about momentum, but day trading is more about volatility. So even if the chart is looking perfectly fine with a good entry from a swing trading perspective, I will not day trade that stock if price movement is not significant.

I only consider day trading those stocks that have gapped up, has just broken out of a range or where there is a volume/open interest spike.

Philip: So your day trading list of stocks is actually from the same pool of stocks that you monitor for swing trades as well?

Nishant: Absolutely. I day trade those stocks from my list of swing trading stocks that show significant volatility.

Philip: Let us summarize the steps you've covered for a moment. Let's say you've done your analysis, found a trading opportunity, identified the ideal entry level, and established a technical stop-loss exit. What is the next step you will take?

Nishant: I practice something called the Fresh Look Strategy. There are only two ways to exit: you either exit with profits or you exit with losses.

Every time I get out of a position whether with profits or losses, I try to look at the chart again as if I am seeing it for the first time and try to see if any trading opportunities might be coming up soon again. I try to put the bias of my recent trade aside when looking for new opportunities in the same chart. I look at it from a completely fresh angle.

The Main Reasons Why Most Traders Fail

Philip: There is this particular saying that more than 90% or even 95% of traders lose money in the long run. What's your take on that? How would you advise a new trader who is demoralized by this low probability of becoming a profitable trader?

Nishant: When I first started TFS, I suggested trading books to everyone. Many people told me that no one would join the group because people just don't want to learn, they just want to get tips. But look where we are now? We have 16,000 members, many of whom are very engaged with the trading knowledge that we are sharing.

The reason why 95% of traders fail is that the industry as a whole disappoints them. You know that to become a doctor, you have a set of prescribed books, a syllabus that you have to cover to become a doctor.

But when you want to become a trader, what does your broker tell you? Your broker tells you to open a trading account with him and trade in derivatives because that's where the big money is. It's not entirely the fault of traders.

The industry as a whole has to take some responsibility for such misconceptions and a high failure rate. That is why I started TFS, to teach people to take responsibility.

I would say that 95% of traders lose money because they don't take responsibility for their outcomes, because they expect too much from trading and because they are undercapitalized.

Many new traders think that they can just bring $500 or $1000 and convert it into $1million in no time. They read *Market Wizards* and saw how Richard Dennis converted $200 into one million. They think that they will be the next Richard Dennis. This is the wrong expectation to have.

Another main reason for such a high failure rate is because most beginners attempt to start with intraday trading and leveraged trading. This is something that I really want to discourage among the beginners.

As I've mentioned above, intraday trading is not something that you start with. Intraday trading is something that you evolve into. I started day trading after three years of swing trading, and I still don't day trade every day now. Day trading is just a part of my business.

I'd like to add a few things about day trading here. Day trading (and leverage) carries a considerable risk of going bust. These are a specialist's job, not a beginner's. I can never go out and blatantly declare that beginners (or even some with experience) should trade in derivatives or day trade.

The fact remains that not many people are wired to day trade. Not many people are knowledgeable and disciplined enough to handle leverage.

Day trading is the highest version of this game called trading. It takes an immense amount of reflexes with split-second decision-making, which is generally a result of years of study and experience. Sometimes, even significant experience in trading cannot make you a day trader. Some specific skills must be present in your overall character.

It's okay if you don't have the attributes to become a day trader. Don't force it. You're in this business to make money, and it doesn't have to come from just day trading.

Of course, many sales-people would tell you that day trading is easy, derivative trading is fun, and all you need to do is to buy their system or whatever. That is an irresponsible act that places new traders in a dangerous situation. If you're a beginner and you wish to trade derivatives or day trade, you have to earn it. You can't just fight your way into it.

A lot of beginners ask me, "Is day trading profitable?" I think the right question should be, "Can everyone be a profitable day trader?" The reason I've transformed the question is that it is never about trading, but always about the trader. Yes, day trading can be profitable but most day traders aren't profitable.

Let's put it this way. If we assume that 95% of day traders lose money, then considering that no new money is generated in the market and only transfer of money takes place, the 5% must be making money. So what 95% lose, 5% make. It's about the attributes those 5% have.

So, yes it is very difficult. When I say difficult, you might think intellect is the solution. But sadly, it's not. It's not about calculations. It's about temperament. Hence, even the most intelligent ones fail badly and lose their shirts.

Day trading is a game of reflexes and managing emotions. Obviously, trading knowledge is essential but reflexes or how subconsciously you can apply your trading knowledge in a changing market without letting your feelings get in the way, is what decides your fate as a day trader.

The reason why most people don't realize this and jump into day trading is that day trading looks easy. I mean, everyone who knows driving cannot imagine that they can participate in an F1 Grand Prix competing with players like Jim Clark, Ayrton Senna, Fernando Alonso, or Nelson Piquet. No one will even dare to imagine that.

But just because opening a trading account and entering an order and exiting an order is easy, everyone who gets into trading assumes that he can participate and compete with highly experienced and shrewd day traders who have honed this craft and their reflexes over decades of hard work and who work their asses off every day in this.

And it's not just participating; our innocent beginner expects to win, too. So, this is the paradox that I always talk about. Day trading is the most challenging form of trading because it looks easy.

I meet, and I talk to many big international traders, and most of them have the same opinion as me, that day trading is part of their business; it's not their only business. So if a beginner follows these four key things, it will be an excellent start for them.

First, follow the bigger timeframe because randomness is lower. Second, don't start with day trading. Third, accept complete responsibility for every trading outcome. And finally, accept the risk; don't trade on a trade-to-trade basis. If a beginner truly accepts these four points, he will already be in that 5% segment of winning traders.

Philip: Before we end today's interview, do you have any final words for the summit participants, especially those new and inexperienced traders? Any inspirational advice you can share so that they can persist through the initial tough learning periods, rather than just giving up, as roughly 95% of the traders tend to do?

Nishant: Sure. My first advice is that a trader should read a lot. You have to read a lot and think a lot too because merely reading will not help. Let me share with you a common analogy about trading. Many trainers say that trading is like swimming and that you cannot learn swimming by reading. I say this is a pathetic analogy.

To me, trading is like performing brain surgery. Of course, you will need practical exposure, but before that, you would need to read a lot of books. So my advice to beginners is to read and think as much as they can.

My second suggestion is to switch off your televisions. If you want to become a trader, you would want to be away from that noise and all the different kinds of analysis out there. Analysis is not the answer. Manage your risks; profits will take care of themselves. And stop obsessing about winning every trade.

And lastly, stay away from "get rich quick" schemes. I so often tell beginners that whenever you come across phrases such as "hidden gems", "100% back-tested strategy," and so on, just run away from that person. There is no such thing as a surefire formula in trading. Remember, trading is not a treasure hunt, but a business.

Philip: Thank you, Nishant, for the time you've spent dispensing your wisdom and your experience to the summit participants. I believe that after watching your interview, they will go back and think about what you said.

Hopefully, they will start reading as well. I would love the chance to interview you again in the future to chat on more in-depth topics about trading, but for now, I wish you the very best in whatever you do and in terms of the kind of vision you want to achieve for TFS.

Nishant: It's a pleasure, Philip. Thank you for having me in the Online Trading Summit!

EDMUND LEE: The Leading Trading Mentor of Philippines' Premier Financial Education Institute

" *Do not compare yourself with other traders. Try to discover what works for you. There are many profitable trading systems out there but not all of them will be a good fit for you.*

Edmund Lee is the President and CEO of the Caylum Trading Institute, a premier educational facility in the Philippines that aims to develop successful traders of global markets.

When I was searching for a trading mentor from the Asia Pacific region to speak and share trading knowledge in the Online Trading Summit, a fellow trader based in the Philippines quickly brought Edmund's name to my attention.

Under the influence of his father Edward Lee, who is the Chairman of COL Financials, the largest online stock brokerage firm, Edmund was introduced to the world of trading at a young age together with his brother Lawrence Lee, who currently runs Citisecurities, a top trading firm in the Philippines that manages over 35 proprietary traders.

Edmund has been a student of multiple international markets since 2011, spanning countries from the United States, Hong Kong & China, Japan, Indonesia and of course, the Philippines.

Prior to establishing Caylum, Edmund was a research analyst for COL Financial and a firm believer that success in stocks must rely on more than just technical and fundamental analysis, and that in order to succeed in this business one must also have a deep understanding of market sentiment and risk management.

His passion and purpose for Caylum is to spread advanced financial literacy to the world and to build a thriving global community of stock investors and traders alike.

In his presentation, Edmund shared a unique FTSR framework that includes fundamental analysis, technical analysis, sentiment analysis, and risk management to pick that one good trade to execute.

Philip: Hi, Edmund. It's great to have you at the Online Trading Summit to share with us your personal trading experience and how you started one of the premier trading institutes in the Philippines to mentor regular people into profitable traders. I'm sure everyone is keen to know how you got started in trading. Could you share with us your story?

Edmund: Sure. Eight years ago, I started my career as a financial analyst. Before the start of my trading journey, I've been an equity analyst all my life. It's something different from the path that most traders take when they start off as a trader. I have a strong background in fundamentals. I received my CFA designation in 2013 and had mostly studied companies from that angle.

However, as an equity analyst, I realized that it was difficult hunting for all those great companies and getting the investments right. Over time, I saw a lot of companies that were moving regardless of their valuations. There were many stocks whose prices reached and remained at irrational levels longer than what most of us believed they should be valued.

As such, I decided to get the best of both worlds and try to see how both fundamentals and technicals could work together to our advantage.

Philip: I'd like you to share more about your trading experience later on. For now, I'm excited to get into the presentation that you've prepared for us. When I first invited you to speak in this summit, you decided to present the topic "Searching for the One Good Trade." Is there any particular reason why you think this is an important topic to focus on?

Edmund: *One Good Trade* is a book written by Mike Bellafiore. He listed all the right criteria he was looking for when picking his trades and emphasized that the most important work as a trader is to keep finding that one good trade.

I honestly believe that there are many trading systems that work. Everybody has their own different systems and setups, and there are many ways to skin a cat, especially in the financial markets.

I believe that a foundation is required for everything that you do, and you have to understand what that foundation is. So I decided to make my topic today more about understanding things from a bigger perspective rather than focusing on the micro-perspective aspects of trading.

There are a lot of opportunities out there in the market, and it's just a matter of laying the right foundation in terms of how you're going to trade the market.

Philip: Great. I'm handing the stage over to you right now, and I look forward to hearing what you've got to share with us, Edmund.

Using The FTSR Framework to Find That One Good Trade

Edmund: Thank you, Philip. As mentioned earlier, I'm going to talk about what I believe are the steps required to find that one good trade. I know that there are a lot of people out there trying to look for that perfect trading system, to find that Holy Grail. Unfortunately, there is no such thing as a Holy Grail in trading.

The reality is that, over time, the more profitable your trading system is, the more you'll notice that the markets become even more efficient. When you become very profitable, people start to learn what you're doing and copy what you do. As such, your system becomes much more difficult to trade. As a trader, what's more important is learning how to be dynamic and flexible.

You might have seen stocks whose prices rose sharply within a short period of time. There are many speculative companies around the world in every stock exchange. It's easy to buy these stocks during the breakout, but the most difficult thing is deciding when to exit the trade. Do I hold my winners? Do I sell now and buy back later? Should I just sell and then step aside? There are no easy answers when considering when to sell.

For example, you might have entered and exited a trade and made an 18% gain in two weeks. It might feel like a great trade to you initially. But imagine if the price doubles in another month's time. Do you now feel terrible because you missed out on that 100% gain within a one-month period? Does your earlier decision to exit for an 18% gain in two weeks still feel like a great trade?

I'm not saying we should try to catch the tops or the bottoms. Our objective as traders is to use technical analysis to find the right time to enter just as the stock is turning around or breaking out. We then try to understand the fundamentals, the numbers, and the stories to figure how far the move could potentially go.

With all of this information and knowledge, we can then have the confidence to hold and ride the profits to maximize our returns.

This is the basic foundation from which we created our trading framework that focuses on fundamental analysis, technical analysis, sentiment, and risk management. I call it the FTSR Framework (see Figure 3.1).

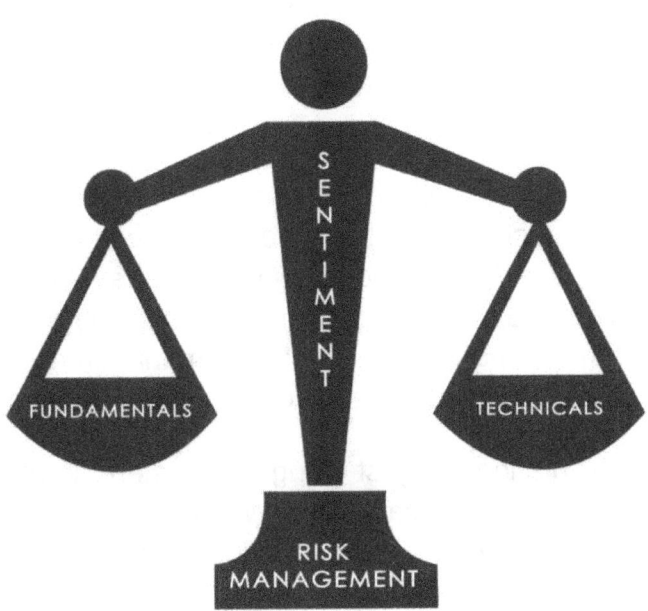

Figure 3.1 The FTSR Framework

We set up this framework through a combination of the books that we've read and what we've seen in the markets over the years.

Let me start off by explaining how I look at fundamentals and technicals. I don't think it's something new to a lot of people. Fundamentals are often concerned about long-term value and understanding companies from a longer-term perspective.

However, in the near term, I believe that short-term earnings or some perception of profits, whether it's speculative or not, will be the one driving companies' stock prices. On the other hand, technical analysis is often used in the short-term to identify entry opportunities.

The other two elements of this framework are sentiment and risk management. And the best quote for me to share with you about sentiment is this: "A high tide lifts all boats".

So if you're looking to make money by buying good companies when the general market sentiment is deteriorating, it's going to be so much more difficult.

And last but not least, risk management is another crucial factor in trading the stock market. You need to know how much you're willing to lose at any given point in time. The next losing trade is always around the corner, so if you do not know how to protect yourself with the right amount of risk management, you can wipe out your trading account easily during a losing streak.

For this presentation, I'm just going to focus on the elements of fundamentals and technicals. When we study the fundamentals of a company, it is important to consider what kind of business stage the company is in.

This is a corporate lifecycle chart that was created by Aswath Damodaran, the founder of Modern Finance (see Figure 3.2). He often explains that companies usually go through five stages in their life, namely, the idea stage, product stage, business model stage, harvest stage, and the endgame.

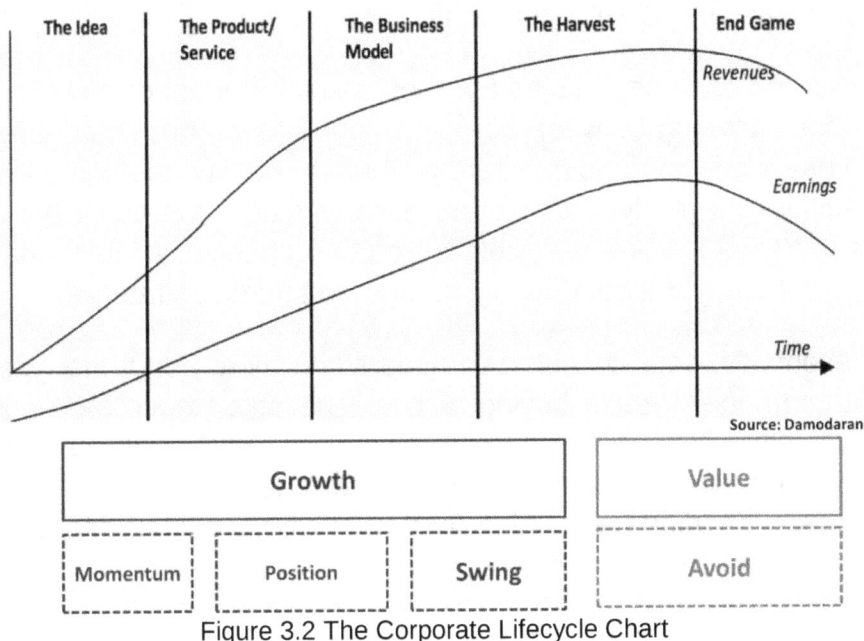

Figure 3.2 The Corporate Lifecycle Chart

Notice at the bottom of this chart that I separated the five life-cycle stages into two main categories, namely, the growth category and the value category.

From a trading perspective, I'm more concerned about picking companies that are in the growth category, when they are still within the idea stage to the early stage of the harvest.

I try to avoid companies that are already in the later stages of the harvest or are already near to their endgame because these companies often or usually trade at lower premiums and have little room for further growth.

So whether you're a momentum trader, position trader or swing trader, having a solid idea of where a company is in its corporate lifecycle stage will help you determine if you're using the right kind of trading strategy on the right type of company.

If the company is still in an idea stage, momentum-trading strategies are usually a better fit.

After the company has established a solid product or business model, growing between 20%–40% per annum, this is the time to use a position-trading strategy. And by the time the company reaches the early phase of its harvest stage, the stock price tends to move around within an orderly channel. At this time, the company will be a perfect fit for swing trading strategies.

Essentially, once you start to understand more about the type of companies you're buying, you will be able to use the right kind of trading strategy on the right stocks. Or if you know what kind of specific trading strategy you want to use, you can then focus on finding companies that meet that corporate lifecycle requirement for your strategy.

People often think that fundamentals are primarily about numbers and that's just not true. If fundamentals are just about numbers, why are companies like Uber valued at 70 billion dollars while making losses of 3.5 billion dollars every year? Why is Tesla valued at a market capitalization of 60 billion dollars when the company is still losing tons of money every year?

The reality is that people are always buying the future. People don't buy the stock of a company for what it is worth today. People are always speculating how much the company might be worth in the future. And the best part about the future is that nobody knows what the future is going to be.

The greater that uncertainty; the higher the volatility and the larger the price inefficiency. This is where smart and alert traders can discover more and better opportunities.

This is the reason why I am always focusing on growth companies for trading opportunities. I suggest that you try to stick to these types of companies as well for your trading ideas. At the end of the day, please remember this: It's not what you think that will move the stock price, it's what the market thinks that will drive the stock price.

Sometimes there are just too many random stories out there for us to filter. This is where I like to use tools to screen for the right kind of stocks and companies.

Typically, people initially screen for stocks for some fundamental data before studying them technically for trading opportunities. But I do it the opposite way. I try to filter for companies that first show signs of technical strength before I analyze their fundamental potential.

For example, if a stock breaks out of its trading range, it is showing me signs of technical strength. I will then figure out whether there is any fundamental story or numbers behind the company to establish whether the breakout move is going to be sustainable or not. That will determine how far we might try to ride the trade if it turns out to be profitable.

In countries like the Philippines or Indonesia, it's straightforward to screen for suitable stocks manually because there is just a limited number of listed companies that we need to be looking at. If I'm trading the big markets like the US market where there are thousands of stocks, I have some filters that I use to screen for the right stocks.

The Five Stock-Screening Criteria to Identify Potential Trading Ideas

The five criteria that I use to screen for stocks are price, market capitalization, volume, three-month price performance, and Relative Strength Index (RSI). Typically, I filter for stocks with a price above $5 per share and a market capitalization between 300 million USD and 20 billion USD. You can exercise some flexibilities if you would like to widen your list of potential trading ideas.

To ensure that there is enough liquidity, it's essential to filter for the trading volume as well.

Usually, I will filter for stocks that have more than 500 thousand shares traded per day. For the three-month price performance criteria, I screen for companies that have moved at least 15% over the past three months because such companies are probably trading way stronger than the index.

Last but not least, I filter for stocks that have an RSI above the 60% mark because that is also an indication of technical strength.

Using this screening method, I can filter down the number of potential stocks from a few thousand into just slightly over a hundred of them. I'll then visually look through the charts of all of these filtered stocks to see if any of them are showing signs of building a technical base, where an overhanging resistance has existed for a while.

As you visually screen through these hundreds of charts, you'll notice stocks at their different stages of price movements. Some might have gone up a lot, some might have gone up too much, and some might still be at the early stages of their initial bases.

Some efforts are required to go through these charts one by one, but that is also how you can indeed find the best opportunities compared to those traders who are too lazy to do this.

I would now like to wrap up some stuff about the screening process with other factors that I consider. The types of companies that I usually look at are in the technology and biotech sectors because these guys are usually in the early stages of their initial bases. This means that there is still more room for these stocks to grow going forward.

If any of these stocks start to break out from their base, I also like to look for trading volume spikes because this proves that there is significant market interest in this stock, which can help fuel further positive sentiments.

Finally, I would like to encourage all the traders out there to do your research. No matter how much research you do, you might not be right all the time. But if you happen to be right and is mentally prepared to take the relevant actions, you will make money at the end of the day.

Out of a hundred trades, you might have seventy or eighty unprofitable ones. But if you are diligent enough to try to understand why they fail and why the rest of the trades were profitable, you'll start to see some forms of similarity and patterns.

Everyone is looking for that perfect trading system, that Holy Grail system that works all the time. The truth is that there's no Holy Grail out there because markets are dynamic in that they become efficient or change over time. So you need to have a system that is going to be flexible enough to adapt to those changes and last you through your entire trading life.

The Top Three Trading Mistakes Made by Traders

I did a survey and asked my trading community for their top trading mistakes so that we can understand the biggest reasons as to why most traders fail (see Figure 3.3).

And the number one mistake and the most common challenge for traders is that they do not cut their losses. When you're entering a trade, always remind yourself that you can be wrong. Pride is not going to save you and ego will kill you.

That's why my number one rule is that I will cut my losses when I am wrong.

1) Not Cutting Losses

2) Emotional (FOMO)

3) Overtrading / Boredom

Figure 3.3 Survey On the Top Trading Mistakes

The second and third top mistakes that traders make is the fear of missing out and not following trading plans.

Similarly, these are mainly emotional and psychological issues. That's why it is so important to build the discipline to trade according to a rule-based system.

Only with a system can you remove as much emotion as possible from your trading actions.

And of course, overtrading and boredom is another common mistake that traders make. And that is due to a lack of patience and discipline. If there is nothing to do, please just sit and wait. Wait for that one good trade before you do anything at all.

Here are the things that can help you to remedy these trading mistakes more easily. Try to keep a trading journal. Learn something new every day and jot down everything about your trades. Why did you buy? Why did you sell? Most people just do a mental review in their mind after they are done for the day but never write down their thoughts and feelings.

I strongly encourage you to write things down because when you write something down, you will remember ten times better. Journaling is not just about recognizing the losing trades but also to recall the profitable trades as well.

Some traders think that losses are bad and winners are good—it's not always the case. A losing trade can be a good trade if you're disciplined enough to cut your losses. A winning trade can be a bad trade if you violate your rules along the way.

That's why you should keep a journal to remind yourself to be objective all the time. Review your journal every day after the market closes. Do more of the right things and do less of the wrong things. Keep searching for that one good trade with the proper process, and you'll get there one day. Thanks for listening and I hope my short presentation was helpful.

Philip: Thanks again for sharing your trading methodology, Edmund. It's refreshing to hear how you incorporate fundamentals and company stories into your trading analysis to find that one good trade.

You mentioned in your presentation that you screen for companies that are forming good initial bases, having good stories, and you will buy when the price breaks out from their bases. Do you advocate getting in straight during the breakout or do you advocate waiting further to see if the price stabilizes above that breakout point?

Edmund: Usually, I buy a stock in three tranches. I typically buy 25% of the intended position when it is still in the base, 25% when it breaks out of the base, and the final 50% after the price starts to experience some kind of pullback.

Managing Your Losses Using The Value-At-Risk Methodology

Philip: You mentioned that cutting losses is something vital. How do you go about deciding when to take a loss?

Edmund: I use this risk management methodology call Value at Risk (VAR). For every single trade that I do, I know the VAR for that trade and how much I can potentially lose. For example, if I have a $10,000 portfolio and I enter a trade with a VAR of 1%, this means that if I cut my loss on that trade, I will lose a maximum of $100.

If I apply a VAR of 1% on every one of my trades, theoretically it means that I have to lose 100 times before I go bankrupt. I usually place my stop-loss level at the bottom of the base and then calculate accordingly how many shares to buy to ensure that my VAR for that trade is contained within my parameter.

Philip: Let's explore a hypothetical situation. Let's say that you found a company with a great story. The price of that stock has just broken out of its base, and you decided to buy the stock.

You established your stop-loss level and then calculated the number of shares to buy according to your VAR methodology. You entered the trade and waited for the trade to do its magic. Unfortunately, instead of running higher immediately, the price fell and touched your stop-loss level.

As a disciplined trader who follows your trading rules, you got out of that trade at your pre-determined stop-loss level with a small loss. You felt disappointed because that fantastic story about the company is still fresh in your mind.

How do you reconcile this psychological conflict? Do you think about getting back into this trade again? Or do you just leave it alone and stay out for a while to avoid letting your emotions run riot?

Edmund: This happens to me a lot of times, Philip. When a stock breaks out of its base, it might just come back into the base again. That is a fact of life we have to accept because it doesn't mean that if a breakout happens, the price is just going to shoot up right away.

That's why I always sell half of my position if the price falls back into the base and will look to redeploy back into the company again when another bullish breakout happens. Don't forget that my original stop-loss is still pegged to the bottom of the initial base. If the price continues to fall and breaks this base low, I will exit my entire position in this stock.

Philip: When that happens, will you just dump the story aside and re-evaluate this stock again just as you would for the rest of the other potential trading ideas?

Edmund: Yes. Price always comes first, and the story comes second.

Philip: Let's say the trade worked in your favor. How do you decide where and when to take a profit? Is it based on a story, a technical trailing stop or a specific profit target?

How to Use Profit Target and Trailing Stop to Exit Profitable Trades

Edmund: There are two kinds of profit-taking exits that I use. The first kind is based on a target price, but my target price is usually very far away.

The second kind is based on a trailing stop using a moving average. Depending on the formation of the price movement, I sometimes use a 10-day EMA as the trailing stop, but in most cases, I prefer to use the 20-day EMA to allow the price more room to fluctuate.

I will typically sell half of my position when the trailing stop is hit and exit the balance if the prices fall through the immediate base. However, if another base has formed just under the trailing stop, I might try to look for opportunities to get back in again if there is another bullish breakout at this new base.

Philip: What are some of the potential downsides and risks a trader needs to think about when trying to implement the trading methodology that you advocate?

Edmund: Yes, a black swan event is what I like to bring to the awareness of any trader. There is always a possibility that things don't go your way or based on what you planned. There will be surprises that you didn't anticipate but can have a significant impact on your positions.

For example, the price movement of US stocks can be so efficient that when a surprise earning report is announced, you might see a sudden price gap down. These are the potential situations that you need to take into consideration.

Philip: You mentioned earlier that you treat each stock as an idea on its own in terms of how you determine the stop-loss and how you size your trade. How would you look at your entire holdings and your open positions from a portfolio perspective? Do you adjust your positions and holdings along the way as any of the trades get very profitable, or do you let each of the trades run fully based on their own potential?

Edmund: I try to scale out as markets become very expensive. Even though the individual stocks may still be showing signs of strength, the strength of the broad market is still what matters the most. Much of my risk appetite is making bets during the early stages of the bases of the global markets. But as the broad market becomes massively overbought, I don't want to establish more individual positions.

Philip: Let's imagine this scenario in which global markets are very bullish. You have fully deployed your capital in the markets that you decided to have exposure in. Somehow another great idea turns up in your filtering and satisfies the entire FTSR framework that you use to analyze an idea.

What do you do? Do you just ignore this idea? Do you exit some of the existing positions so that you have the capacity to take on this new trade? Or do you look into using leverage to take on this new idea?

Edmund: It hasn't come to a point where I have had to do that. But should a stock appear in my screener, and I find that the best opportunity to enter has arrived, I wouldn't mind using margin and leverage to get into this trade.

How to Prepare for The Inevitable Bearish Market Downturn

Philip: Over the past ten years, since the end of the subprime crisis, it has been a boom market for most global markets. As we know, nothing goes up forever. What would be your strategy in anticipating a bearish market downturn or a global recession? How will you trade the market when the inevitable finally arrives?

Edmund: I am constantly monitoring the markets for a key reversal of trend using moving averages as my primary tool. I'm always watching the 50-day and the 200-day EMA and using those parameters as the basis to adjust my trailing stops.

Philip: In a way, all of your individual trades already have some predetermined level that if it starts to roll over, you will automatically get out of the trade?

Edmund: Yep, that's right.

Philip: Let's say 80% of your open positions hit your trailing stops and they got closed out as a result. As this could mean a major change of the trend and tide, do you start to look at shorting the market? Or do you simply sit out and just observe the market as it trends lower from there?

Edmund: To be honest, shorting is not my forte. I don't short because I feel that there's a lot of risks when it comes to shorting. Losses are unlimited when it comes to shorting. I will only consider shorting if I think there is a huge systematic risk happening in the entire market. In the last eight years, I've never shorted anything substantially.

Philip: Edmund, I think we've benefited greatly from your insights about your trading methodology and trading style. Before we end this session, I was wondering if you could share some words of wisdom and inspiration to the traders out there to help them navigate their trading journey more smoothly?

Edmund: Sure. I want to congratulate everyone who has taken the first step to join this summit to learn. I believe that everyone will ultimately have his own trading journey and a trading strategy that works for him.

One thing that I really would like to emphasize is this: Please don't compare yourself with other traders. Learn to find what works for you.

There are so many profitable trading systems out there, but not all of these systems will be a good fit for you. Take your time. I've seen traders who have not been profitable for five to six years, but when they finally discovered a methodology that works for them, they start to become proficient and profitable very quickly after that.

For short-term traders, their learning curve is obviously going to be shorter because they execute a much higher number of trades within a specific timeframe compared to long-term position traders. With five to six months of consistent learning, trading, and reviewing, a short-term trader might get his enlightenment sooner.

The secret to understanding trading and becoming successful is that you need to put in the time, you need to be disciplined, and you need to be patient. The longer you stay here in the market without taking a big hit, the higher your chance of making it in time to come.

If you're losing, just make sure your losses are small. Learn from it and don't be afraid to continue executing your trading plan. Keep a trading journal and review it often. Over time, you will start to learn what are the key things you need to focus on to find that next good trade. Good luck to everybody.

Philip: That's fantastic advice, Edmund. Thank you so much for your time and wish you the very best of luck too!

BRAMESH BHANDARI: The Prolific Trading Mentor Who Runs India's Top Trading Blog

> *As a trader, you need to remember that you are nothing in the face of the market. You cannot control the market but as an individual, you can control yourself.*

Bramesh Bhandari is a trader, educator, analyst, and author who has been persistently sharing his insights on risk management strategies, edge development, strategy construction, and basic market trading education through his blog Bramesh Tech Analysis, which was awarded the best stock blog by the IndiBlogger Awards in 2013.

His prolific trading blog was how I got to know about Bramesh in the first place.

Through his blog, Bramesh facilitates traders with the technical analysis of stocks, derivatives, futures, and commodities, and helps them understand the market dynamics of the trading world with the extensive use of a mechanical trading system. His array of independent analysis and training sessions provide traders with the right framework to make informed and better investment decisions.

Bramesh also actively contributes to the renowned *Futures Magazine* and has garnered appreciation there as well. Apart from regularly updating the blog, he also provides online tutoring to professional traders, stock traders, commodity traders, and beginner or new traders.

His expertise in the area of technical analysis has empowered many traders and organizations to adopt a pragmatic approach towards profitable yet vulnerable markets.

In his presentation, Bramesh elaborated on the numerous trading psychological issues that most traders are burdened with before offering his actionable suggestions on how to overcome them.

Philip: Hi, Bramesh. I'm happy to have you on board this summit to share your expertise on trading psychology with the summit participants. For a start, could you tell us a little bit about your trading background? How did you get started in trading?

Bramesh: I've been trading the Indian market for more than a decade now, and it all started during my college years. Back during the year 2003, the Indian bull market was just beginning, and my father was into stock investing.

That was when I started learning about the stock market from a fundamental perspective. By 2006 to 2007, we were witnessing the mother of all bull runs in India. Everyone was making money as long as they were buying and holding on to stocks. But when the big crash in 2008 happened, people were losing money everywhere.

Generally, I think that fundamental analysis is good because it provides me the confidence to enter a stock. But knowing when to exit is the main criterion for both trading and investing, and for that I didn't think fundamentals are helpful.

During those years, I was also observing the prices of the shares that my father bought. I noticed certain patterns happening in the price movements, and that kick-started my interest in technical analysis.

Over time, I realized that I was not so inclined on the investing side. Rather, I was more interested in the trading side. My interest in technical analysis started evolving from there.

In 2009, I got interested in WD Gann's methodology and have been using it for almost eight years now. It is very complicated, but over a period of time, I found my edge in using that particular strategy. Since then I've been trading indices and stocks.

Philip: I understand you have a very popular trading blog on technical analysis and trading. Why were you inspired to start this blog and did you in your wildest dreams expect that this blog would be so popular now in India?

Bramesh: When I first started my trading journey, I wanted to learn but couldn't find a proper source for that. Reading books was helpful, but it was not enough.

Personally, I felt that I needed a mentor, but unfortunately, I was not able to find a proper mentor in India. Because of this, I had to develop a lot of things on my own. I had to go through the learning curve of losing trades and understanding that these are the major problems that I have.

I know there are many Indians out there just like me, entering the market as beginners but not knowing where to start or what to do. I wanted to help others avoid the problems that I faced. If I can guide even a few people and make their trading journey a little easier, I will be happy. That's why I decided to start a blog to share my personal trading experiences with other fellow traders.

Building The Mental Strength to Take in Whatever the Market Throws at You

Philip: When I first invited you to join this online trading summit, you decided very quickly that you wanted to talk about trading psychology. Why is that the case?

Bramesh: Based on my own experience trading in the market for more than a decade, I firmly believe that 15% of a trader's success comes from risk management, 15% from trading strategy and the remaining 70% from how mentally strong he is. When the market is running in a one-sided manner as it does during a bull run, it's easy to make money.

Trading is the only profession in the world where you can be right just 50 percent of the time and still make money. If you just hit a buy button in a bull market, you will most likely make money. But when the market starts going sideways, that's where your real mental strength is checked.

When the market is volatile or when the market is frequently hitting a trader's stop-loss orders, the trader who is new to the market will think that his strategy has stopped working. It's not that the approach has stopped working; it's just that the market is not willing to give you money then.

Having the mental strength to stay in the market, to accept your losses, to let your profits run over a period of time, that is where trading psychology plays a very critical role.

In the heat of the moment, you have to be in control of yourself and not fall prey to your emotions and do stupid things that blow up your trading account. I believe that psychology plays a very crucial role in the success of any trader in the market, and that's why I want to focus on this for my presentation.

Philip: Fantastic. I look forward to you sharing your ideas, Bramesh. I'll hand the stage over to you right now.

Bramesh: Thank you, Philip. There is this saying that 95% of the traders out there ultimately fail and only 5% become successful traders. To be a successful trader, I believe that our intellect and emotion must work as a team, and trading psychology is the biggest piece of the trading puzzle.

So what is trading psychology? Trading psychology refers to all the human impulses that have an effect on the market. Trading psychology is a necessary discipline that needs to be studied and understood by anyone who aims to achieve long-term success in the financial markets. Self-mastery and emotional control are vital to attaining consistency when trading.

Most of what you do while you trade takes place within your own mind. Trading psychology is more about understanding how our brain works than it is about controlling emotions.

Why are professional tennis players like Roger Federer and Novak Djokovic so masterful in their games? One of the key reasons is that in the heat of the moment of the game, they're able to control themselves. They don't allow their opponents to have a psychological upper hand over them during the game.

Trading psychology is the perception change that you go through once you're active in the markets. The important thing here is that you're trading your own money.

When you trade using a demo account, it might seem easy for you to make money. It looks like it will be just as easy to make money using a live account. But when you start putting on your first live trade, you start to feel indecisive about when to enter, when to cut your losses or when to take profit. This is basically the effect of trading psychology.

As you enter and exit more trades, you start to see your hard-earned money growing and shrinking in your trading account. Because your money is on the line, you begin to feel excited, disappointed, greedy, fearful, etc. And these are the emotions that will cause you to do the wrong things in trading.

You're fighting against hundreds of thousands of other traders out there. You're fighting with institutional traders, and you're competing against those high-frequency-trading algorithms. They're all there to take a bite of your money. You have to protect yourself against them, and the only thing you have control over in such situations is yourself and what you do.

For example, when you're in the heat of a trade and in the midst of losing, what do you have control over? You can choose to hold on to your losses, or you can choose to exit with a minimal loss and look for the next opportunity again. Which will you choose?

As a trader, you need to remember that you're nothing in the face of the market. You can't control the market, but as an individual, you can control yourself. You can control your trading decisions; you can stop being an impulsive trader. You can choose to stop trading when you know that the market is not willing to give you money.

When you can control yourself in such situations, you will then be able to move on to the next level.

Seven Typical Psychological Issues That Traders Face

Here are some of the typical psychological problems that traders face and the bad decisions they might make as a result.

One of the main psychological issues that most traders encounter is the loss-aversion mindset. Loss aversion promotes the irrational actions of cutting trades prematurely and holding on to losing trades longer than necessary.

Most traders tend to close their winning trades too early even though they know their trading setup is solid.

For example, you're fully confident in your strategy, you're fully convinced of your trading setup, but when the trade goes in your direction, you start to worry about giving that profit back to the market. You decide to take your profit earlier than your planned profit target. The psychological issue of "loss aversion in profit" is in play here.

The loss aversion nature in you will also result in your failure to cut your losses when you have the opportunity to. When a trade is not working out as anticipated, you hold on to the position hoping that the market will turn back around and give you a chance to get out at the breakeven level. Because you are afraid to realize your loss, you decide to hold on to the trade.

Another problem that many traders face is the inability to pull the trigger when presented with an excellent trading setup. It might be because his past few trades were losers and that created an impression in his mind that this will be a losing trade as well. This is also a loss-aversion psychological issue.

The next mistake that a trader might make is even worse than the previous one. He adds to a losing position in the hope that the market will turn around and offer him a lower breakeven price to get out.

He believes that the price will not go down forever and when the price recovers, he will reap the benefit of his averaging down. Typically, good traders pyramid on winning trades and bad traders average down on their losing trades.

Fear is another psychological issue that affects most traders. Fear is a negatively charged emotion or feeling often associated with a sense of danger, whether it is real or imagined. Fear doesn't arise from regular activities that you participate in. Fear arises due to events that you are not expecting to happen.

From a trading perspective, fear arises because you have no idea whether you are going to make money or lose money in the next trade. Fear will also be compounded in such situations if you take a large position in that trade.

However, if you enter the trade with the full thought process that this trade can turn into a loss, and if your position size is within your risk appetite, you will not be overpowered so easily by your fear.

Overconfidence is what happens when you enter the market and start making money immediately. Just because you make a certain percentage of return in the first month, you expect to double your profits in the next month. Overconfidence causes you to have unrealistic expectations and take excessive risks. When the tide finally turns, you end up blowing up your trading account.

Please don't have unrealistic expectations of the market. Set a realistic target for your returns and focus on the power of compounding. If you can do that, your account will keep growing.

Hope is the painted positive emotion associated with the expectation of meeting your goals, needs from the higher forces, entities or elements. Hope is a useful mindset to have in normal life, but when it comes to trading, you should never depend on hope because the market does not care about you and your concerns.

Be practical in the market, always stick to your plan and your strategies, and you will be in control of your destiny in the financial markets.

Ultimately, the reason why most traders fail to progress and become profitable in the long run is that they're often stuck in the situation of emotional trading. Emotions are inherent to a human being. If emotions were removed, we would not be human beings anymore.

You can't remove your emotions from your trading, but you can control your emotions. You can start by acknowledging that you have certain emotional issues. If you don't recognize your problem, you won't look for a solution. Once you acknowledge you have a psychological problem, try to understand why you have that issue.

Find the root cause of that emotion so that you can start working on some actions to keep that emotion under control.

The ability to control your emotions will not happen overnight just like you can't build a six-pack on your stomach in one day. You have to develop this competency over time by coming up with a plan, follow the plan diligently, and turn that action into a habit. This is how you can bring your trading to the next level.

Using a Systematic Process to Set Your Trading Goals

Goal setting is essential in trading. I love this particular quote by Brian Tracy: "You can be successful in anything if you set a goal and take action. But you must acquire the knowledge to accomplish those goals." It is ok to have a big goal like "I want to run a hedge fund" or "I want to make a million dollars from trading." But it can be overwhelming if you try to reach for such big goals right from the start.

If you have the goal of building a hundred-story building, you have to lay the foundation first, which usually takes the longest time. After that, you start building the first floor, second floor, and so on. Try to start with a smaller goal and achieve that modest goal first. Lay a strong foundation, and over time keep adding bigger goals until the day you reach your ultimate goal.

Here's a trading system that you can use to work toward your goal through a systematic process.

First, start by learning a trading method. Then back-test the method for as many years back as you can so that you can see how the method is working out across different market cycles and market scenarios. When you're done with that, open a trading account with a small amount of money.

If you're able to see this small trading account grow consistently over time as you trade it live with your trading method, then you can start funding a larger amount.

Once you start to execute trades, this is when the psychological issues that I talked about earlier will come into the picture. If you start your trading journey with a losing streak (which is part and parcel of trading), you start feeling fearful. This is where you need to use mental conditioning to help you overcome your fear.

If you start your trading journey and encounter a winning streak (due to beginners' luck), you become greedy. This is also when you need to apply mental conditioning to control your emotions. Otherwise, you might start to risk excessively and end up blowing up your account.

Despite all these emotions you encounter, if you're able to stay on and just continue to apply your trading method without blowing up your account, that is a great achievement, as you will gradually be on the path to generate consistent profits after that. But if you're not able to handle your emotions, you will ultimately end up blowing up your account.

By then, you can decide whether to fund your account and try all over again, or you can simply choose to close your account if you think trading is not for you.

How to Develop a Conscious Mind to Drive Your Trading Actions

Let's talk about mental conditioning. Most traders have two minds: one is the conscious mind, and the other is the unconscious mind.

When you're a new trader, you trade mainly using your unconscious mind. Your unconscious mind is the driving force that tells you that you want to make a lot of money, you want to buy a lot of fancy things and that trading is not as hard as you think.

You randomly watch charts, enter trades, and exit trades simply by following your unconscious mind's instruction. If you keep allowing your unconscious mind to drive your trading actions, you can never become a good trader.

To become a proficient trader, you have to develop your conscious mind. The conscious mind is like a tutorial as if someone is mentoring you and telling you how you should avoid making mistakes. If you've been trading over some time and have analyzed the mistakes that you made along the way, these personal experiences will also become part of your conscious mind.

Another way to develop a conscious mind is to pay attention to your body signals. For example, if you've opened a trade and you're feeling fear, your hands might start sweating. You might start feeling some gulp in your throat, or you will have butterflies in your stomach. You will not be able to concentrate, and your heart rate will keep increasing. These are all the basic body signals you might experience when you are experiencing fear or greed.

Visualization is a technique that I like to encourage traders to use to develop their conscious mind. Before you start your trading day, try to spend 5–10 minutes sitting in silence. Visualize yourself taking trades, visualize yourself cutting losses and imagine yourself taking profits. Visualize unexpected events happening during your trade and how you handle the situation.

For example, imagine yourself trying to get out of a trade, but suddenly you have connectivity issues to your trading system. Imagine when you have an open position, some big news broke, and your position starts going against you.

Visualize all these possible scenarios and think about how you will handle them calmly and effectively. If you're able to practice this diligently, you will automatically be at peace with yourself during trading. This is how you start to grow from being an amateur trader to a proficient trader.

I think Emotional Quotient (EQ) is very important for a trader. I have an emotions checklist that I run through 15 minutes before trading starts. I will ask myself, "Am I happy about trading or am I stressed about trading?" If you're feeling stressed, you might be feeling unwell, or you might be having some other problems in your life.

The fact is that if you're feeling stressed, you can always stop trading. Not every day is a good trading day.

If you want to become a profitable trader, you need to have the courage to just sit out if you're not in the right frame of mind to trade. Or if you have achieved your goal for the day or the week, you can simply stay out of the market as well.

This is one of the reasons why I started writing a blog. After I'm done with reaching my goal and I don't have anything else to do, I'll start blogging. This prevents me from making impulsive trades because I have time on my hands and there's nothing to keep me occupied.

The next question I ask myself is "Am I alert and energetic while trading?" This is where you need to learn how to take care of your body. Make sure you have good food habits when you start trading. Many of the good decisions you make as a trader are dependent on your energy level and the level of glucose in your body, which depends on how well you have fed yourself.

Have a good breakfast and be very well hydrated so that your glucose level can be at the right level and you can make better trading decisions. When I look back on those trading days when I was not feeling alert and energetic, I often made lousy trading decisions that led me to get hit with significant losses. So nowadays, I make sure I eat healthily and have at least six hours of good sleep.

I will then go on to ask myself, "Am I satisfied or frustrated with my trading?" Generally, there should be a certain level of satisfaction that you have in your trading; otherwise, it's hard to find the motivation to continue.

If you can't find satisfaction in your trading, it could be that your trading goals are too big or too unrealistic. You can try to make your goals more realistic and pat yourself on the shoulder when you achieve those goals.

Finally, I'd like to share what I think is a good trading day for me. Maybe you can use it as a reference to construct the steps to achieve a good trading day for yourself. A good trading day, in my opinion, is a day in which I follow my trading strategy in a calm and confident manner. At the same time, I make sure that I'm managing my money well, whether in gains or in losses.

All of these will, in turn, enhance my profits and consistency and help me become a truly successful trader who can trade for a living. This is my definition of a good trading day. If you can define for yourself what is considered a good trading day for you and focus on doing that, you will be much closer to being a profitable trader. Thank you.

Philip: Thanks for sharing your experiences about managing your trading psychology as a trader. On the topic of managing trading psychology, there is an argument that using a systematic trading workflow is better than using a discretionary trading workflow. What is your take on this?

The Difference Between Discretionary Trading and Systematic Trading

Bramesh: From my experiences, creativity is an essential part of trading. When you're a pure systematic trader, you're just focusing on the system signals. When the market goes into a choppy mode, you might just end up blowing up your trading account.

Personally, I believe that a good trader should be a combination of a systematic and discretionary trader. Systematic trading can help with risk management and money management part, but a discretionary mind is still required to decide what kind of trading strategies to use in what type of market conditions.

Ultimately, whether a trader decides to become a systematic trader or a discretionary trader or both, that is an individual decision. Emotions are not removed from a systematic trader even if he is using a set of rules or algorithms because he can always choose to meddle with his system when he is emotional.

On the other hand, a discretionary trader finds his edge based on his intuition that he develops over time. A discretionary trader also has his trading plan and rules. Because of the strong intuition a discretionary trader has built up over the years, he might make slight adjustments to his rules to take advantage of a change in the market environment more quickly.

Philip: What you mean is that as a systematic trader, there will be times when your system doesn't work, and that's when your psychology will come into the picture again?

Bramesh: Yes. Situations like this will definitely happen. Markets are dynamic; what worked yesterday might not work anymore today. The system that you were following and making money with last year might not work this year.

As a trader, you have to be creative enough to know when things are not working, and you should just stop trading. At the same time, you need to develop that flexibility to re-enter the market when the market becomes conducive again.

The Impact of Trading Psychology On Intraday Traders and Swing Traders

Philip: Do you think psychology has a different degree of influence on a shorter-term intraday trader versus a longer-term swing trader? If I'm starting off as a new trader, which style of trading is easier for me to handle from a psychological perspective?

Bramesh: Trading psychology will impact you whether you're an intraday trader or a swing trader. As an intraday trader, you can enter and exit the trade at any point in time in situations of uncertainty and stress. But in a longer horizon trade or a swing trade, you have to accept the overnight risk.

If you're a swing trader and don't have proper trading psychology, how will you react when the market opens against you significantly or gaps down sharply during the market open? You might end up averaging down on that losing trade.

That's why I feel that trading psychology plays a more critical role when you're carrying an overnight position. Black swan events happen once in a while, but if you don't know how to handle those events psychologically, you might take an even bigger loss.

Whether you're an intraday trader, swing trader, or position trader, what matters is your position size. As an independent trader taking overnight positions, I always ask myself what if my positions open sharply lower and breach the circuit breaker tomorrow? Can I survive that kind of loss? Am I sizing my trades in a way that can withstand such events?

Meanwhile, many intraday traders operate on high leverage without using proper position sizing. If something happens and the market swings wildly against them, it is possible for them to blow up their accounts on the same day.

If you're a new trader, whether you choose to start with intraday trading or swing trading, focus on building up your risk and money management competency quickly.

If you have an optimal position size for all your trades, you will always end up surviving in the market. And if you can survive in the market for one year without blowing up your account, you most likely would have developed a skill set in money management and risk management.

Philip: Do you think it's helpful for a trader to be in a community with like-minded people so that they can continue to encourage one another and to look out for one another? Or do you think that being in a trading community might cause more issues to a trader's trading psychology?

Bramesh: It depends on what kind of people are in that community. There are people who are always there to pull you down.

This might be counterintuitive, but personally, I think that being a full-time independent trader is a lonely proposition. It is difficult to match your bandwidth to another individual trader because you might have a higher risk appetite while the other person might have a lower risk appetite, for example.

Even for like-minded groups of traders, their risk management and trading methodologies might also differ over time. This is why I suggest that you develop your skills on your own and have a few selective trading mentors or trading buddies as your accountability partners. Meanwhile, I encourage you to avoid those social media groups, twitters, financial or news television channels.

Philip: You mentioned that 95% of traders fail and only 5% become successful traders. As a new trader, I might find it a psychological hurdle even to convince myself that I can be in that group of successful traders. How would you suggest a trader overcome this limiting mindset?

Bramesh: Like any other profession, becoming a new trader is like joining a new job, or starting a new business. You can't dream of doing big things immediately. You have to develop confidence and trading skills over time. Your trading skills will come from the hard work that you put in before, during, and after market hours.

If you can develop your risk and money management competencies, if you can control your emotions, if you have a strategy that you believe in, you will stand a good chance of becoming a successful trader.

From my personal experience, most of the people that I see entering the market as new traders are often highly undisciplined guys who don't know what they're doing. These are the people who constitute the bulk of those 95% failed traders.

There's no rocket science behind trading. Follow your trading system, keep doing things that make money, and stop doing those things that don't. If you can keep learning and executing and still survive over a period of time, you'll end up becoming the trader that you aspire to be.

Philip: Before we conclude our discussion, do you have any last words for the new aspiring traders out there?

Bramesh: There is a quote that I like very much and have pasted on my trading desk to provide me with a constant reminder and inspiration. "Failure is an event, not a person. An event fails, a person doesn't."

So never give up because reinvention is the name of the game. You have to keep reinventing yourself. Never say quit, and continue to hone your trading skills in the market. If you can survive in the market, the money will ultimately come.

Philip: Thank you so much for your time, Bramesh. All the best to you, and I hope to chat with you again.

Bramesh: Thank you, Philip. It was very nice chatting with you, too. And the best of luck to everyone.

PART 2
SYSTEMATIC TRADERS

LOUISE BEDFORD: The Most Compelling Trading Mentor from Australia with a Passion for Candlestick Charting

> *" I think sometimes you have to be smart enough to write a trading plan, but dumb enough to stick with it.*

Louise Bedford is one of the leading trading educators in Australia, with more than 20 years of experience in the markets and has trained thousands of people over the years to help them maximize their trading potential.

Together with her partner Chris Tate, Louise has been running The Trading Game and it's trading mentor program in Australia since 2000.

She is also one of Australia's best-selling authors on the stock market for nearly two decades. She has been quoted in more Australian stock trading books than any other trader. Her trading books include *Trading Secrets*, *Charting Secrets*, *Let the Trade Wins Flow*, *The Secret of Candlestick Charting*, and *The Secret of Writing Options*.

Louise is also a highly sought-after keynote speaker. Her presentations are very practical and include time-saving strategies that any trader will need to implement to become a successful trader.

Her key areas of focus are using candlestick charts, trading psychology, pattern detection, the impact of neuropsychology on trading decisions, and trading crisis management.

In her very lively presentation, Louise shared with participants of the Online Trading Summit two unique candlestick patterns that she discovered over the years that have not been widely documented elsewhere. She also divulged a few of her favorite trading strategies using candlestick charts as the foundation.

Philip: Hi, Louise. Welcome to the Online Trading Summit and thanks for taking the time to share your trading knowledge and experiences with the summit participants. Before you start your presentation on how to profit from volatile markets using candlestick charts, I would like you to tell us about your trading journey.

How did you get started in the financial markets and how did you evolve into the trading education work that you are doing today?

Louise: When I was just a teenager, I watched my dad start his trading journey. I saw how we were able to transform our lives from being not very well off, to being able to afford overseas holidays and upgrade our house. That caught my attention and got me interested in trading. So as soon as I was old enough to trade, I started my trading journey as a part-time trader while holding a full-time job.

Five years into my trading journey, I discovered that I had a health issue. I couldn't move my arms for a few years, and because of that, I had to leave my day job as a national sales manager for a big multinational company.

I decided to take a chance on becoming a full-time trader. The transition from a full-time employee to a full-time trader can be very daunting, especially considering I had my health problem at the same time.

Thankfully, I was able to trade profitably by then. Otherwise, I wouldn't have known what I would have done to earn a living. Luckily, I've almost fully recovered now, and I've been a full-time trader since 1996.

Philip: Wow, that was a really long time ago. How long did it take for you to decide to share your experience with other traders and help them along the way to become as proficient and as profitable as you are?

Louise: That thought started when I was still recovering from my health issue. In order to recover the movement in my arms, I needed to go through a series of physiotherapy sessions at the hydrotherapy pool. During those sessions, I got to know a group of patients. We shared our experiences.

Everybody had different issues. We all had disabilities in some way. Many were worried about their financial situations. They could see that I wasn't too worried about my financial situation, so they came to me for advice. That's how I started training people who had disabilities to trade so that they didn't have to stay on welfare. The years have passed, and it has been a lovely journey.

I met my business partner, Chris Tate, a fellow trader, in 1996. I also wrote several best-selling books. Because of the repeat-for-free Mentor Program that I've been running with my business partner for the past 18 years, we now have a beautiful community of traders. We hang out together and hunt for good trading ideas as a pack.

Philip: There are still many questions that I would like to ask you about trading education and community, but before that, I believe that you've prepared a presentation to share with us on how to trade the markets profitably using candlestick charts. I'm going to hand the stage over to you right now, and after that, we'll come back together for the second part of our questions and answers session.

Louise: Fantastic! When I first started trading, I had no idea I would be the most quoted Australian author in other peoples' trading books. I didn't know I'd be quoted in magazines and newspapers, and I certainly didn't expect to be surrounded by so many other traders in the trading community that I've built.

Sometimes I think we underestimate what we can achieve in the long term, and overestimate what we can achieve in the short term. If you're just starting your trading journey, do take heart from my personal experiences that your trading future is still a blank sheet of paper at the moment. If I hadn't started my trading journey back then, I really don't know where I would be today.

Trading has enabled me to buy back my life. Because of trading, I've been able to commit myself to physiotherapy and recover the full use of my arms today. Both my husband and I were able to become full-time parents because of trading.

So if there is only one main thing that you can take out of my presentation, I want you to keep that hope alive that you can use trading to turn your life around. You have no idea what awaits you until you try.

Why You Need to Understand the Nature of Volatile Markets

Now let's get started with today's topic on how to trade volatile markets with candlestick charts. As you've probably guessed, candlestick charting is one of my favorite trading analysis tools.

In this presentation, I'm going to show you some concrete ways on how you can use candlestick charts to trade profitably. First, you need to check whether the charts you are looking at are volatile.

There are different ways of measuring volatility. You might have heard people saying "Wow! The market is so volatile!" You'll hear on the news analysts saying "It's a volatile period." However, this isn't a good way to measure volatility. I'd suggest you start formalizing this.

It's important to look at the peak-to-trough drawdown to see how far things have gone up and down percentage wise. You can consider using a standardized indicator such as the Rate of Change (ROC) indicator or the Average True Range (ATR) indicator to measure the volatility.

Let's say you have a share whose current price is $10 and has an ATR value of $0.10. That means that on an average day, you would expect that share to fluctuate between $9.90 or $10.10 because it's going up or down by $0.10. But is that considered volatile?

Let me introduce to you a concept call ATR percentage. You can try to look for this indicator call ATRV in your charting tool. In some charting software, it's called the ATRVE indicator.

You can then run a 30-period Exponential Moving Average (EMA-30) line over the ATRV line and observe how they are moving relative to each other, as illustrated in Figure 5.1.

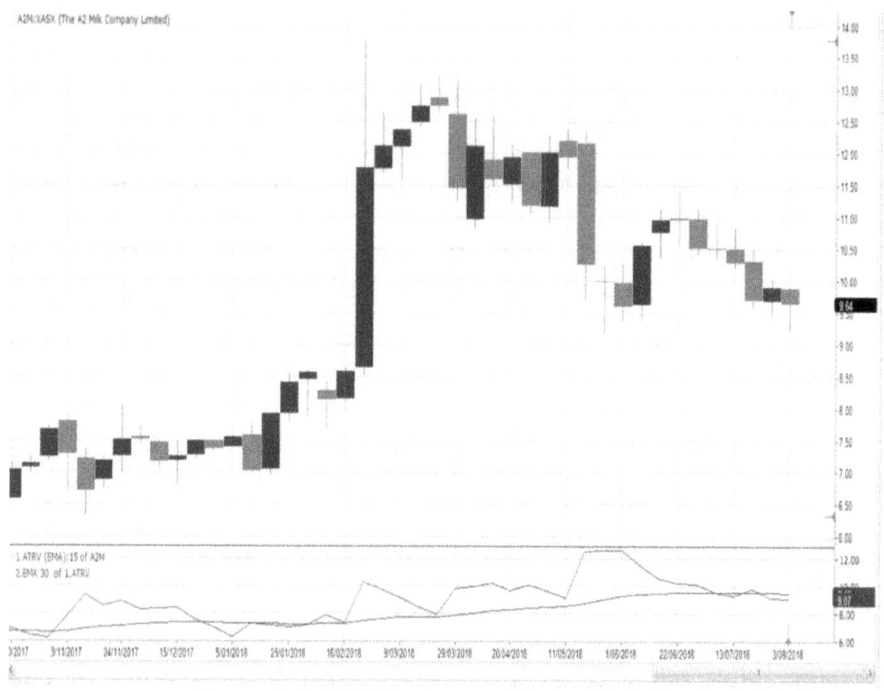

Figure 5.1 ATRV Indicator with EMA-30 line

Usually, the further away the ATRV line is above the EMA-30 line, the more volatile the current price movement is. If the ATRV indicator is hovering below the EMA-30 line, this means the price movement is not volatile.

For those of you who haven't tried this indicator, do give it a shot. It's an easy tool to use, and it is standard in many of the charting tools out there.

Now that we know how to measure volatility, what do we do next? For a start, you need to understand that volatility is not a trend.

As you can see from this chart in Figure 5.2, the price movement is in a lovely uptrend, but the ATRV line is going down.

This is a classic example of a chart trending nicely while its volatility is trending lower. This is the kind of scenario that brings joy to a trader!

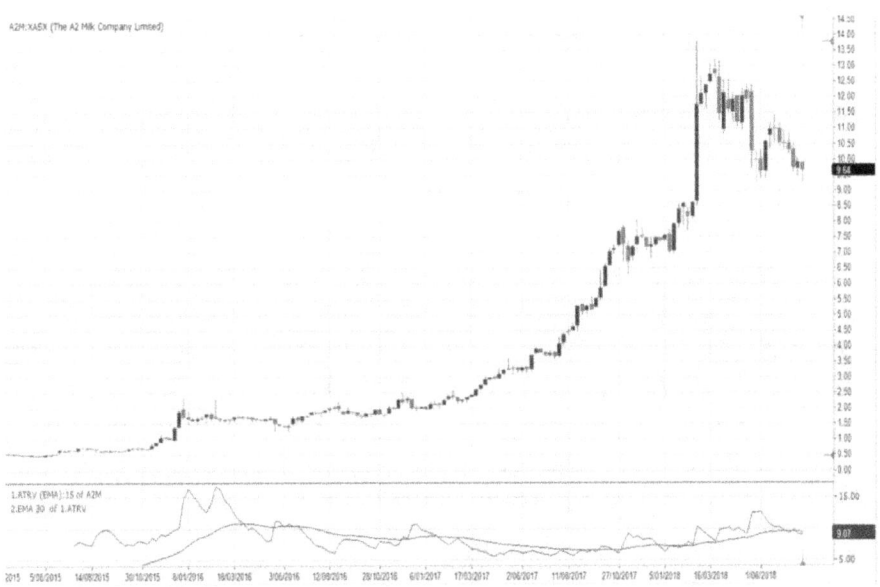

Figure 5.2 Volatility Is Not Equivalent to A Trend

Why is such a scenario important to me? Let me share with you a trading principle. Trading proficiency comes down to specific trading principles that you can use time and time again.

If you understand those principles, you never really have to be concerned about a shiny new idea or strategy interfering with your psychology and mindset.

How to Know When to Seek Risk and When to Avoid Risk

The principle I like to share with you is Risk Seeking versus Risk Avoiding. If a trade is working for you beautifully and you're in paper profits, then you should try to seek risk. So how do you seek risk? You seek risk by pyramiding, by trading more as you make more. However, if you're not in profit, it will be foolhardy to do that.

In fact, if you're making losses in your trades, you need to become risk-averse. The more you lose, the less you should risk. This is called the Anti-Martingale system. Try Googling this term and read more about the concept behind it.

This is a beautiful way to approach money management. If you use this system, your future position sizes will become smaller and smaller as you lose more and more. This will help to protect your capital base during losing streaks so that you have an opportunity to recover when your winning streak comes.

Now that you know the rationale behind risk seeking and being risk-averse, what can you do if the market is volatile? Here are some potential actions you can take. First, longer-term traders should widen their trailing stops during volatile price movements, so that you wouldn't get stopped out so quickly while trying to ride the primary trend.

Second, you can also consider short-term trading during volatile periods because short-term trading can be very profitable during such periods and candlestick charts are perfect for such kind of trading.

Third, you should watch your mindset during volatile periods. I think this is when traders go a little crazy and say. "Oh my gosh, the sky is falling in!" When you're able to remain calm and keep your emotions under control during volatile periods, you'll do very well.

Finally, I suggest that you look to implement windfall profit stops during a volatile period.

Sometimes you might see the price spiking upward in a volatile way. Sometimes it can also spike downwards. When the price climbs very steeply, it is usually unsustainable and will fall as quickly as well after that. As such, you can implement a windfall profit rule in your trading plan when the price spike in the direction of your trade.

Let's assume that you have a long trade and the price spikes up due to a volatile situation and our goal is to take profit quickly on an unexpected price hike, as illustrated in Figure 5.3.

Identify the closing price of the last peak formed and measure four ATR from that level. If the price spikes to that four ATR level, I suggest that you exit one-third of your position and leave two-thirds of your position in to ride the profits.

Figure 5.3 Windfall Profit Example

From my experience, this has been an excellent way to protect my profits by taking money off the table during an event like this.

Once you have formulated your "windfall profit concept" action plan clearly, write it down in your trading plan. Why is there a need to write it down? We do this so that we can honor our commitment to our trading plan.

We like to take shortcuts. We love to make things up on the spur of the moment. We want to think that we know best. However, the best traders are usually the most disciplined ones.

So once you've decided on your trading rules, write them into your trading plan and commit to following through. The best traders that I've trained honor the commitment of their trading plans, and they are also the ones who have achieved amazing lifestyles.

Let's now move into candles. This is my favorite topic in the world. I want to share with you about the specifics behind candles and give you some brand new candlestick patterns that I know you're going to love.

When I started trading, I was first exposed to the bar chart and the line chart. I couldn't relate to them. They didn't have color, and they didn't have movement.

Back in the early nineties, we were still dealing with human brokers, as online trading was not available yet. I remember that I once said to my broker, "I am giving you all of this money for brokerage, but I am not making money. I am sick of it. I need to meet somebody who is trading successfully, and I need to interview them! I need to learn what they're doing. Otherwise, this is over!"

This is a very common phase that most traders go through. Many would have given up there and then.

Fortunately, my broker introduced me to a lady trader that he knows. She used two-minute tick charts to trade, but I didn't have any idea what she was doing when I first got to know her. I asked her, "Oh my goodness, how are you doing all of this? How are you making money and living in this mansion?" She asked me, "Do you use candlesticks?"

I had no idea what she meant as it was so confusing to me. Then she showed me the candlestick charts that she was using and recommended me to do so as well. All of a sudden there were colors, there were movements. It was an enlightenment moment for me, and since then, I never look at other types of charts like bar chart or line chart again.

Now let's have a look to see how we use candles. Candles are a short-term trading instrument. So before you use candles to make your trading decisions, you need to first have a trading setup condition in place.

A trading setup is about determining the medium- to the longer-term trend. As shown in Figure 5.4, these are some of the conditions that you can use to establish the trading setup at any point in time.

 A general environment of conditions that suggest the share is trending. This includes the study of macro patterns such as double tops and bottoms etc.

> → The **Line** family
>
> → The **Moving Average** family
>
> → The **Momentum** family
>
> → The **Volume** family
>
> → The **Pattern** family

Figure 5.4 Trading Setup Conditions

You may choose to use any of these methods to determine a trading setup and then use candlesticks for a trade trigger. A trigger is the specific entry "GO" sign. It's the one that says, "Hey, I'm ready. Enter this trade right now."

You can use candlesticks in any market, whether you're trading stocks, Forex, as long as there are demand and supply and it shows opening, high, low, and closing prices. Candlesticks can help fine-tune your entry methods, and they will give you specific triggers, and that's what I mainly use them for.

The Main Concepts Behind Candlestick Chart Trading

Let me now share with you three concepts behind candlestick charts and then give you some new candlestick patterns that I discovered that you wouldn't find anywhere else.

The first concept about candlesticks is "Indecision." If you see the formation of small candlestick bodies after a significant move, that usually suggests a form of indecision by market participants. Those moments suggest that the chances of the trend reversing have increased significantly (see Figure 5.5).

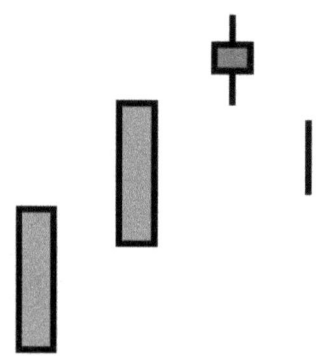

Small Bodies after a Significant Move

Figure 5.5 Indecision by The Market

The second concept is "Decision." This is a candlestick with a long body, and if it's on heavy volume as well, then it might even be called a dominant candlestick.

If you see a long candlestick body appearing as it pushes a vital support or resistance, that is a high-impact event (see Figure 5.6)

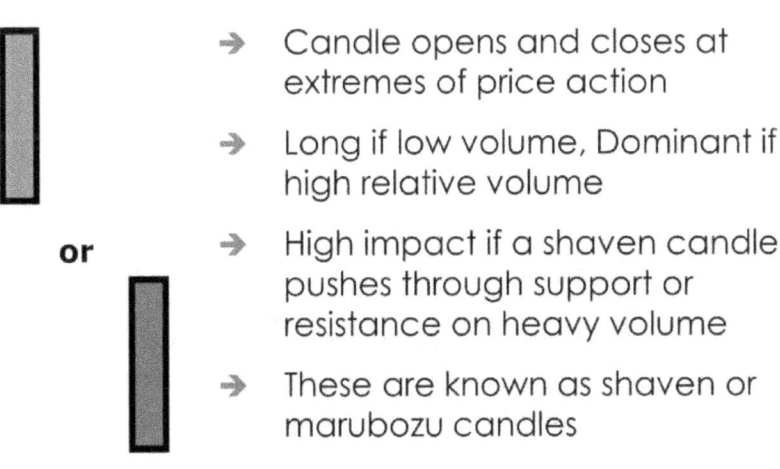

→ Candle opens and closes at extremes of price action

→ Long if low volume, Dominant if high relative volume

→ High impact if a shaven candle pushes through support or resistance on heavy volume

→ These are known as shaven or marubozu candles

Figure 5.6 Decision by The Market

The third candlestick concept is "Rejection". During such situations, you'll observe long lower tails or long upper tails. The tip of the lower tail is where the low of that particular period has been rejected by the market.

Generally, long lower tails suggest that the price is likely to go up while long upper tails suggest the price is likely to go down (see Figure 5.7).

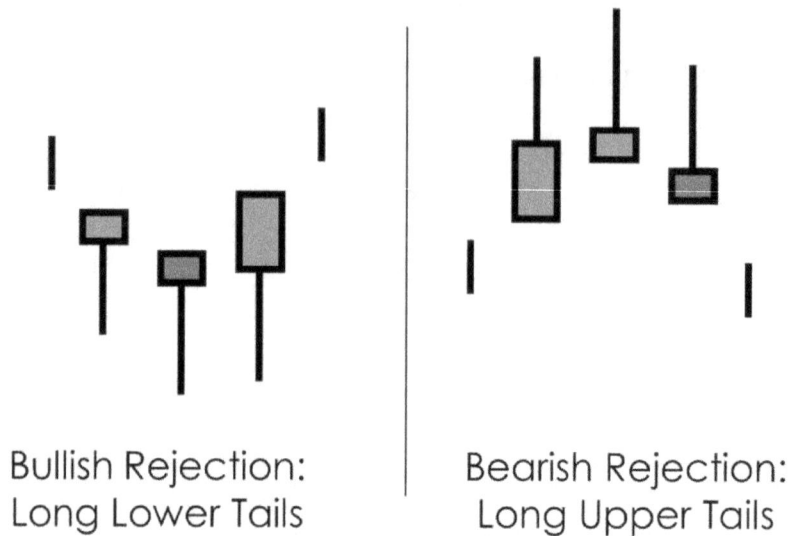

Bullish Rejection: Long Lower Tails

Bearish Rejection: Long Upper Tails

Figure 5.7 Rejection by The Market

Almost every candlestick pattern I know of come from either of these concepts. Even if you can't remember a particular candle pattern, you'll be able to work it out from those three concepts.

There are many ways to use candlesticks. I'm going to summarize my favorite ones, and then we'll go into those new patterns that I told you about.

Bullish breakout is one of those occasions that candlestick can be very useful. If you've got an existing longer-term uptrend and you see the formation of a long green decision candle crossing above a critical resistance level, that can be a trigger to enter on the long side (see Figure 5.8).

- ☑ Breakouts are characterised by a continuation of an existing uptrend, initiated by a green/white candle typically on heavy volume.

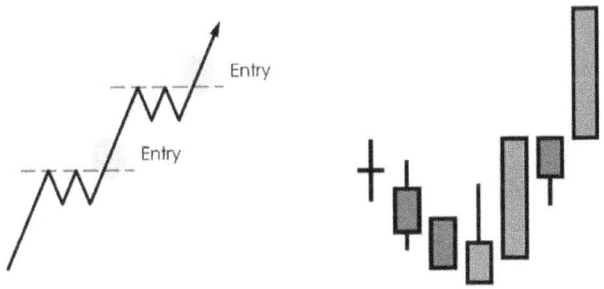

Figure 5.8 Bullish Breakouts

On the other hand, if a long red candle is formed while falling below an important support level in a general downtrend, that is a bearish breakout, and you can consider going short (see Figure 5.9).

- ☑ A continuation pattern of an existing downtrend where a break past support is initiated by a red/black candle.

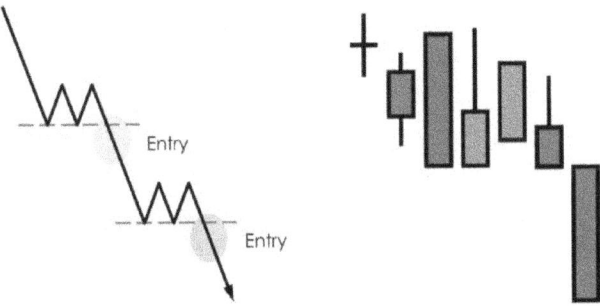

Figure 5.9 Bearish Breakouts

During a bullish retracement, a bottom reversal candlestick pattern can also be used as a trigger to get into a long position during an existing uptrend (see Figure 5.10).

Alternatively, you can also use a top candlestick reversal pattern during an existing downtrend to get into a short position (see Figure 5.11).

- ☑ Trigger into a long position on a bottom candlestick reversal pattern during an existing uptrend.

Figure 5.10 Bullish Retracements

- ☑ Trigger into a short position on a top candlestick reversal pattern during an existing downtrend.

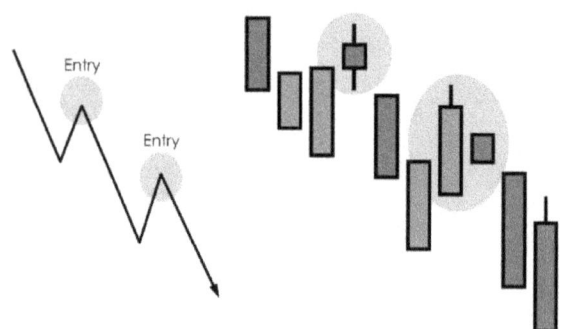

Figure 5.11 Bearish Retracements

Figure 5.12 is an example of a trade that I've taken in the past. You should notice the very clean bullish breakouts with volume increase on multiple occasions. You can use those triggers for the initial entry, or you can use it to pyramid into your existing position.

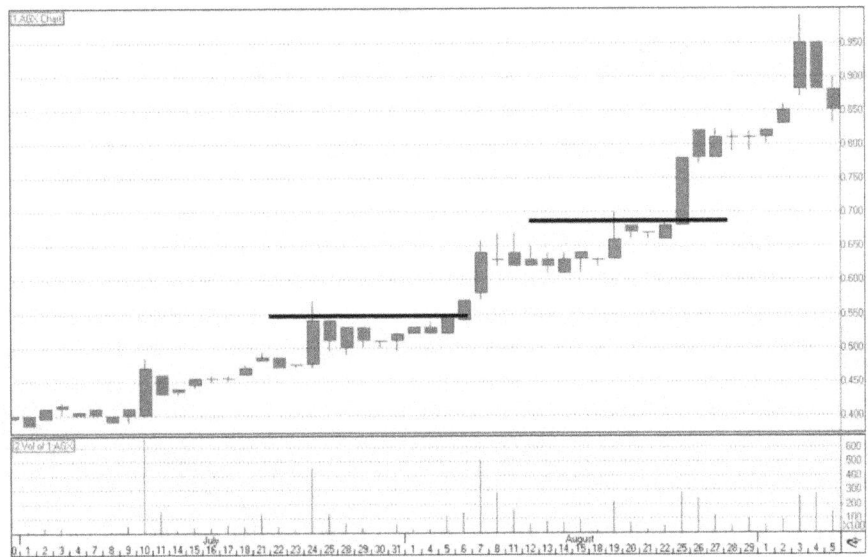

Figure 5.12 Bullish Breakout Example

Remember to take into account the different stages of the market cycle (see Figure 5.13).

In the "Stage 1: Base" and "Stage 2: Uptrend" market cycles, bottom candlestick reversal patterns will be very powerful. Meanwhile, top candlestick reversal patterns can be so punchy during the "Stage 3: Top" or "Stage 4: Downtrend" market cycles.

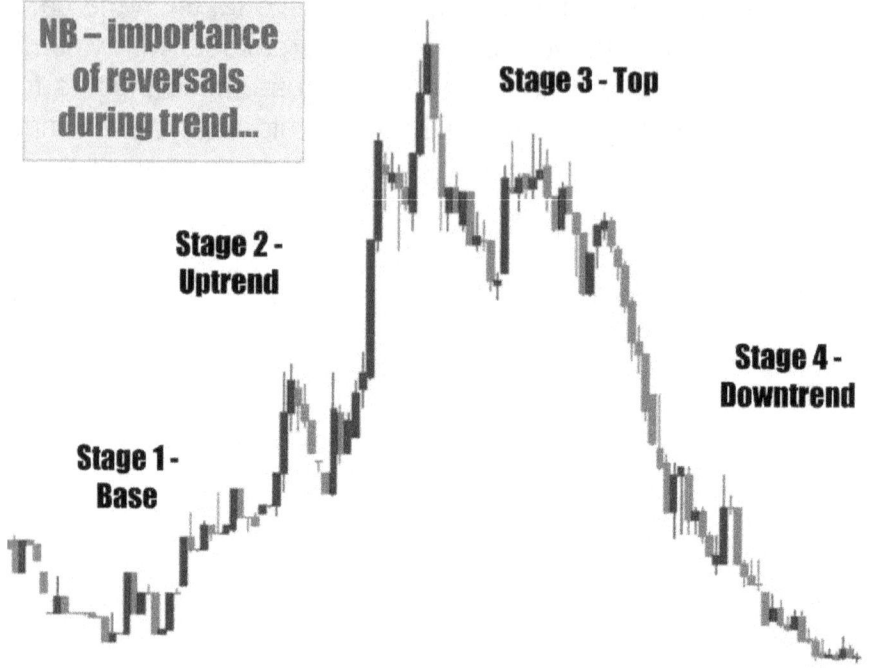

Figure 5.13 Different Stages of the Market Cycle

One important difference to note is that the bulls generally climb the staircase gradually, while the bears usually fall through the elevator shaft quickly. So just be aware that you need to be very sharp and alert during the downtrend stage.

Next, I'm going to show you a list of common high probability patterns (see Figure 5.14). These are my favorite patterns to use on the way up for long trades and on the way down for short trades.

If you're not yet familiar with these patterns, please do some extra studies on them. I've written a book called *The Secret of Candlestick Charting*, and this should be on your "must-read" list. Plus, you'll also enjoy a couple of my other books: *Trading Secrets and Charting Secrets*.

Top Reversals	Bottom Reversals
→ Shooting Stars	→ Hammers
→ Doji	→ Doji
→ Bearish Engulfing Patterns	→ Bullish Engulfing Patterns
→ Dark Cloud Cover	→ Piercing Patterns

Figure 5.14 Common High Probability Candlestick Patterns

The Discovery of 3 New Candlestick Patterns

Right now, I want to share with you three new candlestick patterns that I've discovered that you wouldn't have come across before in other teaching materials out there.

The first one is called the "Inverted Piercing Pattern" (see Figure 5.15). It's one I found several years ago, but I've never discussed it in any of my books.

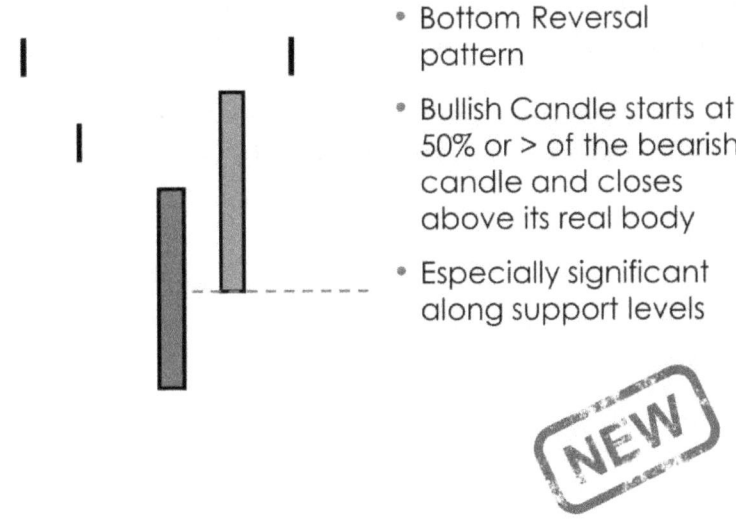

- Bottom Reversal pattern
- Bullish Candle starts at 50% or > of the bearish candle and closes above its real body
- Especially significant along support levels

Figure 5.15 Inverted Piercing Pattern

You might have read about the regular Piercing Pattern where the second candle opens below the closing price of the first candle but rallies higher to end the session at or above the midpoint of the first candle.

However, for this Inverted Piercing Candle, the second candle opens at or above the midpoint of the first candle and then proceeds to rally and close above the first candle's real body.

If you're familiar with candles addition, you will realize that this pattern is actually stronger than a regular Piercing Pattern. Essentially, this Inverted Piercing Pattern adds up to being in the same strength as a Bullish Engulfing Pattern. If you see this pattern forming at an important support level after a significant correction, you can use it as a trigger to get into a bullish reversal trade.

The second new candlestick pattern that I want to share with you is the Inverted Dark Cloud Cover.

The pattern is the opposite pattern of the Inverted Piercing Patter. In this case, the second candle opens around the midpoint of the first candle and fell through the session to close below the body of the first candle (see Figure 5.16).

This is a great bearish reversal candlestick pattern to use and a great one to add into your arsenal of trade triggers.

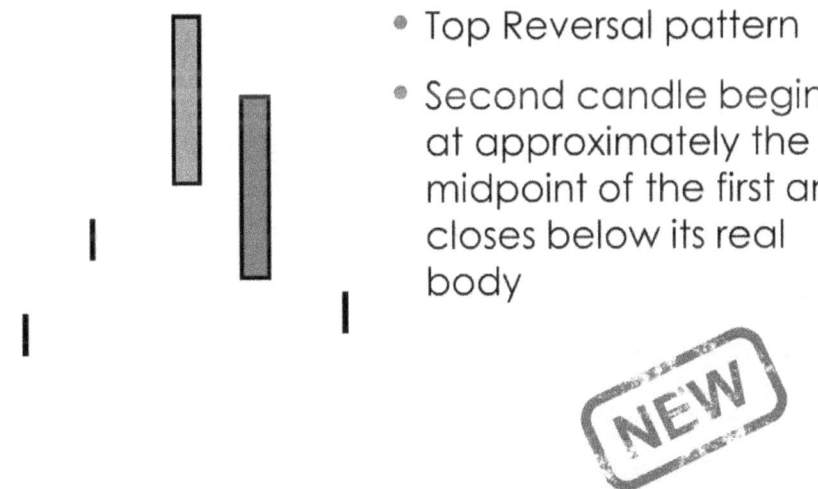

- Top Reversal pattern
- Second candle begins at approximately the midpoint of the first and closes below its real body

Figure 5.16 Inverted Dark Cloud Cover Pattern

The final candlestick pattern that I discovered is the New Money Pattern. This pattern usually emerges as a rejection candle immediately after a bullish breakout from an extended trading range, before rallying higher in the direction of the bullish breakout (see Figure 5.17).

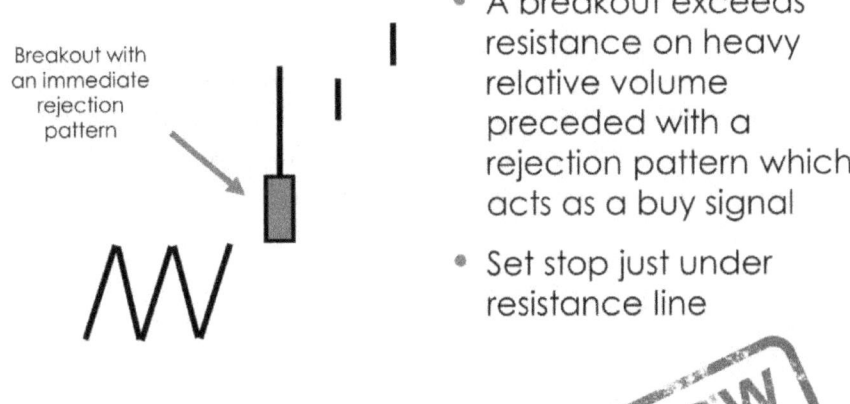

- A breakout exceeds resistance on heavy relative volume preceded with a rejection pattern which acts as a buy signal
- Set stop just under resistance line

Figure 5.17 New Money Pattern

When I first discovered this pattern happening regularly, I was quite confused. Why did the price continue to go higher after showing a rejection signal from the bullish breakout?

Later on, as I tried to understand the market participants' trading psychology in the formation of the New Money Pattern, I started to realize what might have happened.

When a price is initially stuck in an extended trading range, it usually means there are many tired and bored traders waiting for some movements to take profit. So as soon as new money flows in and the price breaks out, these traders who were sick of waiting for an uptick to sell, quickly sell what they had.

This creates the initial rejection candle in the New Money Pattern. However, as more new money floods in, the price quickly recovers from the previous rejection candle and continues on its upward climb. This New Money Pattern is a counter-intuitive candlestick pattern but one worth keeping an eye out for.

Finding Your Personal Bliss Zone Through Passion, Skill, and Money

Finally, I would like to touch on one more topic before I finish up my presentation. This is called the Emotional Distance chart, which was created by Dr. Harry Stanton with whom I jointly wrote the book *Let The Trade Wins Flow* (see Figure 5.18).

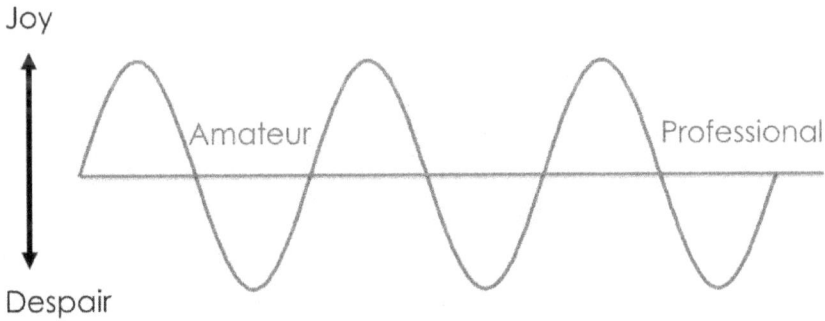

An expert trader displays complete detachment when opening or closing a position.

Figure 5.18 Emotional Distance Chart

Having been in the industry for so many years, Dr. Stanton noticed that the main difference between trading amateurs and proficient traders is that amateurs' emotions swing between joy and despair all the time while proficient traders' thoughts are usually consistent, level, and calm.

As a new trader, it can be very hard as you have so many inputs from the market to deal with. When you're making profits one minute and then taking losses the next minute, it can be challenging to hold on to that clarity and remain level-headed.

So regarding emotional volatility, I'd like to help you smooth that fluctuation. It all starts with your trading psychology. To create a personal bliss zone where you can think and act calmly no matter how the market is behaving, you need to find a combination area that includes your passion, skill, and money.

If you only have passion and skill, but there's no money involved, you have a hobby. For some people, trading starts out as a hobby, and it can take a while before they discover those dollars.

If you have skill and money, but you don't have passion, you are in a zombie zone. I see many people working in their day jobs in this state. They don't seem to have any desire, any purpose or more significant meaning in their life. They have a specific skill, are paid well, and so they decide to stay in their boring job and live like a zombie.

If you have passion and money but no skill, you might have a touch of the "imposter syndrome." But if you ever feel that everybody knows more than you and that makes you feel like a fraud, then you're most definitely feeling the effects of the imposter syndrome.

To smooth out your emotional volatility in trading, you need to have all of these three elements in balance, and that is what I call a "trading bliss" (see Figure 5.19).

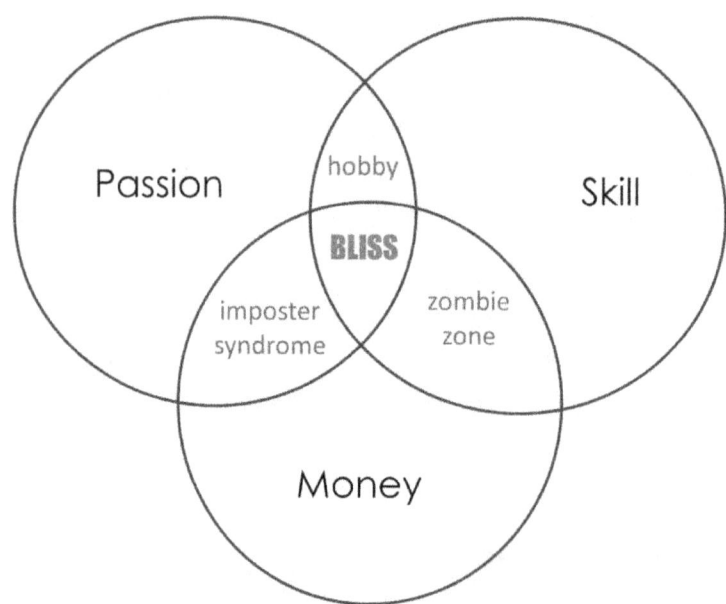

Figure 5.19 Personal Bliss Zone

When you're in a trading bliss, you've got passion, you working with your skills—and you have money coming in. That's the real key to trading well.

You will never overcome your mindset or volatile trading emotions unless you put effort into work on all these three areas. That's even more important than learning how to read those technical charts.

You can investigate further what I've shared with you, throw yourself into the deep end, and strive to achieve the results you've been after. Alternatively, you can ignore me and the rest of the fantastic speakers at this Online Trading Summit. You can choose to remain as the same old you.

Right now, you might be at a crossroad. One path leads to your trading bliss, your way of combining your passion, your skill and your money to achieve a life meaningful to you. The other path leads to the same old way that you've been living your life.

Ultimately, you have to decide which path to take and then live with it. I wish the very best for you, and I'm happy to answer any questions that Philip has for me now.

Knowing When to Cut Your Losses and Take Your Profits

Philip: Thank you, Louise. That was a fantastic presentation. Now, I would like to ask you some questions about your earlier presentation and also to get you to tell us more about your trading workflow and your trading philosophy.

You mentioned that you like to take profit on one-third of your position when there's a windfall profit of four ATR from the previous high. How do you then manage the balance two-thirds of your trading position?

Louise: When there's a sharp rally of price, I exit one-third of my position when there's a windfall profit. For the remaining two thirds that are still in the trade, I just apply my usual trailing stop.

A trailing stop is designed to lock in the profits that you've already captured from that trade, by getting you out when the trend changes direction. By using a combination of these two exit strategies, I get to take advantage of both a windfall situation while allowing my profits to run.

Philip: I have a question about the Inverted Piercing Pattern that you discovered. Let's say that you noticed an Inverted Piercing Pattern emerging during a potential bullish reversal scenario. Do you wait for a third candle confirmation to enter the trade, or would you advocate getting in toward the end of the session of the second candle?

Louise: It does depend on the length of your trading horizon. If you're a longer-term trader, you have more time to react. You have the grace of time on your side. So you can act on the confirmation of that particular trigger.

But if you're a shorter-term trader, you probably should get in on that second candle because the setup is already in place and you don't want the price to run away from you and make your risk-reward ratio less favorable.

Philip: How do you determine where to place the stop-loss for this particular pattern? Are you looking to place the stop-loss somewhere in the mid-body of that first candle or are you looking to set it somewhere below the entire candlestick pattern?

Louise: If you're a longer-term trader you wouldn't want to use this type of stop. You will be stopped out every time there's a tiny little change of trend. If you're a medium-term or longer-term trader, you'll want to stay in while that primary trend is still in place.

Now let's talk about short-term candle-based stops because that's the essence of your question. For some of my very profitable option traders who are very short-term in nature because of the way the instrument is compiled, they'll set their stop at the midpoint of the first candle. They will exit if the price closes below the midpoint of the first candle, and that's quite an aggressive stop to use.

Otherwise, you can consider setting your stop-loss just under the base of the candlestick pattern, where it is usually the apparent immediate support level as well.

If you understand how support works, you will realize that when the price falls to a support level, it will typically experience a rebound and then continue on its way to the next higher high. If the price closes below that support level, it might suggest a high probability that the rebound is not materializing. As such, it might be prudent to take a stop-loss when that happens.

Philip: You mentioned that the New Money Pattern is kind of counter-intuitive, which I do agree as well. So when that shooting-star pattern emerges right after the bullish breakout from the congestion, does the relative trading volume of that shooting-star candle affect how you look at the trading opportunity?

Louise: Not really. For me, the relative volume only matters when I've got a dominant candle (a candle with a long body). With that New Money Pattern, where you'll often see the formation of a shooting star just above the congestion band, the relative volume doesn't really matter.

One thing that I like to add is that for counterintuitive trading setups like this New Money Pattern, I suggest that you wait for a confirmation candle to close higher in the next session before you enter the trade.

Philip: At this point, I'd like to ask you some questions so that we can understand more about how you trade personally. I believe that your trading horizon and the workflow you implement into your daily life can offer some insights to the summit participants.

Would you like to share a bit more about the kind of trading horizon that you prefer and what kind of traders will have personalities more suited to implement your style of trading?

Louise: I like the concept that "there are no old and bold traders in the market." I like to think of myself as a timid cat. I like to think that I'm officially a coward when it comes to the markets, but this is also the main reason why I'm still alive in the markets throughout all these years. I have seen all types of market cycles. I've seen the peaks, I've seen the valleys, and I've traded them all.

There's one personal flaw that I've realized about myself over the years of trading, and that is, the more money I have to trade, the lower percentage returns I'm able to generate on my capital. Because I don't trade well with a large amount of money, I've had to find ways to segregate the bulk of the money from my trading account to keep my trading results up.

As such, I found a way to overcome this by segregating my money into three core buckets.

The first bucket contains the bulk of my capital, which is placed in the superannuation where I've got a few properties in there together with my long-term trades.

The second bucket is for my medium-term trading. Because my husband is a property developer, we alternate the use of the funds in this second bucket between my medium-term trading and his property deals. One thing to note is that I don't use candles for an exit in those long-term and medium-term trades because candles are too short term to be used as an exit tool for these trades.

The third bucket of money is where I do my short-term trading. That's my system development trading. That is my "test out a new system with real money" trading. That is the smallest bucket of all with about 15–20% of my money in there. This is a much smaller bucket because you don't want to test out a new system with the bulk of your money. It's foolhardy.

I keep those three buckets very separated in my mind. After I've executed a long-term trade, I might even walk away from my trading screen. I'll go and make a cup of tea, come back, and then do my short-term trades. I try not to muddy the waters with those three buckets of money.

Philip: For your shorter-term trades, are you more of a systematic trader or a discretionary/visual trader?

Louise: I'm never a discretionary trader. Everything that I do as a trader is system-oriented. My trading plan is sacred. Even though I have my trading plan written down, I know it by heart. I follow it in times of trading pressure.

When you're under the onslaught of the markets, your IQ gets thrown out of the window. You can't think clearly. You do need to follow a written trading plan to protect yourself from making emotional trading decisions.

Philip: Do you in any way try to use like algorithms and programming to configure your trading plans into your trading system, so that you can prevent your emotions and psychology from interfering with your plan?

Louise: I don't use my trading system to enter and exit trades automatically like those algorithm-based trading systems. I use my trading system to scan for high probability trades. If I decide to execute on those trades, I'll execute them manually, or I will set a trade-by-trade contingent order to enter the market for me automatically when some particular conditions are met.

Philip: Let's go back in time to learn more about your evolution as a trader. You mentioned that it took you three years of trading to realize your potential as a profitable trader.

What motivated you to keep going during those three years when you had no idea whether you were going to make it or not? What was that evolution like for you? Were there any "aha" moments that helped you persist through those years before finding success?

Louise: The evolution was horrible! I was often in tears during those years. I was so frustrated. I used to scream as trains went past. I now know that a good trader needs to be calm and not let her emotions run up and down.

Unfortunately, I didn't realize that at the start of my trading journey. It took me a very long time to realize that I had to calm down to think this through and make sense out of my trading.

Back in those days, there were no books on the Australian market written for Australian traders. I didn't even know you could read books about trading. There were no readily visible successful examples in front of me. That's why I begged my broker to introduce me to somebody who was successful.

The reason why I could survive those years was that I was just dumb enough to stick with it. I think sometimes you have to be smart enough to write a trading plan, but dumb enough to stick with it.

For the intellectuals and the smart people, they might struggle with executing according to their trading plan because this might be too mechanical a process to follow through. Sometimes they say, "Well, you know, why don't I just tinker with this; or why don't I just change that?" And guess what? They're usually the ones who don't get results.

I think there's a lot to be said for persistence. Just stick with it. Put yourself in this trading arena for ten years or let me have you for five years. I'm sure I'll be able to change the way you perceive the markets and the results you're getting.

Learning to trade well is a three to five-year process. There is no such thing as a "get-rich-quick scheme" in the markets. You do need to grow into this, be patient, and realize that the results are worth your efforts. There are many great examples of successful traders out there to show you what you can achieve if you put your heart into it. Look to these people for inspiration.

Philip: Let's move forward now to the present day. You probably have coached and educated thousands of traders. Apparently, not everyone is built to be a trader, and not everyone has enough determination to persist through the training phase to become a proficient and profitable trader.

From your experience as a trading coach, what have been the key hurdles and obstacles that have stopped those traders from becoming a good trader?

Louise: The biggest obstacle I find new traders struggling with is that they don't have the support from their family and friends. The lack of support is the hardest hurdle to overcome. Many aspiring traders have spouses who talk them down or work against them. They have family or friends who don't believe in them and therefore don't offer any micro-expressions of positivity to these budding traders.

As such, these traders feel worn down, as they are working long hours at a job and trading ends up being another thing they have to do on the to-do list. Of course, there are many other kinds of obstacles that a trader might face during his trading journey.

I like to share a specific personalized tool that you can use to discover your trading hurdles and obstacles. It's called the Pre-Mortem Technique.

A psychologist named Gary Klein invented this technique. Instead of doing a post-mortem after the event or after a failure, you try to imagine and look forward into the future. You pre-visualize the things that could go wrong, and you try to discover solutions to those obstacles even before they happen.

From a trading perspective, think about all the potential reasons that could make you fail at trading. After that, you scaffold, build and get yourself educated about these reasons. Use your contacts to help you find solutions to overcome those hurdles even before those hurdles occur in real-time.

If you can do all of these consistently, you will stand a much higher chance of graduating as a proficient and profitable trader.

Philip: Thanks, Louise. It has been a great session that you've put up with your presentation and by candidly answering my questions. I'll love to have a chance to interview you again in other areas of trading like risk management, portfolio management, and trading psychology.

Meanwhile, I wish you the very best in whatever you do and hope you can continue to inspire your trading community in Australia and potentially traders from outside Australia as well.

Louise: Thank you so much, Philip, it has been my pleasure!

RAYNER TEO: The Generous Trading Mentor Who Created Singapore's Top Free Forex Trading Blog

" You can't just think about making money. You have to first think about how much you can potentially lose. If you can survive in this trading business long enough, the money will take care of itself.

Rayner is an independent trader, an ex-prop trader, and the founder of TradingwithRayner. He has been trading since his university days in the University of London (UOL), before graduating with First Class Honors in Banking & Finance and was also the valedictorian of his graduating cohort in 2012.

He specializes in studying great research from people who are much more qualified than himself, then applying this information to the real world of trading to find out what works and what doesn't, and, finally, he posts his findings on his blog, so that anyone can learn how to become a consistently profitable trader.

Because of Rayner's willingness to share his trading knowledge and experience freely, he's now the most followed trader in Singapore with more than 75,000 traders reading his blog each month. On social media, he has also attracted nearly 50,000

YouTube followers, 30,000 Twitter followers, and 30,000 highly engaged Facebook group members.

I've known Rayner personally for some years. As we were both from Singapore and had served in the Commandos unit during our National Service days, we naturally developed a strong mutual respect. When I decided to host the Online Trading Summit, Rayner accepted my invitation readily.

During my interview with Rayner, we discussed his two favorite trading strategies: a longer-term, systematic trend-following strategy and a shorter-term discretionary swing-trading strategy. Following that, we went on to address some of the typical issues faced by the traders he mentored and how he went about helping them to overcome those obstacles.

Philip: Hi, Rayner! Thanks for coming on board for this Online Trading Summit to share your experience with the participants about your trading background and all the things that you have learned and done in trading.

When I was browsing through your blog, I noticed your tagline "Saving Retail Traders from Self Destruction." That's an interesting proposition that I haven't seen in any other trading blogs around. Would you like to tell us how that inspiration and purpose came about? Was there any story behind that?

Rayner: As you would have read, I started trading just like how most traders would, by reading trading books and browsing the Internet for trading information. This is now my tenth year of trading.

In my early years of trading, there wasn't much trading related information out there. At that point in time, the trading industry and the education segment of it hadn't really reached its peak or reached the level of where it is at the moment.

I was always looking through books and trying my best to learn about trading, but I found something was lacking. I felt that the trading information that was available wasn't actionable enough and lacked practical insights that I could apply to my trading.

The freely available knowledge that I came across was shallow. For stuff where I wanted to dive in deeper to learn, I usually had to pay to attend trading courses. Those courses typically cost thousands of dollars.

That is the kind of problem that I faced in my early years of trading. I know there are many traders who want to learn about trading, but they just can't afford to spend that amount of money to learn how to trade.

So my goal down here at TradingwithRayner is to equip retail traders with as much knowledge as possible so that they can apply it to their own trading. That's why I share my trading knowledge and experiences freely in the public domains and platforms.

However, should any trader require hand-held mentoring, that's where I charge for my time spent with them. But from the perspective of trading knowledge like trading techniques and strategies, I make them publicly available for anyone to read and learn. I just want to help retail traders get started on the right footing.

Philip: I frequently see trading influencers talking about how they can help traders become very profitable, but yet you chose to use self-destruction as a way to convey your message. Is there any particular reason for that tagline?

Rayner: In trading, everybody wants to make money. But the rite of passage is that before you can make money, you have to play good defense. That's something that Paul Tudor Jones has said.

You can't just think about making money. You have to first think about how much you can potentially lose. I believe that if you can survive in this trading business long enough, the money will take care of itself.

This is where I really wanted to teach and help retail traders to learn how to avoid self-destruction, how to manage their trading risk, and how to survive for the long run.

Transitioning from Day Trading into Swing and Position Trading

Philip: Could you tell us how you got started in trading? How long ago was that?

Rayner: I got started with the financial markets sometime during my army days. I was reading books, and people were talking about investments using Warren Buffett's value investing methodology. So I just followed along and learned how people look at annual reports and arrive at fair values.

After I was done with my national service, I enrolled in the university, took a finance course, and started dabbling in trading.

On one occasion, a broker came to the campus and organized a Forex trading competition. I took part in the competition, and that's pretty much how I got started in trading.

After I completed my graduate studies and received a university degree, I landed a job in a proprietary trading firm, where I was given a portion of the firm's capital to trade. I specialized in the Japanese stock market, the Nikkei futures contract to be specific.

I was with the firm for a couple of years, before I moved on and started TradingwithRayner. Right now, I'm just trading for myself while educating traders about the financial markets.

Philip: What kind of trading strategies did you use when you were working in the proprietary firm back then?

Rayner: At that point in time, I was mainly a short-term trader, basically day trading and even scalping the Nikkei futures. I was trading on the lower timeframe, using three- and five-minute charts to make my trading decisions.

Philip: How did TradingwithRayner come about? Was it some kind of moment that prompted you to start TradingwithRayner? And under what circumstances did you decide to leave your prop trading firm to focus solely on TradingwithRayner?

Rayner: I started TradingwithRayner by chance. When I was still working at the proprietary trading firm, there were many occasions when the market was quiet, and there was nothing worthwhile to trade. I was just sitting there and having nothing much to do, as I didn't watch movies or play computer games.

I preferred to do something that was meaningful and not a waste of time. I had figured that writing a blog and penning down my trading thought process made the most sense. So that's how I started the blog TradingwithRayner.

I started by sharing my analysis of the markets and some basic trading knowledge. Gradually, people took notice of my blog and told me that they appreciated what was being shared.

That was how I realized that I could do more about the blog by sharing more of my trading knowledge and see where that might lead to. This is the reason why I said I started the blog by "chance" or "luck." I didn't really set out to create the website and turn it into what you see today.

Now, the reason why I left the prop trading industry is quite straightforward. Prop trading isn't really a career that you want to be doing for the next 30 to 40 years. In the short run, doing prop trading for about three to five years is fair enough.

But in the long run, I don't think it is healthy to do prop trading for long hours over the long term. This kind of work doesn't really have a good work/life balance, and it's pretty hard to start a family if you're a full-time prop trader.

And that's how I decided that my trading needed to evolve into medium- and longer-term trading. That was why I transitioned into swing and position trading after I left the prop trading firm.

The Most Suitable Trading Strategy for Retail Traders

Philip: What is the main strategy that you think is most suitable for most retail traders and investors out there?

Rayner: There are many trading strategies out there but first, let's talk about trading concepts. If you are like most retail traders, trading will be more of a means to grow your wealth over time.

On average, you might be looking to generate a certain percentage of returns on your capital a year. However, I can't decide for you what percentage is right for you because that depends on your goals and your risk appetite.

But generally based on such a profile, I usually suggest retail traders go with a swing or position trading approach for a start. Hold your trades for days or weeks or even months. Hold it longer term, so that you can catch the larger swing or, the broader trend of the move.

The reason for this approach is that it doesn't require much time compared to day trading or scalping. On top of that, your transaction costs, the commission you pay, will be lesser compared to someone who trades more frequently on a shorter timeframe.

Philip: I read from your blog that you focus a lot on price action and trend following. Are they mutually exclusive or are they a good combination that can be used together?

Rayner: At this point, we can get down to the exact details. So let's talk about trend following first. Trend following originated from the futures market in the form of systematic trend following, for example, buying commodities in the markets during an uptrend and shorting those that are in a downtrend.

Along the way trend following started to branch out into other forms. Besides the usual systematic trend followers, we began to see discretionary trend followers, or traders, who apply the trend-following concept on the lower timeframe and on other asset classes. But all in all, the focus is mainly about trading in the direction of a trend.

I say it's easier for traders to trade with a trend because when you do that, you increase the odds of your trade being profitable compared to if you try to trade against the trend. For a start, I usually suggest that a new trader learn how to read a price chart, learn how to identify a trend and try to trade alongside the trend.

On the other hand, price action is a specific way to read the markets, to understand what the market is doing.

What is the market structure? Where are the support and resistance levels? Identifying what is the stage of the market? Is it in an accumulation stage, distribution stage, advancing stage, or declining stage?

And of course, you also learn how to read individual candlestick patterns, identify price rejection, and stuff like that.

All in all, these techniques actually go hand-in-hand together, especially if you're considering a discretionary trend trading approach. You can also separate the two if you just want to go with a systematic trend-following approach with exact buy/sell signals using a quantifiable method. It really depends on the goal of the trader.

Philip: Basically, you're trying to say that there are many different ways and styles of trading even for retail traders and investors. It's probably more important to decide on a particular methodology or a strategy so that you can become proficient in it and use it with conviction after that.

Can you quickly tell us what your typical trading workflow is like? Is that based on a swing trading kind of style, or is it based on a longer-term position trading style? Your answer might be able to offer the summit participants with some insights about your thought process.

Rayner: Essentially, trend following is the primary trading methodology I use. I have both a systematic and discretionary trend-following trading strategy. Typically, I start my day by using software to download the end-of-day data and then use it to scan the markets for any trading setups or any trades to put on or exit.

That's my systematic trend-following workflow for the futures market, and that takes me about ten minutes a day. If there are any setup, entry, or exit signals, I'll just follow and execute accordingly.

Once that's done, I'll usually spend the next half an hour to an hour to scan the markets manually. I'll try to identify the trading setups that I trade on a discretionary basis. If I find the markets in a trending mode, I'll try to find a place to put on a trade or to manage my existing positions from an earlier trade.

That's pretty much what I do on a day-to-day basis. This entire process typically takes up an hour of my morning. After that, I usually check the charts every four hours or so because I trade off the four-hour and daily timeframe.

Philip: Generally, what's your holding period for both your discretionary and your systematic trading strategies?

Rayner: For the systematic trend-following strategy, my holding period tends to last longer, because I try to catch the longer-term trend for this strategy. If a trade works out, I can be in position for months and for as long as one to two years.

For the discretionary strategy, it's shorter term because my goal for this strategy is to catch the shorter-term and medium-term trends. If my stop-loss exit for a discretionary trade is triggered, I might get out within a day or so. If the trade goes in my favor, I typically hold for about a few weeks to ride out the entire trend in that trading horizon.

How to Implement a Systematic Trend-Following Trading Strategy

Philip: For part-time retail traders who don't have the time or don't want to spend so much time analyzing the market and looking for ideas, your longer-term systematic trend-following approach could be an ideal methodology for them to put their capital to use in the market.

Can you elaborate a bit more on this strategy? Is there any particular signal and insight that you look out for before you get into a trade? Does your system automatically get into the trade and manage the positions accordingly based on some kind of algorithms and rules?

Rayner: The rules for my systematic trading strategy are very black and white, and there is no discretion on my part. When the system says, "buy" it means "buy," and the entry trigger is very simple. I just enter a trade when there is a 200-day breakout.

Once the trade is initiated, I merely follow my stop-loss. If the market moves in my favor, I trail my stop-loss. If not, the protective stop-loss order will get me out of the trade when the trade turns against me.

In my opinion, the "secret ingredient" to systematic trend following is that you must trade this strategy across the right portfolio mix. This means that you have to trade it across Forex, commodities, bonds, indices, energy markets, etc. Spread your strategy out across the different sectors out there.

If you just apply the strategy to a single market, e.g., Forex, it can be disastrous because there will be times when some markets don't trend, and you're just going to get whipped and suffer a very bad drawdown. So the objective is to trade this same systematic strategy across a broad range of markets to diversify this drawdown risk.

Philip: So I supposed you are utilizing this systematic trend-following strategy from a portfolio management perspective. When some markets are trending, the returns from these markets will help offset the losses you made from those markets that you were stopped out because of their non-trending behavior.

Do you apply this systematic trend-following strategy on smaller individual stocks or individual currency pairs? Or do you implement this strategy mainly on macro instruments?

Rayner: Usually I have a similar number of instruments for each of the asset classes. For example, if I'm using this strategy on ten currency pairs, I'll also apply this on ten different indices and ten different bonds for instance. You don't want to end up having a varied mix of ten currency pairs, two bonds, and five indices, as it is not going to balance over time.

Of course, there are hedge funds out there that are more commodity-heavy while some are financial sector-heavy. I prefer to adopt an equal weightage approach across the different markets and asset classes.

Philip: At any point, how many open positions do you usually have based on this systematic strategy?

Rayner: It really depends on the market conditions. At the moment, I have about 24 positions open although I'm applying this strategy across fifty markets. When the markets are trending well, I might have up to 30-plus open positions. On the lower end, my number of open positions is about 15.

Philip: Do you separate your capital base for your systematic strategy as well as for your discretionary strategy?

Rayner: That's right. I separate the two accounts. I don't mix them together.

Philip: How do you typically size your trades for your systematic trend-following strategy? Do you first decide a certain percentage of your account's capital to risk before using that to size your trade accordingly?

Rayner: Yes. I don't risk more than 1% of my capital on any individual trade. This means that if the trade gets stopped out, it will not have cost me more than 1% of my account equity.

That's my risk management parameters for the systematic trend-following strategy. Some people might think I'm risking too little, and some might think that 1% is too much. But this 1% pretty much suits me and the kind of risk I'm willing to take on each trade.

Philip: Let's say you have about 20 open positions each risking 1% of your equity. Does that mean it is possible that your total risk exposure and potential drawdown could be up to 20%–30%?

Rayner: Definitely. Regarding the drawdown based on historical backtesting, it's definitely possible to experience a 25%–30% drawdown. However, it's unlikely that all 20 positions would get stopped out at the same time.

When the same strategy is trading in different directions, different markets, different sectors, some positions will be trending nicely in your favor; some will turn against you and hit your stop-loss.

The overall grand scheme of things and the core idea is that the losers will get chopped off and you will end up riding the winners for as long as the trend lasts. I don't rule out the possibility that all my open positions could swing against me at the same time, but that kind of situation happens only in rare instances.

Philip: Does this mean that you tend to allow a wider stop-loss level relative to your entry price so that you will not get whip-sawed and stopped out that easily?

Rayner: Yes. As this is a longer-term trend-following system strategy, my stop-loss levels are pretty wide relative to the entry. In fact, I use about six times the Average True Range (ATR) on a daily chart as my stop-loss level.

Philip: When you mentioned trailing stop, does that mean that you're constantly establishing your exit level at a distance of six ATR below the current closing price?

Rayner: What I mean is that when the price makes a new high, then my software will calculate six ATR from this high and tell me where my new trailing stop order is going to be.

As you know, the market doesn't go to new highs every day, that's why the trailing stop doesn't need to be adjusted all the time on a daily basis. I just need to scan the market, and it will tell me which trades need to be managed, which trade needs to be exited, and so on. My life is so much easier as a result.

Philip: Assuming a trade is trending nicely in your favor, do you continue to pyramid (stack on more positions) on your trades for this particular strategy?

Rayner: No, I don't.

Philip: So you just open a single trading position and let the course run itself out depending on when it hits your trailing stop.

Rayner: That's right.

Philip: Wow. That makes things way more manageable, and I suppose you don't have to spend much time on this particular system then. Do you at any point attempt to review your system to make any refinements and adjustments?

Rayner: Not really. For systematic trend following, there's no point looking back on hindsight to make those small adjustments. In the grand scheme of things, the essence of systematic trend following is to trade across a wide variety of markets, cut your losses, and ride your profits.

I do track hedge funds that apply a systematic trend-following approach and monitor their performance on a month-to-month basis. As long as I'm generally in line with their performance, I'm not too bothered about making adjustments to my strategy.

Let's assume that February wasn't a good month for most hedge funds that deploy a systematic trend-following strategy. When these hedge funds have a drawdown, and I'm experiencing similar drawdowns as well, I know I am doing okay.

If January happens to be a good month for most hedge funds that use systematic trend following, and I fared well, then it tells me that my strategy is working the way it's supposed to work.

Basically, I'm in the same boat as these funds trading similar strategies, so our performances should be expected to be similar. The only difference is that those hedge funds are trading much bigger sizes of capital and maybe their strategy is a little bit more complex compared to mine because they trade longer term, medium term, and even short term.

Philip: What's the relative portfolio size of your systematic trend-following strategy compared to your discretionary strategy?

Rayner: To be precise, it's about 60% to the systematic trend-following strategy and 40% to the discretionary trading account.

The truth is that as my funds grow, I find that systematic trading takes the emotions out of trading for me.

When I'm doing discretionary trading, there's always subjectivity involved, and I experience stronger emotions. This is the reason why I made a deliberate effort to allocate more capital to my systematic trend-following strategy.

Incorporating A Shorter Term Swing Trading Strategy

Philip: Let's move on to your discretionary strategy right now. You mentioned earlier that your discretionary strategy is more inclined toward swing trading and price action trading. What is the typical trading horizon for your discretionary strategy?

Rayner: My discretionary strategy seldom lasts for months. For this strategy, I'm looking to capture a single swing using the daily charts. In the best scenario, a swing takes at most a few weeks to finish its run. For those trades that didn't work out, I'll usually get stopped out in a matter of days.

Philip: Is there any particular reason why you decided to have another discretionary swing trading strategy, on top of your systematic trend-following strategy?

Rayner: All along I've been a discretionary trader, as I started off as one. It was only recently that I saw the power of systematic trading and started to include that as part of my trading workflow. That's the reason why I'm currently using both types of strategies in my trading.

Philip: Is there something about discretionary trading that excites you? For example, the act of doing visual analysis and discovering an interesting trading idea that jumps right out at you?

Rayner: For me, there's really no excitement in trading anymore. I've been doing this for many years, and the setups are the same over and over again. I don't always know which setup will ultimately be a profitable trade, but I know that all I need to do is manage my risks and I'll be all right.

Philip: For a new retail trader who is starting to get into the journey of learning how to trade, which way do you think would be a better way for him to start? Systematic or discretionary?

Rayner: It really depends on his goal. If you want some kind of intellectual challenge, then systematic trading will not be able to offer you much of that because it isn't something that's very deep and complicated. You follow your rules, you buy, and you sell, that's it.

For discretionary trading, it does provide an intellectual challenge. Although every trader says he wants to make money, there's always a secondary reason to why they want to trade. Some of them might say that they like the intellectual challenge.

You have to be honest with yourself and ask yourself why are you getting into trading? If one of your key motivations is about the intellectual challenge, the gaming aspect, the feeling of winning, then maybe discretionary trading is something that you can start with.

But if your sole purpose is just to get on with life, grow your wealth systematically in the most cost and time-efficient way possible, then a systematic approach would be an approach you might want to start with as there is little to analyze in this strategy. You just follow a set of rules, do it over the long run, and the result will show for itself.

Philip: Let's get back to the discretionary trading strategy again. Can you share more about how your discretionary trading strategy works? Does it in some ways adopt the trend-following approach that you use in your systematic trading strategy?

Rayner: Yes. The idea is pretty much the same. It's just that instead of trading 200-day breakouts, I also trade pullbacks in the direction of the major trends as well as the different reversal chart patterns during those pullbacks. Generally, the core concept of my swing trading strategy is pretty much the same as my systematic trading strategy, just that the way that I enter and exit a trade is slightly different and based on a different trading horizon.

The Proper Way to Building a Trading Workflow

Philip: Can you tell us how your trading workflow works, all the way from idea generation to the reviewing of a closed trade?

Rayner: First and foremost, I look at a chart and ask myself what is the current stage of this particular instrument's price trend? Prices typically move between the four stages. The accumulation stage happens when the price has been trending lower previously and then starts to go sideways into a range.

That is a potential accumulation stage because at this point not many people want to enter, as they are still worried that the price will continue to fall. When the price starts breaking out of this range on the upside, that's where we think it could be the start of a new uptrend or what we call the advancing stage.

At the advancing stage, we will see prices moving to a higher high and a higher low. As we know, the market cannot go up forever. At some point, it will get tired and wear down. The advancing stage will have to move into a distribution stage.

A distribution stage looks very much like the range trading that I mentioned earlier on, except that this happens after a prolonged uptrend move.

Eventually, when more and more people continue to take profit with short sellers coming in, the price is going to break down. That's when the distribution stage transitions into a declining stage.

Once you have an idea about how these four stages look like and based on the chart that you are looking at, you need to ask yourself what stage the price movement is in right now?

Define the stage and decide whether it is accumulating, advancing, distributing, or declining. If the price is moving somewhat randomly such that it is hard to define the trend, just move on and look at other instruments for trading ideas.

Let's say the price is in a potential accumulation stage right now, and I think there's a chance it could move into an advancing stage soon. What I look for now are the signs that the price will break out higher out of that range.

For example, the price could be coming into a resistance and consolidating for the past four to 10 days on very tight-range candles. When the price finally breaks above resistance, I'll be looking to buy the breakout and see whether it moves on into the advancing stage that I just shared earlier on.

Typically, that's how I analyze the chart. Classify price movement into one of the four stages, find the logical place to place an entry, set a proper stop-loss, and give the trade room to run. That's the core idea behind it.

Philip: Do you use a trailing stop as well for this discretionary trading strategy?

Rayner: That's right. I'm using a trailing stop as well for this strategy. But I don't do six times ATR, which is what I do for my systematic trading strategy. I use a shorter-term trading trailing stop-loss for this discretionary swing trading strategy.

Philip: Do you like to scale in and out of a winning trade? Or do you just hold on to a single position when you trade an instrument?

Rayner: I used to scale in and out previously, but I don't do that anymore.

Philip: Why is that the case?

Rayner: The main reason is that I'm already trading a portfolio of instruments that have a certain correlation with one another. It doesn't quite make sense for me to scale into instruments that already have a similar trend bias or trend direction as another instrument in my portfolio.

If I were to do that, I might end up scaling into multiple positions or correlated trades at the same time and have a significant exposure on those correlated trades.

For example, I might have a long position in both AUD/USD and NZD/USD at the moment. If I scale into or go long more the Aussie dollar, I'm just basically exposing myself more to the USD.

Philip: What kinds of instruments do you use for this discretionary trading strategy?

Rayner: I trade mainly the FX and futures market, similar to my systematic trend-following portfolio of markets. There are some markets that I don't trade because the broker for my discretionary trading account does not offer as many instruments as the broker who I'm using for my systematic trend-following account.

Philip: What are three of your favorite setups that you try to look out for in your discretionary trading ideas?

Rayner: The first trading setup that I like to look out for is a trend-continuation trade. For example, the market is trending on a longer timeframe and does a weak pullback in the next shorter timeframe. That is a pretty straightforward setup that I like to trade.

The second trading setup will be what I call a false-break market. The price breaks out of a resistance or support, followed by a 180-degree reversal and goes back into the range. That's another setup that I trade.

And the third trading setup is the typical breakout trade after the price has been in a tight range for a long time. I will enter a trade when the price finally breaks out of the trading range.

Philip: I understand that on top of doing your independent trading, you also coach traders as well through an online-based arrangement. Can you share more about that?

Rayner: Yes, I provide training and coaching services to traders using only online services, and I think it's quite natural since I have a trading blog. Readers of my blog started requesting for more coaching and help. That was how it led me down the road to start offering online mentoring programs.

Philip: How many traders have you mentored in this program? Are they generally based in Singapore, in Asia, or around the world?

Rayner: I've mentored about 250 traders to date. Approximately 40%–50% of them are from Singapore, and the remaining are pretty much around the world, from places like US, UK, India, the Philippines, etc.

The Two Most Common Issues That Retail Traders Have to Deal With

Philip: I supposed that you have a first-row seat to understand how retail traders typically think since they will share with you their trading issues during your mentoring program. Without naming anyone, can you share with us the common issues that these traders typically bring up to you for mentoring help?

Rayner: One of the core issues that keeps coming back is that many of them just don't have a trading plan.

Let's use this interview that I'm doing with you right now as an example. In this interview, I discussed the many different ways to trade a market, and many traders will come across this interview and try to apply what they've learned. They will go back home excited, look at the chart and attempt to start trading without diving in deep to try to understand the core concept of why it works.

So when a losing streak comes, the trader is going to give up and move on to the next "interesting" strategy. This is one of the biggest problems that I see. Most traders just don't dive deep enough into a trading methodology to study why it works, how it works, and then apply it consistently with confidence.

Another common issue that I've seen is that traders give up too easily. For example, trend following is simple to execute, but it's not easy to trade because of the drawdown that comes with it. Sometimes, you might have drawdowns for months and years on end, and not many traders can swallow it during those losing periods.

Philip: So how do you go about helping them to overcome this kind of obstacle? Is this a hurdle that a mentor like you can help, or do they simply have to overcome it by themselves?

Rayner: As a mentor, I will share with them the facts of what trend following is like. I will share with them the year-by-year breakdown, the month-to-month breakdown—and explain to them that that's the reality of trading.

By letting them know that they're on a similar path as other trend followers or even the hedge funds that deploy trend-following strategies, I'm able to help them fine-tune their psychology in some ways. If those big boys who are managing billions of dollars have a down year or a down month similar to you as an independent trader, you kind of know that you are still on the right path.

On the other hand, if you're making money while most of the other industry players executing similar strategies lost money, you should be a little worried. You need to ask yourself why you're making money when most other trend-followers are losing money.

It's fine when this happens occasionally, but if such situations happen repetitively, it's a cause for concern because you might not have implemented your strategy correctly. In other words, you are making money simply from riding on your short-term luck instead of leveraging off your long-term edge.

So in summary, I think that it's helpful to keep track of how the industry players are doing, especially if they are applying similar strategies as you are.

Philip: For a retail trader who wants to start with long-term position trading, it usually takes a long time to feel confident about his strategy, as significant time is needed for most of the positions to work themselves out.

During those times, you might have drawdowns, you might doubt yourself, or you might even wonder if your strategy has an edge or not. But for shorter-term swing trading, traders can get feedback about their strategy sooner and potentially learn faster.

From this perspective, do you think a new trader should start with shorter-term trading or longer-term trading?

Rayner: I think there are two ways to look at it. The first way, which I think is the easiest way to overcome, is to use a software program to do all the back-testing work, especially for those long-term systematic trend-following strategies.

If you do proper backtesting on your planned strategy, you can use the historical performance to build your confidence in using them even during drawdown periods.

For traders who aren't systematic or don't have access to back-testing resources, they can trade the shorter-term strategies and get feedback faster. But at the same time, the emotional level may be quite different compared to longer-term trading.

Regardless of whether you're planning to trade in a shorter or longer timeframe, you must at least understand why your strategy makes money in the first place. If you can't answer that question, there is no point trading it at all because when the drawdown comes, your confidence and everything that you believed in will be thrown out of the window.

So it's very important to understand why your strategy makes money. Once you understand why your strategy makes money, you will have the confidence to trade it in the future whether your account is in a drawdown or not. There is no shortcut. That's why it takes years for someone to develop and grow to the point of becoming a profitable trader.

If you trade on the daily and weekly timeframe, it might take one or two years to get enough feedback to know how you are faring. If you think that's too long, you can go down to a shorter timeframe like the one-hour and four-hour charts. Try it and see how it works.

Of course, you have to bear in mind that things will move so much faster in the lower timeframe and you might be more prone to errors and mistakes.

Philip: What do you think is the easiest and the hardest thing to apply in trend following from your personal experience and your mentoring of your students?

Rayner: Let's first talk about the hardest thing. The hardest thing about trend following is definitely about having the conviction and discipline to continue with the strategy in a period of drawdown. It is difficult to keep pulling the trigger when you have losing months, but you just have to do it anyway.

If you skip any of your trades, then any long-term positive results that you've received from your backtesting will be voided because you're not even following the rules of your strategy in the first place in the short run.

The easiest thing about trend following is that the concept is straightforward to understand. Strategy-wise, it is not difficult, and anybody can do it. Executing the strategy consistently over time is what makes this trend-following approach so difficult for most traders.

Philip: Rayner, you've given us some great insights. As a conclusion to this interview, do you have any last advice for a trader who is looking to get into trend following? Is there a personality type that might be a better fit for trend-following strategies? Is there any book that you will suggest a trader to read to build up his knowledge?

Rayner: I don't know what type of personality will best suit the trend-following methodology. Generally, to be a consistent trend follower, you have to be comfortable losing and you have to be comfortable being wrong.

If you're the type of person with a big ego, or if you want to be right most of the time, then trend following is not for you. In fact, with that kind of character trait, trading as a whole might not even be for you.

If you want to get started on trend following through reading, you can head to my trading blog TradingWithRayner, as I have written and published many free articles on that. With regards to books on trend following, I think *Following the* Trend by Andreas Clenow is a good book. *Trend Following* by Michael Covel is another good book to start with.

You can read about the Turtle Traders as well, even though the exact strategy doesn't seem to work in recent times anymore. However, the concept and principles behind the turtle traders' strategies are still pretty much valid.

So if you're keen to learn more about trend following, there are many books out there that can expose you to it. Read them, and understand why trend following works and why it's so important as a trading methodology. After that, start formulating strategies and draft your trading plan so that you have a systematic way to take advantage of this phenomenon in the markets.

Philip: Thank you so much for your time today, Rayner. I wish you all the best in any upcoming endeavors that you have.

Rayner: Thank you, Philip. The pleasure is mine.

ADAM GRIMES: The Practical Trading Mentor from the United States Who Is Out to Fight Trading Scams

" *It is easy to fund an account and execute a trade, but it is not easy to become a truly competent trader. The market is an environment that is constantly evolving to make you do the wrong thing at the wrong time.*

Adam Grimes has over two decades of experience as a trader and system developer. He's worked for small firms and big firms, from the farmlands of the Ohio Valley to the trading floors of the New York Mercantile Exchange.

In addition to his work with MarketLife, he is also the Chief Investment Officer and Managing Partner of Waverly Advisors, an institutional research and advisory firm for which he writes daily market commentary. On top of that, he also contributes his writings to many publications on quantitative finance and trading, and is much in demand as a speaker and lecturer.

Adam is fascinated by the limits of human knowledge and peak performance—specifically, how do we get there and stay there, and how to teach others to do the same? His relentless focus on trading excellence and self-development through financial markets have created a unique body of work that has helped many traders move along the path to trading success.

I got to know about Adam from the excellent technical analysis book that he wrote, *The Art & Science of Technical Analysis: Market Structure, Price Action, and Trading Strategies*.

Subsequently, when I got to learn about his motivation to provide tons of free education to the public to counter-trading scams and unethical trading educators out there, I knew I had to invite him to the Online Trading Summit to share his thoughts and experiences.

In his presentation, Adam talked about what trading edge is about and how to go about finding it. He also spoke about why trading psychology and discipline is the key to implementing a trading plan consistently.

Philip: Hi, Adam. Thanks for coming on board to share your trading experiences in this Online Trading Summit. Before we get into the presentation that you've prepared for us, could you tell us how you got started in trading and what was the journey like for you through these years?

Adam: I started my trading journey like most other retail traders. I probably had no idea what I was doing when I first started trading in the mid-1990s. In those days, scams were still conducted through the mail rather than through email that we often see today.

I remembered I received a trading course brochure in my mailbox that promised to teach me how to corner the cattle market with just a few thousand dollars. At that time, I had no trading experience and definitely didn't receive any education about the financial markets.

But I thought the course sounded kind of fun, so I bought the course, went through the training, opened a small trading account and started to trade. Needless to say, I blew my trading account soon after. I absolutely had no comprehension of risk or leverage or how the whole mathematics of trading works.

But something about that experience grabbed my attention and got me wondering: "I think I can figure this trading thing out although it might be a lot harder than I thought." Basically, that was how I started my trading journey, which I carried on until today.

Just to provide a little context about my background, I was a musician by training before I became a trader professionally. But what was unusual about me as a musician was that I was very much into science and quantitative models as a kid.

When I went to college, I was in a bit of a dilemma because I was not sure whether I wanted to learn music or to study hard science. Ultimately, I decided to study music.

And the outcome of that was that I didn't go through any rigorous quantitative thinking in college although I had some idea how to think scientifically. I taught myself subjects like statistics and learned how to look at numbers and information to figure out probabilities. Along the way, I had some help from some mentors who were very important to me.

Subsequently, I decided that I wanted to work in the financial markets, so I earned myself an MBA and went to New York to work. I spent a few years working on the New York Mercantile

Exchange before I went on to trade for a big prop firm after that. Following that, I launched an institutional advisory service and have since then operated that for almost ten years to date.

One thing that is unusual about my trading background is that I've probably traded every liquid market out there, whether it's stocks, options, futures, or currencies. I've done very short-term trading, and I've also built long-term portfolios.

Besides analyzing the financial markets and trading, I also enjoy teaching. That's the reason why I blog about the markets and wrote books about trading. There's a lot of hard work involved, but I find the work pleasant and get a lot of satisfaction from it.

I find that when I teach, I'm forced to articulate my ideas more clearly and it helps me understand myself better as well. Personally, I believe that if I'm able to write down and tell people exactly what they should do, it's less likely that I will do anything stupid that violates what I teach.

So when I teach people about trading best practices, that naturally filters into my trading, and I find that a virtuous cycle.

Over the years, my work has helped a lot of people. Almost every day, I receive messages from somebody saying, "Your work made a difference for me." Knowing that I've been able to help someone who struggled for ten years to ultimately achieve success is enormously gratifying for me.

Philip: I totally agree with you, Adam. I too enjoy the challenge of taking complicated principles and topics and translating them into easy-to-understand analogies.

Before I go on to ask you more about your personal trading experiences, I'm eager to hear about the presentation you've prepared for us. During my initial discussion with you, you mentioned that you wanted to focus your topic on some of the most challenging things about trading. How did that thought come about?

Adam: Actually, I felt a little conflict in my mind when I wondered whether to talk about this topic. If you focus too much on why it's difficult, you risk focusing on negativity. But at the same time, I think that it's important to be honest about how difficult trading really is.

There are many educators out there telling you that you just need to learn this pattern and you can make money. Or you can just learn this super-secret combination of moving averages or learn to use Fibonacci numbers, and you can become a profitable trader. They want their students to think that trading is simple and easy.

Over time, those who survived long enough realized that it doesn't really work like that.

Let's say that I'm trading patterns on a one-hour currency chart. I'm looking for simple patterns to initiate a trade. It takes me just a few seconds to notice a tradable pattern or idea. I know immediately where my risk is, where my exit is, and this all seems to be very simple for me. I could write it down on a small piece of paper. But if I give that to somebody else, he wouldn't be able to replicate that easily.

Trading might appear to be as simple as putting on a trade and exiting a trade, but if you wish to become highly skilled, it's not as easy as it seems.

The Motivation Behind Providing Free Trading Education

Frankly, there are a lot of scams out there when we talk about trading education. People are literally paying ten to fifteen thousand of dollars for trading courses that contain nothing more than a book you could buy. The shelf behind me is filled with them, and they cost about $50 each. With so many dishonest courses out there, I decided to take a stand.

That's the reason why I decided to produce a massive free trading course, which contains more than 30 hours of video that I've recorded over the years. I did this to counteract a lot of what I saw as abuses in the trading education industry.

Many of the big online trading education companies have tried to buy my course or hire me because they don't like competition and they don't want something as extensive as my free course out there in the market.

Many of the trading educators that I know were former insurance salesmen, former car salesmen, former brokers, and even people who worked in back offices. They were very experienced in attracting capital but had not really managed money before.

I always believe that the person you want to learn to trade from should be someone who has cried and bled and has had the experience of putting on trades and taking trades off.

Besides that, the ability to teach effectively is another skill that needs to be mastered. Just because someone is a proficient and profitable trader doesn't mean that he's also a good trading educator. Trading is a skill, and it can be difficult transmitting the essence of that skill to another person.

So in this upcoming presentation, I'm going to try my best to transmit my understanding about trading to the summit participants. I'm not going to talk about sexy patterns. I'm not going to talk about how you can easily buy and sell and make a lot of money. I'm just going to discuss how you can use my experiences to find trading success for yourself.

Philip: Sure, Adam. I'll hand the stage over to you right now.

What A Trading Edge Is and Its Importance

Adam: Great, thanks. I've titled this presentation "Trading: Winning the War through Statistics, Psychology, and Risk Management". There are good reasons why trading is hard, but the biggest problem is that people make trading even harder than it has to be.

This is mainly due to fundamental misunderstandings people have about trading. Newbies don't understand how vital psychology is and they don't know what trading success really looks like. This is what I'll be focusing on in my presentation.

First of all, let's consider what a financial market is. Today, it's straightforward to pull out a price chart or price quote from any financial website. It's hard listening to the news on the television without hearing somebody talking about the financial market and market prices. Where do market prices come from?

Market prices are set by traders buying and selling something in the market. In the financial markets, everyone is trying to gain an advantage over others in the market or at least find a "fair" price for what he hopes to buy or sell. No rational person goes to the market and says, "I want to lose a lot of money."

That's why markets are incredibly competitive and why many of the smartest and well-capitalized people are attracted to the financial markets to figure out how to make money.

How then can we win the game? We have to accept that there will always be bigger traders who know more than we do. We also have to admit that there will always be smarter people than us in the markets. Despite these facts, it is still possible to win if you're able to find a trading edge for yourself in the markets.

So what is a trading edge? It's merely a higher probability of something happening compared to something else.

Directional edge is one of the purest forms of trading edge. When you have a directional edge, it means that the direction of your trade has more than a 50% chance of being right.

Another form of a trading edge is a volatility edge. You might have no idea which direction a trade might go, but you still do have an edge if you think that there is a 55% chance that the price will bounce around a lot over a specific timeframe.

There is another non-directional edge that deals with the magnitude of a move. For example, "I don't know which way this thing is likely to move, but when it does move, it is likely to move a lot." That is what I call the "magnitude of move" edge.

I don't want you to get stuck in the idea that an edge offers a clear sign whether the market is going up or down. At best, an edge is only going to give you a probabilistic tilt. Besides, there are multiple forms of edges and not just directional ones.

Ideally, we should be able to define an edge clearly. At the same time, an edge could also include some kind of skills that you can't quantify.

For example, I know of a prominent spread trader who made consistent money over a long period of time but was unable to explain what he was doing at all and where his edge was. He was able to react to market conditions naturally and instinctively, but of course, that came from the decades he had spent trading those markets.

As a developing trader, you want to be able to define your edge clearly, and if you can't do that, you probably aren't ready to start. Besides defining your edge, you should ideally focus on an edge that is repeatable.

An example of a non-repeatable illegal edge is insider information and trading. This is considered a once-off illegal edge that you might be able to bet big and make a killing, but if they catch you, they're going to put you in jail. So it's probably not worth taking advantage of such an edge anyway.

The kind of edge that we're looking for is something that we can do hundreds, thousands, or tens of thousands of times. There are many different ways and places that people find edges.

The commonly known edges include fundamental valuations, technical patterns, inter-market relationships, specialized information, etc. The key thing to know about edges is that most markets are so competitive and efficient that whatever edge there is, it's usually tiny.

Many well-educated academics and researchers spent a lifetime researching data and conclude that the markets are too random and efficient for anyone to find an edge. We need to respect their views, but I happen to disagree with those views.

I can show you many reasons why I disagree with that, but more importantly, the views of these academics certainly offer us a sobering reminder that it's tough to find an edge in the markets. This is one of the main reasons why trading is so hard.

Another important point I want to share with you is that your trading results aren't always tied to your actions. When you're learning a musical instrument, it would be effortless for me to show you the right things to do with your body to produce the right sound on the instrument and then you can do it over and over again until you become good at it.

You can quickly evaluate your result and know whether you are getting the exact outcome that you want from your actions. This is also true in a lot of sports; this is the idea of feedback in learning and allows us to do deliberate practice for improvement.

However, this is not true in trading. Any idiot can go into any market, execute a trade and get lucky.

Personally, I know of a kid who, for a while, was able to pay for his college by buying crazy out-of-the-money options. He took a few thousand dollars and ran it into a few hundred thousand dollars in the course of a few months. He started to think that he was a genius trader.

He racked up an incredible amount of arrogance about his trading ability and that translated into his trading actions of taking excessive risks. Finally, when his luck turned, he bled badly until his father had to cut his trading off.

I want you to understand that you can have good results by doing bad things. And of course, you might also encounter bad results despite doing good things. This is because most people don't understand the reason for their success and failure in trading.

As a developing trader, you might find an edge, develop a system, go into the market, follow your trading plan and then get hit with five consecutive losses.

You're doing the right things and taking the right steps—but your losing trades could merely be due to bad luck. If you continue to follow your trading plans, things might turn around. There is a high possibility that you can be back in the black again as you accumulate more trades.

The truth is that an edge is difficult to test and quantify. But that doesn't mean that if you can't define an edge scientifically, you take it as a proof that there is no edge.

Many people lean heavily on trading tools like Fibonacci ratios, for example. I've researched a lot of these kinds of mystical approaches, and they're quite difficult to quantify as an edge.

Some people think these techniques are rubbish and there are people who swear by them. I'm sure there's a subset of people who are lying about such methods because they're trying to sell something.

But there's also a subset of traders who believe that they are profitable because of such strategies, although there is a possibility that their trading edge wasn't due to such strategies but due to some other reasons.

When you don't truly understand the real reason why you're successful, it will be impossible for you to teach others. If you don't understand why you're able to do something, then you're not going to be able to explain to someone else what you did. I think it is quite a huge problem in trading.

How to Build Trading Consistency

One of the greatest paradoxes that a trader has to deal with is that he wants consistent results when the markets are noisy and highly random. You have to accept that your trading result is not going to move in a straight line.

In the early part of my trading journey, I used to have this fantasy that I would sit down in front of the computer, trade an hour a day, and draw money out of the market like it is an automated telling machine. That was a pretty naive thought.

Over a long period of time and over a large number of trades, you have a high probability of becoming a proficient and profitable trader if you keep doing the right things. But even so, there will always be surprises here and there. You will have drawdowns, and you will have losing periods, and so the consistency in your trading results will be limited.

So how do we work toward getting that consistency in our trading results? The only way to move toward that consistency is to act with consistency. And this is why the good traders are always talking about being disciplined.

Discipline is one of the most important traits a trader needs to have. Let's recap on what I've talked about. I mentioned that markets are very competitive. If there are edges to be found in the markets, they're likely to be very small and thin edges. And finally, if we want to get consistent results from markets, we need two things: a trading edge and the discipline to apply that edge with consistency.

But knowing all of what I've just shared is not enough to take people to success. Why? Most novice traders who start getting into the market will discover how overwhelmingly emotional it becomes. This was indeed my experience. Before I began to trade, I used to think that I was a pretty relaxed person.

As a performing musician, I could get on stage in front of hundreds of people, and I had no anxiety. In fact, I tend to perform better with a little bit of anxiety. Sometimes, I even go to the extent of creating that anxiety for myself backstage. I will try to imagine all kinds of things that might go wrong just to help create that little bit of tension.

But that calmness when performing as a musician didn't translate to an equivalent calmness when I first started to trade.

When I put on my first trade, I had an incredible and physical emotional reaction. My blood pressure went up, I was breathing heavily, and I was feeling nauseous. I didn't know what was going on, but soon, I realized that I was encountering a strong physical response to the anxiety that I was having with my first trade.

As such, it is not rare to see a trader doing stupid things and making simple mistakes although he might know what the right thing to do is. It is usually the emotions and the anxiety that causes such negative behavior.

Last night, I received an email from one of my blog readers who's been trading for many years.

This was what he said: "My problem is emotional. It's not that hard. You could teach the basics to a kid. I know I have great workable strategies for trading. I just can't follow through due to fear and anxiety. I experience very uncomfortable feelings while I have open positions. I get out too soon, win or lose."

I bet most of us can relate to this trader. And if you still can't relate to it, you'll probably experience that sooner or later at some point in your trading career.

And the point that I want to emphasize is that having such trading anxiety is normal. This is just natural human behavior. Some traders might think, "What's wrong with me? Am I hopeless? Am I stupid?" No, you're not. You're not hopeless, and you're not stupid. You're perfectly normal.

Remember what Andrew Lo said in his Adaptive Markets Hypothesis, which is that you have to understand that participating in a competitive market is like living in an ecosystem or a natural habitat, where you will find both predators and preys.

And if you think from an evolutionary perspective, you'll usually find a predator that's really good at hunting the prey for food. As time goes by, the prey evolves, develops better camouflage, or develops a poison to deter the predator.

At the same time, the predator will evolve as well to be able to hunt other preys that it couldn't previously. You might realize by now that evolution is simply an ongoing arms race between the different animal species over a long time. This is what's going on in the market all the time.

You might find it very easy to fund a currency account with a few dollars, push a button and make a trade. But that ease of starting has in no way equipped you with the necessary abilities to deal with this harsh trading environment that you've walked into. The market is an environment that is continually evolving to make you do the wrong thing at the wrong time.

You buy something, and it goes down. You get angry, you buy more, and it goes down more. You get really mad, you sell it, and then it turns around and goes up. You go into a fit and punch your monitor.

What has just happened to you is not some random thing, and it's not because you're stupid. It's because the market encodes all of these intense emotions from all the traders out there. You happened to behave like a prey while those who made money behaved like the predators. That's the trading environment that we fight in.

The good thing is that this is not a hopeless situation. In the financial markets, a prey can become a predator, and a predator can become a prey. Once you understand this possibility, you can then start to think about ways and strategies to overcome your initial limitations.

The Role of Trading Psychology in The Evolution of a Trader

Trading psychology plays a vital role in this part of your evolution as a trader. You might have discovered your trading edge, you might have formulated a good system, but you still can't do it. This is where we move into the realm of trading psychology.

Personally, I think it's a mistake to believe that you should work on your trading psychology first. This is because trading psychology has no value if you don't yet have a trading edge and a trading plan in the first place. Trading psychology is just a tool to help you go into this twisted market environment and to help you understand what's happening and stick to your plan with discipline.

People don't understand that discipline is an outcome. It is the result of you having your trading edge, having your trading plan, and then following the plan. Discipline is about how well you follow your trading plan but only if the trading plan makes sense.

For example, you might have a trading plan that says, "I'm going to buy the euro against the US dollar every day at 10:05 AM." That's probably a stupid trading plan because there is no edge in that plan. And if you execute this plan with discipline, you're likely to lose it all ("luck" is not going to save you).

Basically, what I'm trying to say is that if you haven't identified a trading edge, there's no point having a trading plan. And if you do not have a viable trading plan with an edge, there's no point having the discipline to execute your plan.

You've got to have your edge. You've got to have your trading plan. And then we focus on how well you execute the plan. And that's where the discipline comes in. You might not believe this, but I've seen traders without an edge, consistently executing their trading plan with perfect discipline, until their trading accounts were destroyed.

Sometimes people ask me what the most important thing in trading is. And the short answer to that is that all of these things matter. I hate those social science equations where people say that skills plus time plus whatever equal success. They are mostly made-up equations to illustrate an over-simplified concept. In trading, the parameters should multiply rather than add.

If any one of those parameters is zero, your outcome is still a zero. If you're a disciplined trader, have good risk management, are well capitalized, but lack one single piece of the puzzle, the whole equation still multiplies to a zero.

Let's summarize what we've talked about today. The answer to how you can win the trading war is that first, you've got to have a trading system with a positive edge and expectancy.

Then you need to verify that edge until you're confident enough to crystallize a trading plan around that edge. The trading plan will say precisely what you will and will not do in the market.

Then you start to follow and execute your plan as flawlessly as you can. This is where trading psychology and discipline becomes essential.

Along the way, you review your trading, fine-tune your trading plan, and work on your psychological and emotional issues as they appear.

That's it. I hope my presentation has been helpful.

How A Beginner Can Find His Trading Edge

Philip: Thank you so much, Adam. It has been a beneficial session. I liked the part where you mentioned that trading success is a multiplication equation and not an addition equation. In your presentation, you spent a significant amount of time talking about finding a trading edge.

Let's assume a relatively new and inexperienced trader is asking you this question, "Adam, what would be a viable way for me to find that trading edge?" How would you answer that question?

Adam: I think the most basic way a new trader can try to find his edge is to learn about pattern recognition on the charts. Most people might think that the charts are highly subjective, but if you understand how markets move, you'll realize that the market keeps repeating a certain kind of structure regarding how prices move.

For a beginning trader, the two core concepts that you can investigate are the idea of pullbacks and the idea of mean reversion. Pullbacks occur when the market starts to consolidate after a trending move. The details of that will be too much for me to cover today, but that is one key idea where a trader can explore to find a trading edge.

Mean reversion is what happens when the rubber band gets stretched too much. It could be a massive single-day move or an extended move away from some average price levels. I think these two concepts are good starting places for a trader when thinking about having a trading edge.

Philip: Does that mean that some types of edges are pretty timeless? Regardless of how things change, those edges based on certain principles will always be there?

Adam: That has been my experience. I've researched a lot of these ancient time series. We have commodity prices from the Middle Ages; we have barley and other commodities prices from Europe in the 1400s.

We even have some of those Phoenician clay tablets of price records made by merchants. Back then what they did was something like a point and figure chart. The merchant did not record the price every day, but when there is a significant price change, the date and the price would be recorded.

In those days, they were already trying to filter out market noise. Based on what I see in the data, I think there's a very high probability that you could have traded commodities in Europe in the 1400s with pullback patterns. I know that you could have traded stocks in the 1800s with pullback patterns.

Basically, what I'm trying to say is that there are elements of price behavior that are timeless. Everyone is now very focused on using AI to take away all of the edges. High-frequency trading is often talked about today. Technology and market will keep changing, but some things will still stay the same in some ways. There are some edges that come and go.

Arbitrage opportunities should be an obvious example. Interest rate relationships in currency trades might also shift when macro perspectives change and evolve. But I do believe that the core of a robust technical approach toward trading these relatively simple price patterns is more or less timeless.

Philip: Do you think such edges appear due to human behaviors? And because human nature has not changed that's why these edges are timeless as well?

Adam: Just a few days ago, I had this idea that the financial market is just a fundamental expression of the human spirit. It's one of the basic things that a human does.

Whether we're standing under the camel skins in the desert under the hot sun bartering over the price of some spices or trading some other commodities on a computer screen from the comfort of our home, we're still mainly the same humans feeling the same emotions, having the same cognitive biases and making the same mistakes.

So yeah, I suspect that the timeless nature of these edges has something to do with our cognitive machinery, which hasn't really changed since the beginning of human civilizations.

The Synergies Between Visual Discretionary Trading and Algorithmic System Trading

Philip: I understand that you consider yourself a system developer, who typically tends to focus more on algorithms and mathematical formulas. At the same time, you wrote a book on technical analysis, which focuses more on using visual patterns to trade. What's your take on the difference between a visual discretionary trader and an algorithmic system trader? Are there any conflicts between the two?

Adam: I think there are more synergies than conflicts between the two. When I published my first book on technical analysis, some people basically thought they were too smart for charts. Personally, I think that the price chart is a very useful heuristic.

I can look at a chart and notice things about the time series that your risk management system cannot see. I quickly get a sense of whether the trading is continuous or discontinuous by just looking at the chart. I know how the price volatility evolves with just a look on the chart. Basically, you can get a quantitative perspective from a somewhat casual inspection of the price chart.

Generally, visual discretionary traders tend to be sloppy with their analysis and trade execution. By quantifying your strategy into a precise rule set that can be executed systematically and algorithmically, you stand a better chance of not falling prey to that sloppiness.

There are definitely some advantages to systematic trading, but my experience as a visual trader is that I can outperform in some areas versus trying to quantify things systematically.

At the same time, I would also argue that systematic trading is not as purely quantitative as what many people might think. As a systematic trader, you're still making decisions. What parameters do you use? When do you turn the system on and off? Ultimately, a systematic trader is still a human providing discretionary inputs into his systematic trading system.

Some traders might say, "I'm not disciplined, that's why I want to be a systematic trader." I think that is just a case of running away from the issue rather than addressing it. If a trader chooses to become a systematic trader because he's not disciplined, he's still going to fail as a systematic trader because it's entirely possible for a systematic trader to override his system in all kinds of harmful ways.

Ultimately, you might decide that you want to be a purely discretionary trader or a purely systematic trader. There's no right or wrong on this, but generally, I think the more you know about the different ways people trade, the more experience you'll gain and the better off you'll be.

Philip: Let's assume that I've found a strategy with an edge and have also backtested it. Obviously, the next stage is about building a trading plan around the strategy. From your personal experience, how would you go about implementing a trading plan? Is there a step-by-step process?

Adam: Building a trading plan shouldn't be complicated because what you need to prepare is merely a document. Your written trading plan might look like a 14-page legal contract with points and sub-points. If your edge is a discretionary chart pattern, you might have issues defining that pattern and turning it into a specific trading rule. Still, you need to try your best to define it and write it down in your trading plan.

After you complete your trading plan, try to forward-test it. Go through the process and execute your trading plan using a simulator or demo account. Try to develop a set of maybe 20 to 50 trades.

Depending on your trading horizon, this process might take you several weeks or months. Of course, you might think that you don't have the time to do this or you don't want to wait. You can skip this forward-testing stage, but you're probably going to pay for it with real money somewhere down the road if you do.

You might also consider forward-testing your trading system by trading with real money in very small position sizes. In some markets like commodity futures, there's a limit to how small you can trade, so this method might not be realistic. If you're trading commodity futures on daily charts, you probably need to risk thousands of dollars per trade. With currencies or stocks, forward-testing with small position size will not be a problem.

Why do I suggest that you forward-test with a small position size? At this early stage, you want to have the capacity to lose for weeks and months without blowing your trading account. You're probably going to be frustrated and discouraged with all of these losing trades, but at least you're not badly hurt financially.

If you rip through your trading account by trading too big with this first forward-testing that failed, you will have a severe problem because you're not going to be able to trade after that. If you've gone through this process by trading small and discovered that your edge didn't work, at least you'll still have the capacity to try to look for some other edges.

Here's where the granularity of the risk matters. If your forward-testing results with small position sizes look good, you can increase the risk more until you're trading a meaningful position size. There are four main stages: the back-test, the forward-test, the actual trading with small size, and the actual trading with significant size. There are learning opportunities in each of these stages.

For example, your forward-test might look good, but when you start to trade with small size, your results deteriorate. Why is that the case? Is it because your forward-test simulator didn't account for the trading spread? How is the real world trading different from your forward test simulation?

When you find the answers to all these questions, you can make adjustments and improve. You might even discover that you don't have an edge after all and need to go back to the drawing board again.

Philip: That's excellent advice, Adam. Before we conclude today's session, do you have any last words of inspiration for those aspiring traders who are just starting out?

Adam: Many trading gurus like to show themselves at the beach, with a nice sports car or swimming in pools with beautiful models to "inspire" those newbie traders to take action and learn from them. I think most educators who present such trading lifestyles are feeding the wrong kinds of expectation to new aspiring traders.

You might have realized by now that my work and my focus is kind of anti-sensational. I really believe that trading can potentially change your life for the better.

Trading is a skill, and there's nothing magical about it. If you have had any formal training in any discipline, the chances are that you've probably learned and done something that's intellectually more difficult than trading. The financial rewards can exceed your wildest dreams. But you need to be prepared for the arduous journey. You need to be aware of the reasons you struggle and the reasons you will fail initially.

Once you start to understand the reality of trading, you will realize that good trading can be boring. And that trading is not going to be the exciting, glamorous event that you thought it was supposed to be. If you can embrace all of these, the journey of becoming a proficient and profitable trader is absolutely worth your efforts.

Philip: Perfect. Thank you so much again for your time, Adam. I wish you the very best of luck in your endeavors and hope for an opportunity to chat with you again.

Adam: All the same to you, Philip. Thank you very much for having me here at this summit.

JET MOJICA: The Systematic Trading Mentor from the Philippines Who Embraces Quantitative and Visual Analysis

> *" In a bull market, market exposure is more important than market timing. The market will leave you behind if you are too obsessed about timing your entry levels.*

Jet Mojica is an independent portfolio manager and the founder of BoH Society, an online community of Filipino stock investors based locally and abroad.

Since 2014, Jet has strategically positioned BoH into a one-stop source of trading solutions, independent market research, and technical analysis training for institutional investors and avid traders in the Philippines.

Before starting BOH, Jet was an associate portfolio manager for BPI Asset Management and Trust Corporation, one of the largest asset management firms in the country.

As a portfolio manager, he managed segregated client equity portfolios in excess of US$45 million. Jet was also a securities dealer for the Financial Markets Group of BPI, and the head of research and risk officer for Multinational Investment Bancorporation.

I was first introduced to Jet by a trader who was based in the Philippines. What caught my eye about him was that he specializes in quant-based models for momentum trading.

Compared to a typical trader who looks for pure discretionary trading ideas for execution, Jet's trading approach from a quantitative and portfolio-management perspective was unique and refreshing.

I felt that his methodology could offer a different angle and bring fresh insights toward trading, and that was why I decided to invite Jet to present his trading methodology in the Online Trading Summit.

Philip: Hi, Jet. Thanks for joining the Online Trading Summit to speak about "Momentum Trades Selection Workflow Using Quant and Data Visualization Techniques." Before we proceed with your presentation, I was wondering if you could share with us how you got started in trading and how has your trading evolved since then?

Jet: I started studying the financial markets when I was still an undergraduate. I did a lot of academic research work on the financial markets in those days. After I graduated, I continued to pursue my craft in the investment research field. Over time, I was given the opportunity to lead as the research head for one of the oldest investment banks in the Philippines.

Philip: Were you mainly using fundamental analysis and value investing as your research model? Or did you move into technical analysis and quantitative trading right from the start?

Jet: My background is in economics, so my original approach was from a macro point of view. I started off as a global macro analyst before transitioning into the technical side of things after that.

Philip: How did you get into the technical side of things?

Jet: When I was still the head of research at the investment bank, I was tasked to put together a proprietary equities trading desk. Because of this, I had to research, plan, and carry out the entire process of setting up the trading team.

After the desk was set up, I had to plan the entire investment process from stock selection to portfolio construction and trade-planning execution. Along the way, I learned about technical analysis and quantitative trading. That was how I discovered my strengths and interest in this field and eventually shifted toward this model.

Philip: Fantastic. Before I go on to ask you more about your trading experiences, let's hear what you have to share with us about your topic on trade selection using quantitative models and data visualization.

Jet: Thanks, Philip. In this presentation, I'll be talking about my workflow and how I use simple quantitative models and data visualization techniques to identify momentum stocks to trade.

This trading approach was developed while I was a portfolio manager at one of the largest asset management firms in the Philippines. Previously, I applied this model mainly on the Philippines equities, but over the past few years, I've started to apply this model to Forex, US equities, and cryptocurrencies as well.

Quantitative analysis wasn't commonly used in the Philippines until about 2007. For the longest time, equity portfolio managers in the Philippines had focused solely on studying company fundamentals and building relationships with top management of those publicly listed companies. That was the primary methodology that they use to get the required information to make their investment decision.

But after the global financial crisis in 2007–2008, more foreign fund managers started to come into the Philippines market. They brought in a more quantitative approach toward their trading methodology, and we figured that we needed to study how we can use those models to improve our trading edge as well.

That's when I started to research and evolve into this quantitative model in our trading process.

Subsequently, I left the investment bank and set up BOH Society because I wanted to introduce this model to retail traders and level the playing field between them and the professional money managers. Through BOH Society, I was able to introduce my process-based trading methodology to the regular folks out there over the past five years.

How to Identify Market Leaders and Laggards

A key focus for me when educating retail traders is to drill into them the importance of buying leaders and selling laggards. This is a trading principle based on William O'Neill's research, which was published and popularized in his book *How to Make Money in Stocks*. He's the founder of *Investor's Business Daily*, and they specialize in relative-strength rankings where they map out leaders and laggards and then publish that research to their subscribers.

We know that we should be focusing on leaders and avoiding laggards, but we don't really know how to go about doing it systematically. Whether you're trading equities, currencies, commodities or cryptocurrencies, the preferred way is to always trade with the trend and trade with the leaders.

Somehow, this is a concept that most retail traders struggle with. At the same time, we often hear people discussing momentum strategies, but we don't really hear about their workflow.

In my presentation, I'm going to share with you my momentum strategy workflow. I will then talk about the ranking models and data visualization techniques that you can use to optimize the way you pick stocks to trade. Finally, I will introduce to you the concept of momentum efficiency.

Ranking Securities by Price Momentum

So what is momentum? The momentum I'm talking about now is not the momentum measured by your technical indicators like the RSI, MACD, or Stochastic. I'm talking about the price action momentum that illustrates a rate of change of price over a specific time horizon.

Let's first define a few momentum metrics so that you have a better context to my explanation later on. First, a 12-month change is the percentage change of the current closing price versus the closing price 12 months ago.

For example, if the close for today is $2 and the closing price 12 months ago is $1, then the value of the 12-month change is 100%. Besides the 12-month change, I'll also be using the three-month change, the five-day change, and year-to-date change metrics later on.

A typical momentum strategy focuses on buying the top 30 performing securities and selling the bottom 30% securities based on the 12-month change of the lists of stocks in the entire universe.

This is essentially a ranking mechanism. If you have a list of 100 stocks in your universe, you're basically ranking those 100 stocks according to their individual 12-month change, to identify which are the leaders and which are the laggards.

Based on my experience, a more straightforward momentum strategy is to rank securities by their year-to-date change, by using the percentage change of the current closing price versus the opening price on the first trading session of the year.

What I've found is that the rankings tend to be more stable and the returns tend to be higher when using this year-to-date ranking versus the 12-month rolling metric.

There are other advanced ranking systems, but the above two basic strategies will help you get started. These simple ranking strategies are missing in the analysis process of the majority of retail traders out there. Most retail traders spent the bulk of their effort on market timing the entries and exits of individual stocks.

Most do not realize that they could have improved their trading edge further if they had used these simple ranking models to help them narrow down the best stocks to trade before trying to applying market timing strategies on them.

Ranking Trades by Year-To-Date Returns

Let's discuss the methodology of ranking securities based on year-to-date (YTD) returns. What are the advantages? What insights will you gain from ranking securities using YTD returns? How will it help you if you refresh this ranking every month, every week, or every day to see which leaders are emerging?

Essentially, the basic principle behind this ranking framework is that the leader for the first three months of the year is also likely to be the leader for the rest of the year. If you've been tracking the YTD performance of all of the stocks in the universe since the start, you would have been able to prioritize your trades on the leaders throughout the year.

At the same time, when you pull out the price charts of these YTD leaders, you will notice that their charts tend to have the most beautiful trends. These are the stocks that usually have well-defined entry levels, well-defined momentum, and show very sustainable moves.

One example I want to highlight to you is a US stock called Herbalife (HLF). If you had run the YTD filter in February 2018, you would have realized that this stock was already one of the top 20 performing stocks in the investment universe. This leading stock was up 23% by mid-February and continued to trend higher for another 25% gain over the next five months.

Herbalife is not the only stock that showed such inclination. Many other stocks emerged as leaders in the first two months of the year and continued to outperform over the next five months.

Once you have a ranking model like the one I just mentioned, you can then use your typical technical analysis methodologies on these leaders to identify optimal entry and exit points, followed by the rest of your trading plan regarding execution and risk management.

I'm often asked this question, "How will you know that the momentum leaders that you filtered during the first few months using the YTD ranking approach will continue to outperform the market for the remainder of the year?"

To answer this question, I did some research where I broke up all the Philippine stocks into four groups based on their respective market capitalization (see Figure 8.1).

Figure 8.1 Market Capitalization Groups (Stocks in The Philippines)

There were 42 stocks in the micro-cap group that has a market capitalization of less than USD 60 million. The small-cap group has 44 stocks of market capitalization between USD 60 million to USD 200 million.

Meanwhile, the mid-cap group with a market capitalization of between USD 200 million to USD 1 billion has about 43 stocks. Finally, there were about 51 stocks in the large-cap group with a market capitalization of more than USD 1 billion.

Once this was done, I tabulated the YTD benchmark returns for the different market capitalization groups (see Figure 8.2).

Large caps can gain 10% to 30% per annum

Mid caps can gain 30% to 100% per annum

Small caps can gain 100% to 200% per annum

Micro caps can gain 200% to 400% per annum

Figure 8.2 YTD Benchmark Returns Based On Market Capitalization

Based on this study, we observed that Philippine stocks in the large-cap group could generate returns of between 10% and 30%. There will be one or two stocks in that basket that will generate more than 30%, somewhere between 50% and 70% a year.

When we continue to drill down, we noticed that mid-caps could generate anywhere between 30% and 100% per annum. Small-cap stocks can generate anywhere between 100% and 200% per annum and then finally micro-caps can generate anywhere between 200% and 400% per annum.

There will always be outliers in each of the groups that defy this benchmark returns that we've compiled over a nine-year study. There will be stocks that will break that 400% return per annum upper limit for micro-caps, and those stocks tend to become unicorns. They have a good chance of generating 1000% return once they break that 400% per annum upper limit.

Please note that this benchmark study was done for the Philippines market. The outcome for the same kind of studies will be different for US equities or other equity markets. Interestingly, this YTD approach can be applied to other asset classes as well. For example, if you're trading Forex, you can rank the different currency pairs in terms of YTD returns and identify the leaders and the laggards.

The insights that you get from the rankings can help you prioritize which currency pairs to run your trading systems on. If you directly apply your trading "long" setups on the top 20% leaders, you should see a strong performance in your portfolio.

Likewise, you can also run your trading "short" setups on the bottom 20% laggards, which means you should be able to generate significant profits from their price decline.

The rankings force you to look only at the charts of the leaders and laggards to identify the optimal point of entries and exits. This should help you improve the overall edge of your trading system.

Do note that all securities' YTD returns will be reset to 0% at the start of each year. In short, it's a level playing field, and any security can be a momentum leader from a YTD scorecard approach.

The scorecard approach is beneficial specifically during the first three weeks to three months of the year because it's straightforward to track the performance of all of the securities in your investment universe during that window.

The basis of the YTD approach is that once a security has an established trend specifically over the first three weeks of the year, that indicative trend during those first three weeks will usually help you to generate returns over the next three months. It starts to get tricky after the first three months because by then, you will need to deal with momentum rotation among the different trades.

That's when you need to tweak your approach and use more sophisticated models to capture the momentum rotation tendencies across the investment universe.

Ranking Trades by Multiple Duration Returns

That's basically how the YTD return scorecard can be used to shortlist the instruments to look at for potential trading opportunities.

In addition, with YTD rankings you can also incorporate shorter duration rankings such as the three-month, one-month, five-day, or even one-day returns to compare the relative performance over the different periods (see Figure 8.3).

Ticker	Name	Close	1DCHG	2DCHG	5DCHG	1MCHG	3MCHG	12MCHG	YTDCHG
USDTRY	US Dollar Turkish Lira	4.890	0.67%	0.76%	0.08%	6.48%	10.78%	40.36%	29.17%
USDINR	US Dollar Indian Rupee	68.645	0.03%	0.06%	-0.44%	-0.34%	1.28%	7.18%	7.50%
USDZAR	US Dollar South African Rand	13.148	-0.32%	-0.24%	-1.04%	-2.88%	5.70%	-0.42%	6.25%
EURSEK	Euro Swedish Krona	10.246	-0.54%	-0.59%	-0.55%	-0.03%	-0.32%	7.64%	4.06%
USDCAD	US Dollar Canadian Dollar	1.302	-0.38%	-0.28%	-1.05%	-0.89%	1.10%	3.67%	3.47%
EURAUD	Euro Australian Dollar	1.581	0.31%	0.37%	0.39%	0.11%	0.63%	5.87%	2.74%
GBPAUD	British Pound Australian Dollar	1.774	0.08%	0.12%	0.13%	-0.95%	-1.16%	9.49%	2.38%
USDCHF	US Dollar Swiss Franc	0.988	-0.60%	-0.64%	-0.55%	-0.51%	-1.32%	2.36%	1.40%
EURNZD	Euro New Zealand Dollar	1.715	-0.05%	-0.10%	-0.17%	-0.45%	0.19%	4.89%	1.27%
EURCAD	Euro Canadian Dollar	1.525	0.11%	0.20%	-0.81%	-0.69%	0.99%	3.24%	0.99%
GBPNZD	British Pound New Zealand Dollar	1.924	-0.27%	-0.35%	-0.43%	-1.28%	-1.60%	8.47%	0.91%
GBPCAD	British Pound Canadian Dollar	1.711	-0.12%	-0.04%	-1.06%	-1.52%	-0.81%	6.77%	0.62%
EURGBP	Euro British Pound	0.891	0.24%	0.26%	0.27%	0.85%	1.71%	-3.36%	0.37%
NZDCAD	New Zealand Dollar Canadan Dollar	0.889	0.15%	0.30%	-0.64%	-0.25%	0.78%	-1.58%	-0.29%
USDNOK	US Dollar Norwegian Krone	8.133	-0.71%	-0.67%	-0.56%	0.89%	0.67%	3.69%	-0.94%
EURCHF	Euro Swiss Franc	1.158	-0.13%	-0.16%	-0.30%	-0.30%	-2.08%	1.63%	-1.04%
GBPCHF	British Pound Swiss Franc	1.299	-0.36%	-0.40%	-0.57%	-1.14%	-3.83%	5.10%	-1.39%
AUDNZD	Australian Dollar New Zealand Dollar	1.085	-0.36%	-0.47%	-0.56%	-0.34%	-0.43%	-0.92%	-1.46%
USDJPY	US Dollar Japanese Yen	110.970	0.03%	-0.07%	-0.21%	0.32%	0.56%	1.78%	-1.51%
AUDCAD	Australian Dollar Canadian Dollar	0.965	-0.22%	-0.17%	-1.19%	-0.58%	0.35%	-2.50%	-1.73%
EURUSD	Euro US Dollar	1.171	0.48%	0.49%	0.25%	0.64%	-2.28%	-0.90%	-2.40%
GBPUSD	British Pound US Dollar	1.314	0.25%	0.30%	-0.02%	-0.64%	-2.69%	2.68%	-2.75%
CHFJPY	Swiss Franc Japanese Yen	112.310	0.65%	0.58%	0.35%	0.84%	1.86%	-1.03%	-2.89%
NZDUSD	New Zealand Dollar US Dollar	0.683	0.52%	0.57%	0.41%	0.65%	-0.99%	-5.35%	-3.64%
AUDCHF	Australian Dollar Swiss Franc	0.732	-0.45%	-0.52%	-0.68%	-0.19%	-2.70%	-4.01%	-3.70%
EURJPY	Euro Japanese Yen	130.000	0.49%	0.42%	0.05%	0.52%	-0.26%	0.57%	-3.89%
GBPJPY	British Pound Japanese Yen	145.850	0.28%	0.18%	-0.23%	-0.32%	-2.05%	4.01%	-4.22%
CADJPY	Canadian Dollar Japanese Yen	85.270	0.41%	0.22%	0.86%	1.23%	-1.23%	-2.57%	-4.82%
AUDUSD	Australian Canadian Dollar US Dollar	0.741	0.16%	0.12%	-0.15%	0.31%	-0.83%	-6.25%	-5.04%
NZDJPY	New Zealand Dollar Japanese Yen	75.780	0.53%	0.52%	0.20%	0.96%	-0.47%	-4.14%	-5.09%
USDMXN	US Dollar Mexican Peso	18.531	-0.49%	-0.52%	-1.85%	-3.56%	-5.32%	4.53%	-5.73%
XAUUSD	Gold	1,223.190	0.05%	0.01%	-0.17%	-2.72%	-5.31%	-4.69%	-6.16%
AUDJPY	Australian Dollar Japanese Yen	82.230	0.18%	0.05%	-0.35%	0.62%	-0.89%	-5.01%	-6.47%
XAGUSD	Silver	15.514	0.15%	0.06%	0.15%	-3.38%	-5.30%	-9.17%	-8.77%

Figure 8.3 Relative Performance Summary Table

With this table, you can potentially identify a good counter-trend trade despite there being a sharp decline in their YTD returns.

189

Or you can use the table to identify swing-trading ideas by focusing on instruments that have strong YTD returns but are currently showing a short-term one-month decline in returns.

These are some examples of how you use a relative performance table that incorporates multi-duration returns and rankings based on your specific trading strategy. However, it might not be easy for most people to analyze these comparison data in such a table format because it can look overwhelming.

Simplifying Momentum Trade Selection Using Data Visualization

This is where we bring in data visualization techniques to help us graphically analyze the table of data, to identify the best momentum opportunities.

Generally, when we use data visualization techniques, what we're trying to do is to look for outliers. We're trying to look for instruments that stand out and can differentiate themselves from the rest of the investment universe.

One example of such a data visualization technique is to plot the instruments to compare a short duration return (e.g., three-month returns) against a long duration return (e.g., YTD returns).

With this technique, we're able to create four quadrants to visually identify lagging instruments, improving instruments, leading instruments, and weakening instruments (see Figure 8.4).

Part 2 – Systematic Traders / Jet Mojica

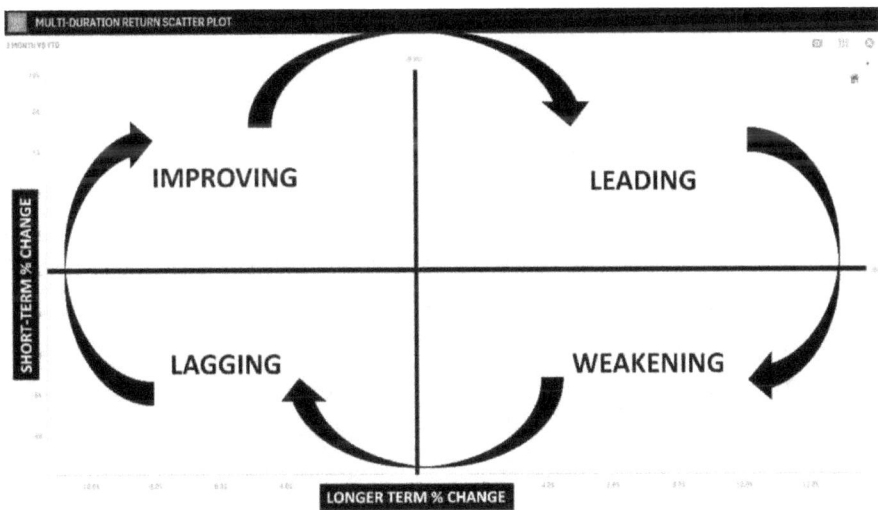

Figure 8.4 Multi-Duration Return Scatter-Plot

On the first day of the year, all the instruments start at zero, at the bottom left corner of the scatter-plot. Gradually, the instruments will begin to spread themselves across the different quadrants.

Some instruments will advance quickly toward the top right "leading" quadrant and become the leaders of the pack. Some of the instruments will start lagging immediately at the start of the year by remaining at the bottom left "lagging" quadrant.

Meanwhile, some instruments will move into the top left "improving" quadrant, meaning their short-term trend is improving, but the long-term trend is still negative. Lastly, those instruments that move into the bottom right "weakening" quadrant show a positive long-term trend with a deteriorating short-term trend.

If you keep reviewing how the various securities move through a multi-durations scatter-plot, you'll notice some of the leaders weakening at some point and fall back into the "weakening" quadrant.

If the weakening continues, these securities might even drop into the "lagging" quadrant and become the new laggards. The true leaders, however, might fall into the "weakening" quadrant briefly before recovering their upside momentum and head back into the "leading" quadrant again.

Typically, my preferred parameters for the multi-duration return scatter-plot combinations are the three-month return versus the YTD return because that's the timeframe which I base my trading system on (see Figure 8.5 for an example of a scatter-plot I did for NYSE and NASDAQ equities).

Figure 8.5 Sample Scatter-Plot of NYSE and NASDAQ Equities

However, if you have a different trading horizon or trading style from me, you can consider using other combinations of the scatter-plot for your needs.

For example, if you're a scalper or day trader, you can use the two-day vs. the five-day return scatter-plot to identify the instruments in the ideal quadrant for your type of day trading strategy.

If you're a swing trader, you have a longer trading horizon compared to a scalper or day trader. You're better off looking at the five-day vs. the one-month scatter-plot.

If you're a trend follower and trying to buy into pullback, then your best bet is to look at one-month versus three-month scatter-plot. Focus on instruments that are pulling back on a one-month return but still maintain their three-month uptrend.

Finally, long-term position traders use the three-month vs. 12-month, or YTD scatter-plot for big-picture trends and pullbacks.

Let's recap what we've covered so far. We've talked about how to generate ideas using a YTD scorecard model. The model is very helpful in identifying leaders, laggards, and themes.

We've covered how to track momentum rotation using a multi-duration table and scatter-plot model.

We have also covered how scatter-plot models are not just useful for momentum trades and also how you can use the visualization model to generate ideas regardless of your trading style, trading preference, and trading strategy.

However, momentum is not the only factor that you need to consider. Volatility matters too!

Finally, I want to introduce to you the concept of momentum efficiency. Momentum is the parameter that determines your return. However, volatility is what defines your risk. Profitable trading is never just about momentum and returns. Other than momentum, other factors, especially volatility, need to be considered as well.

I'm now going to share with you how to use the momentum efficiency framework, through a combination of momentum and volatility data, to generate a watch list or a model portfolio that you can eventually use to execute trading ideas on.

So what is volatility? Volatility is a measure of the variation of returns of a security over a specified time horizon. A typical high-volatility security will have a lot of wide peaks to trough swings in the shorter term although its longer-term movement might show a very clear uptrend (see Figure 8.6).

Generally, we don't like this kind of security in our portfolio because our portfolio returns will be subjected to wide swings as well. We prefer to have securities in our portfolio that has a smooth uptrend and are not swinging too much in their price movements because smooth price movements are easier to trade compared to high-volatility ones.

If you're a swing trader, obviously you want to trade those stocks that have high volatility. But if you're putting together a portfolio for the long term to capture excess returns or to generate alpha, you want to focus on instruments that are trending in your preferred direction but low in price volatility.

Volatility is a measure of the variation of returns of a security or market index

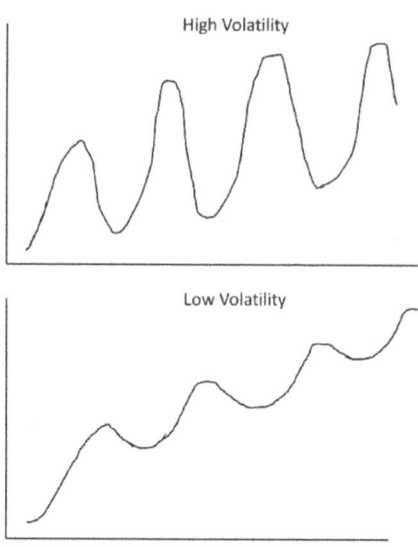

Figure 8.6 High Volatility Return Versus Low Volatility Return

This is where the momentum efficiency model comes into the picture. This model is based on the Efficiency Frontier framework introduced by Harry Markowitz.

Markowitz put all the individual securities in his investment universe into a scatter-plot and then compared their individual expected returns against price volatility.

Now the problem with this approach, when applied to stocks, is that it's reliant on your estimates of expected returns. Estimates that are based on fundamental analysis and fair value estimates can be very cumbersome to compile for use in the efficiency frontier framework.

Instead, I decided to use price momentum as a replacement for fair value estimates, and use it to compare against price volatility. This is how I came up with a momentum efficiency frontier model (see Figure 8.7).

Compared to fair value estimates, price momentum is a more stable, more predictable proxy for expected returns.

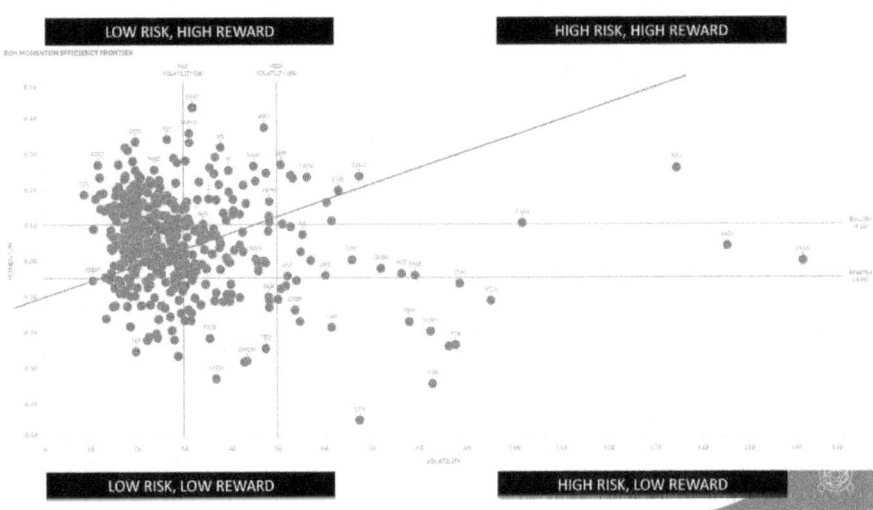

Figure 8.7 Momentum Efficiency Frontier Scatter-Plot

With the momentum efficiency frontier chart, you will be able to deduce which individual securities are efficient, or which securities are rewarding you for the risk you took on them.

Do note that the relationship between risk and returns is non-linear. Just because you're taking risks, it doesn't mean you're going to be automatically rewarded.

This is a common misconception that many retail traders have. They tend to believe that the only way for you to generate excessive returns is to take on excessive risks.

Once you start looking at the momentum efficiency frontier scatter-plot, you'll begin to realize that even if you're taking on excessive risk through high-volatility stocks, you might not be equivalently compensated with a high-momentum stock.

Ultimately, it really depends on what you're trying to capture. Are you trying to capture more momentum? Are you trying to capture more volatility? With this momentum efficiency scatter-plot, you'll be able to consider your options. Again, this framework can be applied to different asset classes and different sectors to find the best opportunities in the specific segment that you like to trade in.

Let's summarize what you've learned so far.

We started off with momentum strategies by ranking securities based on their YTD performance or across other timeframes. This ranking model helps us to systematically look out for leading stocks to long and lagging stocks to short.

Next, we learned about data visualization so that we can compare short-term momentum returns vs. the long-term momentum returns.

By using the scatter-plot using two different timeframe returns, we can find the ideal stocks to trade based on our specific trading strategies. Lastly, we talked about the momentum efficiency frontier that can help us combine momentum and volatility in a unified framework. With this framework, we can focus on capturing potential trading ideas that can give us the best possible risk-adjusted returns.

That's the end of my presentation, Philip. I'm happy to answer any questions that you might have for me.

Philip: Thanks for the great sharing, Jet. You're right. Many traders constantly look to time their trades but seldom put enough thoughts into the kind of stocks they should shortlist to trade.

Earlier in your presentation, you talked about the range of returns between stocks of different market capitalization. To many retail traders, it might seem like an easy and straightforward way to generate higher returns by just focusing on the leaders in the small and micro-caps. Is there any downside to concentrate on only those categories of stocks?

Jet: You're right. One of the findings of my studies is that if you want to generate higher returns, you need to move away from the prominent large-cap companies and look into the speculative ones like small-caps and micro-caps. However, that's just one aspect of the equation. The underlying factors like risk and volatility are what you will need to consider and accept as well.

Philip: Based on your YTD returns ranking model, you mentioned that after the first three weeks of the year, we will be able to see the leaders emerging. Does that mean that we should avoid trading for the first three weeks of the year and start looking at potential trading ideas from the fourth week onwards?

Jet: That's right. That is how I do it. By waiting for the leaders to emerge during the first three weeks, I'll be able to target the outperforming and high-momentum stocks, which will likely provide me a higher probably returns over the next three months.

Philip: If I attempt to buy a leader that has strong YTD returns, as well as solid returns over both the prior three-month period and prior one-month period, do I risk buying at the top of that leader's uptrend?

Jet: That's a good question. There are two factors that you need to consider further here. First, you can use the "market capitalization benchmark" returns numbers to see if the stock that you're buying has already reached the upper limit for the year.

For example, if you're looking to buy a large-cap Philippine stock and it is already up 30% for the year, the likelihood is that the stock has already reached its peak for the year. The probability of you generating more returns from this stock for the rest of the year will be lower unless that stock turns out to be an outlier kind of leader.

Secondly, financial research literature has previously established that for prices that have been in a trend for three months, it will likely remain in that trend for the next six to ninth months before encountering a choppier and volatile price fluctuation. So that is another factor you can use to see whether it's worth taking a chance on that strong leader as well.

Philip: I'll like to discuss your trading workflow beyond the initial shortlisting of potential stocks. Let's say you have used both the momentum ranking model and the momentum efficiency frontier model and shortlisted a few instruments that you think have high potential. How do you go about deciding which ones to trade, when to trade or whether to trade all of them?

Jet: It depends on my view of the general market sentiments. When I'm bullish about the broad market, I tend to be fully invested at all times on those leaders in my watch list. I will try to deploy as much and as quickly as I can into those leaders because cash will be a drag on my performance if I don't deploy them.

In a bull market, market timing for me becomes a secondary consideration.

As long as my stock selection process is intact and I am bullish about the market, then I should be safe because I'm already holding the strongest leaders in my investment universe. However, if my view on the broad market is bearish, I tend to be very selective and trade just a portion of my portfolio rather than being fully invested, or rushing into the stocks in my watch list.

Philip: Once you decide to buy a stock based on all the parameters we've discussed earlier, do you also have a stop-loss for this trade in case you're wrong or if the momentum reverses suddenly towards the downside from that point onwards?

Jet: It depends. When the market is bullish my usual process is to review my positions every three weeks and re-balance accordingly.

I do have stop-losses on individual positions. But as long as my portfolio's equity curve is well behaved and not affected by a particular stock's underperformance, there are instances when I will keep those positions even if the stop-losses get hit. I typically hold out and rebalance the portfolio at the end of the three-week review period.

However, if the broad market is bearish, I have very tight stop-loss rules that I will exit the trade once it is hit. Also, I'm usually not fully invested during a bearish market environment.

Simplifying The Asset Allocation Strategy and Balancing the Portfolio

Philip: How do you size your trades? How do you allocate your capital among the different positions?

Jet: I just simplify the asset allocation process and equal weight to everything. Applying equal weights is the simplest way to allocate your investment capital and is known to outperform portfolios that used more sophisticated optimization strategies.

But regardless of the portfolio allocation rules you use, you need to understand that the number of securities you hold in your portfolio will depend on your portfolio size. Here are some basic rules of thumb:

For portfolio sizes US$200,000 and up, optimal holding is seven to 11 securities. For portfolio sizes US$60,000 to US$199,999, optimal holding is five to seven securities. For portfolio sizes less than US$60,000, optimal holding is three to five securities.

The above rules of thumb are just guides and should also depend on your trading experience. If uncomfortable with the prescribed rules, move one or two bullet points up until comfortable. In my experience, there's no point to holding more than 11 securities unless you're managing a sizeable portfolio or managing other people's money.

An equal-weighted portfolio for a US$200,000 portfolio size would mean an allocation per trade of between 9.09% and 14.24%.

Philip: Let's say one of your stocks has outperformed significantly and that stock is now occupying a big part of your portfolio value. During your review stage, do you rebalance your portfolio by selling a portion of this stock and re-allocate the capital to other stocks to equalize your portfolio?

Jet: If that stock is already trading at the upper limit of the benchmark returns of its market capitalization group, I'll trim some and put it back to its original size during the review stage.

If that stock is not yet trading at the top end of its range, then I will let it be and continue to ride on the profits that this stock has accumulated. For those under-performing stocks in my portfolio, I'll just yank them out and replace with other potential leaders.

Philip: Is there any downside risk a trader needs to be aware of when using this quantitative and visualization model?

Jet: When using this quantitative and visualization model, one key thing you need to pay attention to is the context of the market. You have to take a view on whether the overall market condition is bullish or bearish. If the market sentiment is bearish and you're trying to trade those momentum leaders, their trends tend to have a shorter duration and a shorter lifespan.

Philip: So what you are trying to say is that before you even use the model to identify leaders to trade, you should already have a view on the broad market trend?

If that's the case, do you also attempt to plot the global stock indices to identify the global market leaders and laggards before you drill down to the individual stocks? Or do you have other ways to determine broad market sentiments?

Jet: There are two ways to determine broad market trends. The first method is to use traditional technical analysis.

For example, you can study the stock index and compare the price against the 200-day moving average. If the price is above the 200-day moving average, it means that the board market is likely bullish. You should only engage in the market if it's above the 50-day moving average or above the 200-day moving average.

The other method to study broad market sentiments is to count the number of stocks with positive returns versus the number of stocks that have negative returns. Either of the above methods should be able to indicate to you the health of the broad market and whether your momentum strategies will work under these conditions.

Philip: There is this saying that getting into a trade is not nearly as important as when you get out. Based on what you have just shared, it has mainly been about what to get in and when to get in.

Do you have a model regarding when to liquidate your positions? You can't possibly wait until those stocks in your portfolio become laggards and fall back into the bottom 30% before you get out, right? How do you decide when to get out of each trade to stem losses and to maximize your profit?

Jet: That's a very good question. I always tell my students that in a bull market, market exposure is more important than market timing. The market will leave you behind if you're too obsessed about your entry levels.

On top of the review process that we do every three weeks to rebalance our portfolio, we also try to protect the profits that we've made by having trailing stops for all our individual positions. When the trailing stops get hit, I will get out, even if the planned review and rebalancing process is two weeks later.

Philip: Let's say one of your leaders hit its trailing stop and exited the trade. Is there any possibility that you might get back into this stock again?

Jet: I need to re-evaluate this stock before I consider re-entering again. My trailing stops are pretty liberal, so if a stock triggers its trailing stop, this means that there's a good chance that the stock has started to roll over into a major downtrend.

Philip: Jet, thanks very much for your wonderful sharing. I'm sure your data and visualization models will offer the traders out there plenty of ideas on how to improve their trade selection edge. I hope we'll have opportunities to exchange pointers again!

Jet: The pleasure is mine, Philip. Thank you very much.

PART 3
ALGORITHMIC TRADERS

ANDREA UNGER: The Renowned Trading Mentor from Italy Who Won the World Cup Trading Championship Three Times in A Row

" You have to risk and trade small, in fact much smaller than you can imagine, because the losing streak is always around the corner.

Andrea has been a full-time professional systematic trader since 2001 and an honorary member of SIAT, the Italian Technical Analysis Organization member society of IFTA (International Federation of Technical Analysts).

I got to know about Andrea when I read about his prolific achievements in the global trading competition arena.

He is renowned for being the only trader to ever win the World Cup Championship of Futures Trading titles three years in a row, with returns of 672% in 2008 (futures division), 115% in 2009 (futures division) and 240% in 2010 (futures & Forex division). In 2012, he won the competition for the fourth time, becoming the only four-time winner of World Cup Trading Championship.

A frequent speaker, Andrea has been invited to speak at IFTA world conferences in Sydney 2016 and Milan 2017, and other important financial events around the world.

Andrea is one of the very few algorithmic trading educators out there, whom I've noticed is able to translate potentially complicated algorithmic trading strategies and processes into easy-to-understand trading knowledge for the layman.

So when the opportunity came along, I knew I had to invite him to contribute his trading knowledge in the Online Trading Summit.

In his presentation, Andrea told us how he got started in algorithmic trading and illustrated his comprehensive six-steps process to building an algorithmic trading strategy that will help any new trader lay a strong foundation in systematic trading.

Philip: Hi Andrea, welcome to the Online Trading Summit. We're honored to have you here at the Summit so that you can tell participants about your trading experience and knowledge. For a start, could you tell us how you got started in trading? How long ago was that and how did your trading evolve since then?

Andrea: Sure. I got started in trading a long time ago. In fact, that happened in the past century, sometime around 1997. I had a Master of Science Degree in Engineering and was working as a mechanical engineer in a multinational company. At that time my colleagues and I were interested in making some extra money, so we started investing in the stock market, mainly based on rumors.

We even purchased the shares of the company that I was working for. We did make some money at the very beginning, and because of that, I felt that I was very smart! As usual, after I ran out of beginner's luck, I lost all that money and more. However, I didn't quit after that because I didn't like to lose money and I didn't like being a loser. I still felt that I was smart enough to figure out how the market works.

So I started studying and tried to understand how markets really work. I discovered technical analysis and learned about all the standard tools like moving averages, indicators, and oscillators.

I was still losing money although I felt I was growing and learning as a trader. An important turning point happened when I discovered some price inefficiencies in some of the instruments in the Italian market. Those instruments were "covered warrants," which were some kind of options quoted by market makers.

The market makers had slow software, so their quotes were coming out a bit late. Their warrant and option prices were about five to thirty seconds slower than they were supposed to be based on the underlying price updates. As I was pretty strong with my math, I made some quick calculations and figured that there was room for me to conduct arbitrage trades.

So I started making money through these arbitrage trades. I resigned from my day job and became a full-time trader. I knew that I would be able to easily find a job in one to two years if trading didn't work out for me in the end, so I was pretty relaxed when I started this adventure.

As time went by, I realized that the banks and the market makers would not stick with such poor software for long and that very soon I would run out of opportunities to do these arbitrage trades.

I knew I needed to prepare myself for the future. I started to dive deep into other aspects of trading. I understood that the best form of trading for me based on my mindset and skill sets was to find my path in automated trading.

As I have a mathematical mind, I found that developing trading systems based on numbers, backtesting, and fixed trading plans was the best option for me. So I started developing my trading system by putting the rules that I thought were "common sense" into the machine. It was a disaster.

Then I started trying to mix all sorts of indicators to find the best setup, and that was another disaster. So I began to think that it might be impossible for me to find my way in automated trading. But I didn't want to quit.

Fortunately, I had a friend who spoke to me on one occasion, "Look, I know you're a smart guy. I want you in my team to help me develop trading strategies." He passed a simple piece of code over to me and said, "This is the starting point. We started developing on this; now you help me continue on that."

"How could it be that simple?" I wondered to myself. And it turned out that it was supposed to be that simple. It all started from that tiny piece of code. I built the entire environment you probably have heard about today from that starting point.

I realized that it was possible to develop strategies based on a simple process where you put things together brick by brick, just like how you build a cathedral.

You formulate a plan. You start stacking the bricks one on top of another and in the end, you will have your building, your cathedral or whatever you prefer to imagine. After I designed my first profitable strategy, I was able to continue my work in trading with a more relaxed attitude. I knew I already had something that worked and I just had to think of other ways to find and build profitable trading systems.

So year after year, adventure after adventure, I found other models to build trading systems, and I'm still using them today. I have some basic models that I put strategies on, followed by layering trading rules on top of that. It's not that difficult once you find the right way to get started.

I decided to go with systematic trading because I believe that it helps me psychologically. Once everything is in the machine and running, it means you have made all the decisions in advance, and as such, it's easier to stay in the markets.

If you're a discretionary trader, you have to make decisions during the market activity, and that can put you under significant stress. Whether you're losing or making a lot of money, you feel stressed about your trades, and the pressure doesn't help you in making the right decisions.

In systematic automated trading, you first measure your idea with backtesting. Once that is done, and you believe you have a good strategy that works, you just turn it on and let the machine do the job for you. Also, the computer can handle many tasks at the same time but human beings cannot.

For example, a human trader can trade in only one to three markets at any one time while the machine can easily trade more than thirty markets at the same time.

I remembered an incident that happened when I was still a trader manually managing my trades. I was trying to purchase some shares, and I entered the market with a supposed size of

10,000 shares. At the very moment when I clicked on the mouse button, the stock price jumped. I was thinking to myself, "Oh! I am so good. Look! I've just bought the shares, and it rallied immediately!"

The next moment, I noticed something weird. I realized that I was the one who made the share price jumped. I had entered 100,000 shares instead of the 10,000 that I was planning to buy. So it was my 100,000 purchased shares that sent the share price to the sky!

I tried to get rid of those extra shares while trying to minimize any losses. It was a struggle, but I somehow managed to do that with some patience. If I had used a computer to execute my trade automatically, this would not have happened. Once you program the size into the machine, it doesn't add a zero to the number of shares to purchase.

Philip: Was this automated trading system implemented even before you joined the World Trading Championships? Did you utilize your trading systems during the trading competition?

Andrea: I won the World Cup Trading Championships in 2008, 2009, 2010, and 2012, and I achieved that using trading systems. In the first edition of the competition, my trading ideas were generated by my system on my computer, but the orders were still placed manually because automated execution technology was not as good ten years back compared to today.

However, during the competition in 2010, I implemented an automated structure from idea generation to execution of the trades. Those years of competitions helped me a lot in developing my trading skills because I learned a lot on how to react to the changing markets.

For example, the behavior of the markets in 2008 was completely different from the behavior in 2009, 2010, or in 2012. As each of the trading competitions had a one-year window, it was essential to understand that the markets were changing continuously.

I had to react to find the right solution quickly because I was expected to generate the best performance within a 12-month period. As such, I was able to improve my adaptability to react to the changing market conditions.

In the trading competition, we have a small but real trading account of USD15,000. You can't try fifty strategies. You have to choose the strategies you believe should be those that will do best in that competition. Competitions are helpful because they help us to stay in touch with the markets.

So I suggest that anyone should try participating in a trading competition to improve your skills in terms of making the right trading choices.

Philip: That's inspiring! I'm looking forward to having you share with us the trading methodology that you used that helped you achieve those kinds of world-class results in your trading competitions. I'm going to hand the stage over to you right now, Andrea.

Building a Trading System with The A.T.T.E.M.P.T Process

Andrea: Sure. Now I will show you my step-by-step process to building an automated trading system. I like to call this process the ATTEMPT Trading System. ATTEMPT is an abbreviation to help you remember the different steps you have to go through to build an automated trading system (see Figure 9.1).

Analysis
Testing
Tuning
Evaluation
Money
Management
Portfolio
Trading

Figure 9.1 The ATTEMPT process to build a trading system

"Analysis" is what I do to design a trading strategy.

"Testing" is what I do to check to see if my trading strategy has proven to be profitable in the past.

"Tuning" is what I do to improve on a trading strategy that has worked in the past.

"Evaluation" is what I do to check if the trading strategy is a good fit for my trading personality and psychology.

"Money Management "is what I do to properly size my trades to keep risk under control while maximizing the potential of the trading strategy.

"Portfolio" is what I construct so that I can trade a variety of different trading systems to diversify my risks and returns.

"Trading" is what I input into my computer to let it automatically execute trades for me based on the trading rules that I code into my system.

Analyzing The Characteristics and Behavior of your Target Market

Let me first elaborate on the Analysis process. Each market needs investigation. You have to investigate every single market that you want to trade.

For example, you need to find out if the market that you wish to trade has enough liquidity. You have to understand the main characteristics of every single market you're interested in. This is very important. Some trading lecturers say that a robust systematic trading strategy has to work on every market and in every timeframe. I don't believe that such a strategy exists.

Markets are divided into two categories—the category of trending markets and the category of mean-reverting markets. In a trending market, the typical behavior is such that when there is a breakout, the market tends to continue moving in the direction of the breakout.

In a mean-reverting market, the market tends to fade the breakouts. Instead of breaking out above a resistance or below a support, a mean-reverting market tends to reverse its move as it comes close to the resistance or the support.

Over the long run, markets usually trend. Some markets might be going up; some markets might be going down. How can we decide the characteristics of a market? Let me share with you a simple way to test if a market has a trending characteristic or not.

Use a daily chart and program your backtesting software to automatically buy the breakout of the previous day's high and sell the breakout of the previous day's low: no stop-loss, no profit taking. Just keep reversing the trade whenever either of the above two conditions is met.

Leave the commission component out of this simple backtesting. We are not trying to study the profitability of this strategy. We just want to use this simple backtesting strategy to analyze the trending behavior of a specific market.

If the market that you're applying this backtesting on has trending characteristics, this simple strategy should show you some profits. On the contrary, if a market is in a mean-reverting condition most of the time, this basic approach should probably show you losses on your backtesting.

Let's take a look at some of the results that I've compiled and ranked using this backtesting strategy on the futures market over a certain testing period (see Figure 9.2).

Strategy	Symbol	Period	FromDate	ToDate	Net Profit	Max Drawdown	Profit Factor	Trades	Avg Trade	Win%
BuySell	RB3-067	Daily	03/01/2000	End of Data	€ 377.982	(€ 50.709)	1,31	1.705	€ 222	41,3%
BuySell	NG3-067	Daily	03/01/2000	End of Data	€ 334.630	(€ 33.470)	1,26	1.732	€ 193	39,4%
BuySell	GC3-067	Daily	03/01/2000	End of Data	€ 205.350	(€ 36.050)	1,27	1.705	€ 120	39,9%
BuySell	PL3-067	Daily	03/01/2000	End of Data	€ 185.265	(€ 20.725)	1,30	1.753	€ 106	41,0%
BuySell	GX-067	Daily	03/01/2000	End of Data	€ 173.063	(€ 73.550)	1,09	1.786	€ 97	38,1%
BuySell	HO3-067	Daily	03/01/2000	End of Data	€ 171.028	(€ 64.819)	1,13	1.749	€ 98	36,9%
BuySell	SI3-067	Daily	03/01/2000	End of Data	€ 147.350	(€ 126.600)	1,12	1.791	€ 82	35,8%
BuySell	CL3-067	Daily	03/01/2000	End of Data	€ 138.420	(€ 45.890)	1,13	1.719	€ 81	40,0%
BuySell	HE-067	Daily	03/01/2000	End of Data	€ 117.510	(€ 14.600)	1,37	1.695	€ 69	41,5%
BuySell	GF-067	Daily	03/01/2000	End of Data	€ 104.738	(€ 29.213)	1,22	1.810	€ 58	37,2%
BuySell	CT-067	Daily	03/01/2000	End of Data	€ 91.970	(€ 19.505)	1,19	1.768	€ 52	37,6%
BuySell	CC-067	Daily	03/01/2000	End of Data	€ 82.490	(€ 8.660)	1,27	1.715	€ 48	38,1%
BuySell	ZS-067	Daily	03/01/2000	End of Data	€ 81.850	(€ 28.988)	1,14	1.780	€ 46	37,2%
BuySell	IFS-067	Daily	03/01/2000	End of Data	€ 68.675	(€ 78.525)	1,04	1.832	€ 37	37,7%
BuySell	KC-067	Daily	03/01/2000	End of Data	€ 68.081	(€ 38.119)	1,08	1.773	€ 38	36,6%
BuySell	LE-067	Daily	03/01/2000	End of Data	€ 45.440	(€ 13.080)	1,14	1.808	€ 25	37,0%
BuySell	SB-067	Daily	03/01/2000	End of Data	€ 43.826	(€ 13.888)	1,16	1.757	€ 25	37,3%
BuySell	VX-067	Daily	03/01/2000	End of Data	€ 42.250	(€ 36.150)	1,07	1.431	€ 30	34,9%
BuySell	ZC-067	Daily	03/01/2000	End of Data	€ 42.200	(€ 12.988)	1,15	1.777	€ 24	38,4%
BuySell	ZW-067	Daily	03/01/2000	End of Data	€ 36.175	(€ 23.025)	1,08	1.759	€ 21	37,2%
BuySell	G6N-067	Daily	03/01/2000	End of Data	€ 33.970	(€ 36.970)	1,09	1.265	€ 27	38,4%
BuySell	G6B-067	Daily	03/01/2000	End of Data	€ 29.169	(€ 34.875)	1,05	1.768	€ 16	38,1%
BuySell	DX-067	Daily	03/01/2000	End of Data	€ -11.530	(€ 47.935)	0,98	1.866	€ -6	36,3%
BuySell	G6E-067	Daily	03/01/2000	End of Data	€ -14.225	(€ 97.850)	0,99	1.820	€ -8	36,6%
BuySell	ZB-067	Daily	03/01/2000	End of Data	€ -18.344	(€ 51.156)	0,97	1.784	€ -10	37,7%
BuySell	EBI-067	Daily	03/01/2000	End of Data	€ -21.250	(€ 42.660)	0,95	1.827	€ -12	36,9%
BuySell	G6S-067	Daily	03/01/2000	End of Data	€ -24.763	(€ 83.288)	0,97	1.795	€ -14	35,7%
BuySell	EX-067	Daily	03/01/2000	End of Data	€ -26.130	(€ 47.110)	0,93	1.696	€ -15	36,0%
BuySell	G6A-067	Daily	03/01/2000	End of Data	€ -26.200	(€ 61.440)	0,96	1.811	€ -14	37,2%
BuySell	G6C-067	Daily	03/01/2000	End of Data	€ -41.670	(€ 54.120)	0,91	1.781	€ -23	36,7%
BuySell	NQ-067	Daily	03/01/2000	End of Data	€ -48.015	(€ 90.025)	0,93	1.839	€ -26	37,4%
BuySell	G6J-067	Daily	03/01/2000	End of Data	€ -49.125	(€ 93.013)	0,93	1.808	€ -27	36,2%
BuySell	ZN-067	Daily	03/01/2000	End of Data	€ -55.016	(€ 59.672)	0,88	1.874	€ -29	36,7%
BuySell	HG3-067	Daily	03/01/2000	End of Data	€ -92.975	(€ 118.175)	0,90	1.839	€ -51	35,7%
BuySell	ES-067	Daily	03/01/2000	End of Data	€ -108.713	(€ 120.638)	0,85	1.898	€ -57	37,0%

Figure 9.2 Back Testing Results to Study the Trending Behaviour of the Futures Market

From the backtesting result, it's evident that the different instruments don't show common behavior under this simple trend-analysis approach. Those instruments at the top made a lot of money while those at the bottom were a disaster.

From this analysis, we can see that gasoline, natural gas, gold, platinum, DAX, crude oil (at the top of the list) are the markets with typically trending characteristics. So if I want to trade using trend-following strategies, I probably will choose one of these markets to develop my trend-following trading system on.

On the other hand, those instruments at the bottom of the list tend to have mean-reverting characteristics. As such, I will never put my efforts into developing a trend-following strategy on these instruments.

This backtesting result does not tell us the true profitability and viability of this simple trading strategy, but it gives us a good idea about the behavior and the enormous diversity of the different markets.

Next, let's consider a matrix from which we shall base our trading decisions on (see Figure 9.3). Generally, I break it up into four different steps, namely the Why, the When, the Which and the Exceptions.

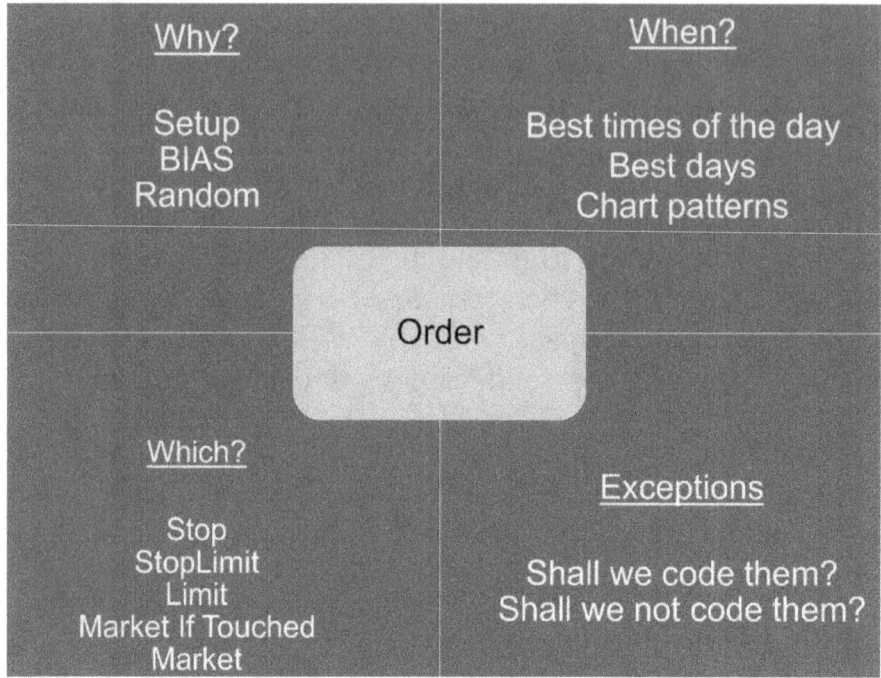

Figure 9.3 The Four Steps of the Analysis Process

Firstly, you need to ask why you are entering the market. One answer for this might be that you have a specific trading setup and that setup has been triggered for you to execute a trade on. Another reason could be due to bias. A bias could be based on the seasonality of a market.

For example, if you discover that a market has a specific tendency to turn bullish or bearish during some periods of the day, you might decide to add long or short positions depending on your trading strategy.

After you know why you are entering a market, the second step is to find out when is the right moment for you to enter the trade. Maybe the session opening is the best time of the day to enter a trade or maybe three hours into the session might be a better time. You might also consider which are the best days to enter and which days are not.

Chart patterns can be another tool to help us decide when to take a trade. Chart patterns tell us something about the recent moves and the behavior that follows after that, so using that information to determine when to enter a trade might be helpful as well.

Let's now consider the third step for placing the right types of orders. There are many different types of orders out there. For example, there are stop orders, stop-limit orders, limit orders, market orders, and so on.

Depending on the type of strategy you use, you might need to consider and decide which type of order will serve your needs. Generally, classical trend-following strategies use a stop order or a stop-limit order, while mean-reverting strategies tend to use a limit order.

Finally, let's consider some of the potential exceptions and decide if we might want to trade them or code them into our trading system or not. One typical exception for me is that I never enter a market during the main economic data release or during the employment data release dates in the United States.

I don't want to enter because there is too much volatility and uncertainty on how the market might behave. I will code and instruct my system not to trade during the first Friday around data release.

Meanwhile, an exceptional event like Brexit is something that I can't code or something that I want to make use of but doesn't make sense to code because an event like this probably happens only once in a lifetime. Instead of writing codes into our system to factor the impact of Brexit, we merely switched off our trading system the day before and stayed out of the market.

Verifying Your Trading Edge by Testing and Tuning Your Trading Strategy

We've just gone through the first stage of our ATTEMPT process: the analysis part. Once that is completed, we go into the testing stage. In our earlier analysis phase, we discovered that the mini S&P 500 has a mean-reverting characteristic.

Let's try to implement a mean-reverting trading strategy on the mini S&P500 and backtest it. Let's use a breakout of the highest high or the lowest low of the last five days as the setup.

Five days is a very important window of time because five days is a week of activity in the markets. When the mini S&P500 experiences a bullish breakout of the highest high within the last five days, we go short. If it encounters a bearish breakout of the lowest low of the last five days, we'll enter long. I coded these rules into my backtesting software and ran the test between 1997 and 2012.

As expected, we had good backtesting results where this trading strategy on the mini S&P500 between the years 1997 and 2012 showed pretty strong profitability. This was a winning strategy, and it confirmed that counter-trend trading is better than trend following for this instrument.

But when we take a look at the equity curve of this strategy, it seems that the drawdown is quite substantial and unstable (see Figure 9.4).

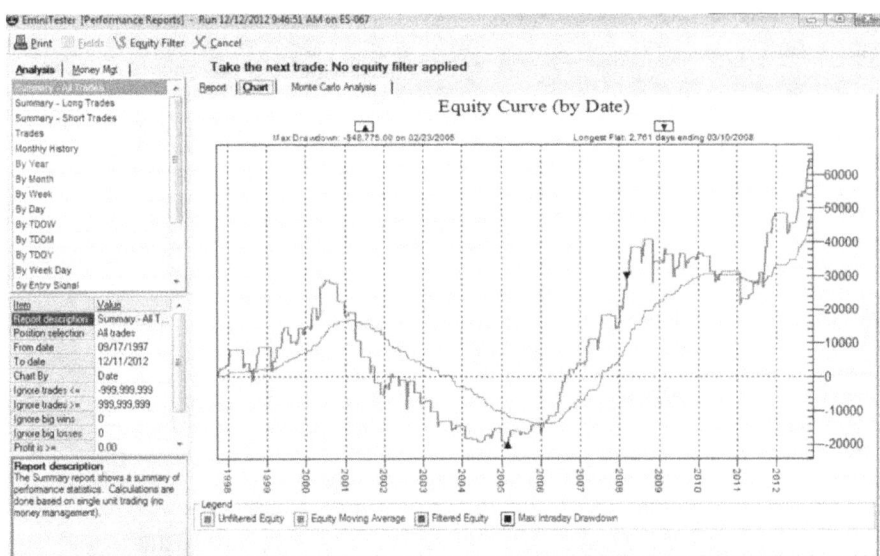

Figure 9.4 Equity Curve Before Adding a Stop-Loss Rule

This is where we add more basic rules to improve the strategy and the equity curve. Let's say we add a stop-loss since I always trade with a stop-loss.

After adding a stop-loss to the rules, we see some improvements to the equity curve. Drawdown is not as deep as before because we now have a stop-loss to protect us from experiencing significant losses (see Figure 9.5).

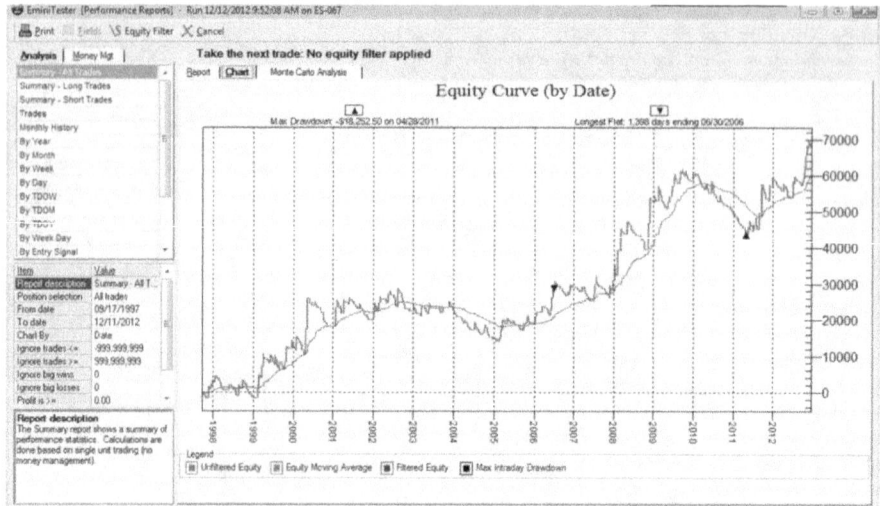

Figure 9.5 Equity Curve After Adding a Stop-Loss Rule

Now our strategy is almost ready. We have a setup, an entry, and a stop-loss. This is where we head into the tuning stage, the third stage of our ATTEMPT process. This is where we try to improve things, to clean up what we've done so far and to see if we can get something even better.

Let's see if any specific day or days of the week might be more conducive for trading. Personally, I believe in bias and agree that not every day is a good day to trade.

For example, if we study the results of a strategy, on single days of the week, we might see that Monday, Tuesday, and Wednesday are more profitable compared to Thursday and Friday. You might also realize that long trades work better on some days while short trades work better on other days.

After you've done such tuning, you can try to run the backtest again to compare the results. After the tuning, the profitability of your system might have improved, and your equity curve might look even nicer now. You might realize by now that curiosity is very important. This is what leads my development because I'm always curious about the markets.

Other elements that you can fine tune includes which part of the day to run your system on. For example, the mini S&P500 is open 23 hours a day with a day session and a night session.

Generally, I believe that the behavior during the day session gives me a much more realistic picture of what the market is doing because that is the period when all the big players are trading the market. If you try to set up the rule for the system to run only during the day session, you might notice an improvement in your backtesting.

The Importance of Evaluating Your Trading System and Firming Up Your Money Management Rules

After we are done with tuning our strategy and rules, it's time for us to do an evaluation, which is the fourth stage of our ATTEMPT process. We need to ask ourselves these questions.

Do the backtesting reports show good results? Are the results consistent over the years? Are the results replicable under normal conditions? Can the strategy work in real time? Are the results real or might there be a software bug that gives you a false positive? Is this trading approach and strategy in line with your personality and beliefs?

This is very important because if you don't like to go against the trend, you will find it hard to implement and stick to a counter-trend strategy.

Psychological and financial strength are important considerations as well. Do I have the financial and mental strength to trade this strategy? Do I have enough money to go through the drawdown periods? Do I have the psychological strength to go through a $10,000 drawdown?

You have to write all of these questions down and answer them with utmost honesty and sincerity. Please don't cheat yourself.

Let's move on to the fifth stage of the ATTEMPT process, which is money management.

Previously in our analysis, testing, tuning, and evaluation stages, we used just a single contract to study how our strategy performs. In reality, there is no limit to how many contracts you can use for each trade. You can buy one contract, 10 contracts or 100 contracts depending on how much capital you have. This is what we call position sizing.

Position sizing can dramatically affect the result of your strategy and how your equity curve behaves (see Figure 9.6). Examples of position sizing include fixed fraction sizing, fixed ratio, and more. I'm not going to elaborate on those here. I suggest readers study more about these sizing methods before using them.

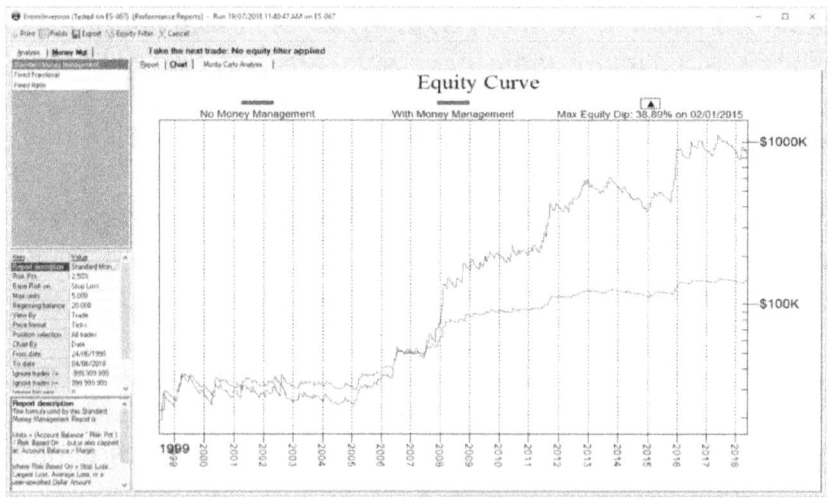

Figure 9.6 How Position Sizing Affects the Equity Curve

Build Your Portfolio of Strategies and Establish Your Trade Execution Rules

The sixth stage of our ATTEMPT process is portfolio. Earlier on, we focused only on one specific strategy on a particular market. Generally, to diversify risks and have a smoother equity curve, you should have a mix of different sectors in your trading systems.

The different sectors might include instruments like indices, energies, currencies, metals, stocks, bonds, and more. Depending on the suitability, you might also want to consider applying a mix of trend-following or counter-trend strategies in the different sectors.

Trading horizon is also an area where you can think about diversifying your portfolio of strategies. You might have a mix of intraday, medium-term, or long-term trading strategies in your portfolio.

The final stage of the ATTEMPT process is trade. This is where you finally think about how you're going execute your trades.

As there are many trading platforms out there, and their features are constantly changing and improving, I'll leave it to you to find out which might be the best fit for you. But as a guide, I will share with you some of the things you need to consider when selecting the right platform to use.

They include factors like the number of markets covered, length of historical data, ease of programming, technical support, integration with your preferred broker, price of the software, is the software buggy, user experience, programming language used, backtesting capabilities, portfolio testing capabilities, learning curve required, real-time trading, and its trading community.

You also need to ask yourself how much money you have to run your trading business. This doesn't include just the amount of money that you're going to put into your trading account. You should also consider the amount of money you need to invest in your trading business, for example, the infrastructure costs such as software, data feeds, and cloud VPS.

If you have a small capital base, you can consider trading Forex because of its small contract size and also its scalability as your small accounts grow into a large account.

That's it for my presentation. I hope I've provided you a good insight into the different stages of building an automated trading system. I'm happy to answer any questions that you might have for me, Philip.

Philip: Thanks, Andrea. That was a fantastic session. For someone like me who hasn't ventured into systematic or algorithmic trading before, what you have shared offers an excellent overview of the different stages of building an automated trading system. I'm very curious about how you won the World Trading Championship on multiple occasions. What were the key elements of your trading system that helped you win those trading competitions?

Andrea: I had to build a plan on which strategies to use and how to use them from January to December during the run of the competition. I already knew how my different strategies were supposed to perform, as I had already done backtesting on them.

In my first competition, I mixed four strategies together. For the intraday trend-following strategies that I have, I used it on the DAX futures, the Italian futures, and the Euro FX futures. I also had an intraday counter-trend strategy on the mini S&P 500.

As such, I was able to have some form of diversification using this small portfolio of trading strategies and markets. As we only have USD15,000 of trading capital to start with, I couldn't diversify significantly.

Because of my backtesting, I was able to have a rough idea of what could happen. I could also measure my trading results during my competition and monitor if things were going properly as planned or if there was something that I needed to change along the way.

Philip: Can the strategies that you used in your competition be replicated in real life trading in other asset classes and instruments as well?

Andrea: You can use the main approach in other asset classes and instruments, but you can't just use the same strategy on other instruments because the exact model was tweaked specifically for the market that I was trading in during the competition.

Philip: Are you advocating that we should always start with analyzing the characteristic of a specific instrument first before coming up with the particular strategy to trade that instrument?

Andrea: Yes. My approach is to understand every single market as much as possible and then to tailor suit the strategy for that market.

Philip: There is this saying that when traders use systematic and algorithm trading, there is always a tendency for them to curve fit. As such, the backtested results might appear very beautiful but might not be robust enough to remain profitable in the future in the long run. What is your take on that?

Andrea: Some kind of tuning is okay if you're just trying to clean up the minor details, but doing too much adjustment or adding too many conditions is wrong. When you do that, you get the best, appealing backtested numbers on hindsight, but it only breaks down in real-life trading.

You have to find a good compromise, which is not easy. There is no rule to say that you can't have more than ten conditions in your trading system. It's based on common sense and experience. That's the reason why I said earlier on that the more perfect your equity curve looks, the more dangerous it is because you probably have put in too many conditions and constraints into your trading system.

Philip: I suppose that together with risk management and position sizing, events like winning and losing streaks will have a massive impact on your equity curve. Based on the systems that you have developed over the years, were there any occasions where you had such long losing streaks that you could have faced the risk of ruin if you sized your trades too large?

Andrea: Yes. I've had many strategies that lost their edges over time. So the proper position sizing where I limit the risk of each trade is the best way to protect my trading account. Even when things go wrong, I'm still losing no more than what I can afford to. That's the key.

You have to risk and trade small, in fact much smaller than you can imagine, because the losing streak is always around the corner. The risk of ruin is something that is very far from my imagination, but that's because I risk very small. I always take just enough risk and never leverage too much.

In my trading account, I usually use only a third of my margin at most. I am very conservative with my use of leverage. You have to stay humble. When you think you've got what it takes to become rich, it's usually that moment when you'll start losing. You have to ask yourself, "How much can I afford to lose?"— and then based on that, you calculate your position size.

Knowing When to Overhaul Your Trading Strategy

Philip: Earlier on, you mentioned that you had many strategies that went broken. How do you know if your strategy has broken down? How do you judge when the time is right to review, fine-tune, or overhaul your strategy?

Andrea: There is no one single way to do that. In the past, I typically ran a Monte Carlo simulation to see what the average drawdown and its standard deviations could be for a specific strategy based on historical data. If the real-time drawdown experienced by that strategy exceeds two standard deviations of its average historical drawdown, I will shut the strategy down.

However, this method is not realistic when I have fifty or sixty strategies. Nowadays, I simply build a ranking of performance for the different strategies that I have. From this ranking and some conditions, I have an automated selection of strategies to trade for the next upcoming period. The rest of my strategies will be stopped and rested.

When a strategy has clearly become weak or is not working anymore, I think it's better to throw it away rather than try to tweak it. When you take a failing strategy and try to tweak the parameters, you might get better performance, but that's usually the result of curve fitting.

Philip: I've heard from systematic traders that they have to keep thinking about new ways, new ideas or new strategies as the market changes, as the trading environment changes, and as technology changes. Is this something that you do on a regular basis? How do you come up with new trading ideas and strategies?

Andrea: It's not really about coming up with new ideas. You might try new setups or more likely new approaches. When you look at the markets every day, you might notice something sometimes and ask yourself, "Hey, I notice something here. Can I take advantage of this?"

Generally, you have to explore new markets and try to understand more about what's going on there rather than trying to find any rocket science ideas.

For example, you might have noticed that for a particular market, entering a trade between noon and 1:00 pm might offer a higher probability of being right.

The discovering of new ideas means that you notice something and you test what you noticed to see if that thing can make money. Then, you check if this new idea is too correlated with the other strategies that you're already using. If the correlation is too high, you might want to use less of this new strategy because you're merely doubling your risk exposure by using two strategies that are highly correlated.

Philip: In your opinion, what would be some of the reasons why certain systematic strategies might lose their edge over time?

Andrea: It is usually due to a loss of the edge itself. Strategies often base their profits on inefficiencies. The higher the number of traders exploiting an inefficiency in a market, the more efficient the market will become because there's always someone out there who tries to anticipate and make a move first, causing the rest of the slower traders to miss out on that profitable move.

Such a situation causes the inefficiency and the edge to disappear because you have too many people trying to do the same thing.

For example, you might notice a big sale at the shopping mall. The bigger the number of people who know about the sale, the faster the discounted items will run out. If you're too slow or heard about the sale too late, you won't find any discounted items left because everything was sold out.

Philip: So does that mean that in order to find a strategy that still has got an edge, that strategy has to be contrary from a certain perspective? If everyone is pursuing the same strategy using the same rules, the edge will start to disappear, right?

Andrea: Let's say there's an opportunity to make a hundred pips. Soon, other traders notice that opportunity and come in to exploit that edge. As time goes by, the hundred pips opportunity becomes 90, 80, or 70 until the point where that opportunity is no longer enough to cover your costs or to compensate you for your trading efforts.

When that time arrives, that edge and that opportunity are gone. You will then have to move on to somewhere else because there's no more real advantage in trying to do something that everyone else is doing as well.

Philip: In recent years, it seems like artificial intelligence (AI) and machine learning has become a very hot topic in trading. It now seems possible that AI and machine learning can be used to analyze the market and develop some kind of trading strategy on its own or at least to improve on a strategy. What's your take on that?

Andrea: I'm not a fan of AI or machine learning. I think that they're mostly curve-fitting tools. I firmly believe in the human action behind the tools we are using.

I analyze with software, I put numbers together, but again it's still me making the final decisions on what to put together. I don't use things that I don't understand. If I don't understand the reason why something could work, I will not trust trading it because it could merely be a coincidence.

In my opinion, we're not yet that advanced to delegate every trading choice and decision to the machines. So far, I have not really seen any successful AI trading guys out there.

Philip: Right now, in your usual daily trading, do you still encounter anxiety even though you are already using an automated trading system? For example, when President Trump says or does something drastic that might move the markets, do you fear and do anything differently with regards to your trading system?

Andrea: No, I don't experience that a lot. Of course, I have temptations to behave differently sometimes, but I try to stick to a routine as much as I can. I will change something only when it is acting strangely or if there is something technically wrong with it.

Even in situations of a losing streak, I will still keep my strategies alive because I am supposed to stick to that routine. Over the years, I noticed that making decisions to change things under such circumstances usually produce poorer results overall compared to just sticking to the original plans.

Philip: If there are overnight Black Swan events, or financial bubbles and crashes, you will continue to run your trading system as usual?

Andrea: That scenario is slightly different. My systems are based on the nature of markets, so if the markets are disturbed and start to behave differently, then I will not continue to trade that market until it returns to its old nature.

For example, if you go out and drink too much and become drunk, then you're not Philip anymore. You're a different version of yourself, and it isn't very productive to discuss trading with you until you have become sober again, right?

It's the same case with the markets. During events like the Brexit or others, the nature of some of the markets might change for a while, maybe for a few days or perhaps a few weeks, so it makes sense to pull the plug on those markets temporarily.

Now, if the event is something like the Fukushima nuclear accident or some kind of disaster, I usually will keep everything running as per normal because the effects of such events exhaust quickly.

Philip: Andrea, it has been a truly wonderful discussion with you. Before we end today's session, will you be able to offer your top three ideas or recommendations to any trader who is looking to go into systematic and automated trading?

Andrea: First, my general advice for any trader, not just a systematic trader, is to stay humble. Stay humble when you're losing and especially when you're winning. When you're making a lot of money, stay humble and be careful.

When you're winning too much money, you might be doing something wrong. You're probably over-exposed. Occasionally, you might do very well, and that's okay, but always be careful because it will reverse, sooner or later.

Second, don't underestimate the power of automated trading because it can help tremendously in your trading if you know how to use it properly. At the same time, don't overestimate what automated trading can do because obviously, it isn't the ultimate miracle and solution to trading.

Don't think that just because you're trading using an algorithm that you will definitely become profitable. The machine is smart, but not so smart to put money in your pockets.

Automated trading can be a way to overcome some psychological issues, or to help you plan according to your trading style, but it's not something that makes you the George Soros of tomorrow.

I chose this systematic and automated approach because I have a mathematical mind. So if you like it, you can approach it. You don't need to be a very skilled programmer to start automated trading. There is some basic knowledge that you need to learn, but you don't need to be a computer wizard to do it.

Finally, you need to have a passion for trading. Please don't trade for money. Trade for passion, because if you trade for passion, you will do it happily and you will overcome the bad periods.

If you just want money, there might be other ways out there to make money while giving you less stress. Making money is not easy, and in my opinion, trading is probably one of the most difficult ways to make lots of money.

Philip: That's great advice, Andrea. I think what you said will bring many traders back down to earth regarding the kind of high expectations they might have about trading. And that is precisely what we're trying to achieve with this Online Trading Summit, to help traders understand that there is no Holy Grail in trading.

Thank you again so much for your time, Andrea. I am very sure your teaching is going to impact many traders out there.

Andrea: Thank you for inviting me, Philip, and I wish the very best for everyone. Stay humble and be careful!

GARY YANG: The Humble Trading Mentor from Singapore Who Trades for A Living as A Home-Based Independent Trader

" *Regardless which trading rules you were taught or which book you read, you ought to test it for yourself. Don't take anyone's word for it.*

Picture this: You're sitting in a deck chair by the white powdery beach looking out in the direction of the Pacific Ocean. Armed with a notebook computer on your lap, you punch in some numbers on your keyboard and guess what? Some 30 minutes later, you are $1000 richer in your trading account.

This is a dream that you might have had before. This is also the dream sold by many trading gurus to their dreamy audience, so as to sell their expensive trading courses easily. Guess what? At the end of the day, these trading gurus are the ones at the beach enjoying life instead of you—and most likely, they aren't holding on to any notebook computer either.

I'm not saying that the above dream isn't possible, but it definitely is way tougher to achieve than how it has been portrayed by those trading gurus. For a start, a realistic goal that any beginner can start to aim for is to become a profitable stay-at-home full-time trader at least.

I got to know one such guy during my years of being in this industry. He doesn't trade from the beach during his holidays but definitely is running his own little trading business from the comfort of his home.

His name is Gary Yang, and in this interview, I attempted to draw out insights from him to understand his trading journey from a part-time trader who lost his entire trading account multiple times, to a full-time stay-at-home trader who is now living the kind of lifestyle that works for him.

Many trading experts featured in this summit trade from home as well, but what differentiates Gary from the rest of the speakers is that he doesn't teach trading for a living. He doesn't sell courses to generate a secondary income. He simply trades for a living.

In my interview with Gary, he told me the story of how he blew up his trading accounts twice as a part-time retail trader before finally getting the enlightenment he needed to become a proficient trader.

He also has plentiful advice for anyone who is looking to turn full time. So if you've always been dreaming about quitting your job to become a full-time, stay-at-home trader, this interview is for you.

Philip: Hi, Gary. Welcome to the Online Trading Summit.

Gary: Hi, Philip. Thanks for inviting me to participate in this summit. I've been waiting to do this recording. I hope I can share something of value to part-time retail traders who are looking to take the same path that I did.

Philip: Yes. Definitely. One of the main reasons why I decided to invite you to share your experience was because you're one of the very few independent traders that I know that simply just trade for a living. So I thought it might be fascinating for the summit participants to be able to understand from your perspective what it takes to become a full-time independent trader.

But before we go into the details of how you became a full-time, stay-at-home trader, I'm interested to hear how you got started in the financial markets. How long ago was that and what was that experience like?

Gary: I got started in the financial markets with SGX shares back in 2004. Like most other retail traders, I started out by going for trading courses. Those were weekend courses, where you pick up some skills here and there, but I didn't really quite get the hang of stock trading.

During a random chance, I attended another Forex trading course by Nicholas Tan. He turned out to be one of my first real trading mentors. He was a retired bank trader, and with his teachings, I started to pick up trading. I began to discover for myself what was suitable for me and what wasn't based on my personality.

At one stage, I busted two trading accounts over a two-year period. But I didn't give up, and over time I started to see more consistency in my trading. Like many of my friends who I was trading together with, I just wanted to learn to trade well and generate side income.

But as time goes by, as my side income from trading started to grow to the point where it was slowly able to replace my full-time job salary, I started exploring the real possibility of becoming a full-time trader. At that time, I didn't have any significant family commitments, so I thought to myself why not give it a try.

So the agreement that I had with my wife was that I would give myself one year to try it out using a certain amount of fixed capital that I'd saved up over the years. If I were to bust that account within that one year, I'd just look for another job. And that was how I became a full-time independent trader in July 2012.

Philip: I see. Before we go on to that part of your trading journey, I'm really interested in understanding your experience busting up two accounts before that. So what happened? What were you doing wrong that you ended up busting up the account? Were you trading on a part-time basis then?

Why Beginner's Luck Is Detrimental to A New Trader's Journey

Gary: Yes. I was trading part time. I was mostly using the daily chart and thought I had a pretty lucky start to my trading journey.

And as you know, most beginners start to get cocky after they have like maybe nine wins in a row. I thought I had mastered the market, but then it is usually at those times that the market will come back and haunt you.

When I started to think that I had conquered the market, I started to over-risk. I began to risk a lot more and refused to cut my losses because I thought I was better than the rest in understanding the market. And I did this even as the positions went against me.

As these huge money-management and risk-management issues started building up, I built up a position so big that I eventually got my margin call. That was my first account, and it was about $10,000.

Philip: So you lost everything during that particular margin call?

Gary: Almost everything. I think I was left with just about a thousand dollars. To me, that was as good as blowing up my account. But due to the earlier series of trading successes before this margin call, I thought this was just a once-off event, so I wasn't too afraid and concerned. I went on and topped up my trading account to twice the amount that I had in the first account.

Within a month, I busted the account again!

Philip: Was it due to the same reasons again? Did you bust your second account due to one single trade or was it attributed to a series of losing trades?

Gary: Yes, I busted my second account due to a single trade. I opened multiple positions, but they were all linked to the same trade in which I was averaging down on. I refused to admit that I was wrong although the price was heading lower and lower.

At that point, the market was starting to rotate to the downside. I could have gotten out, but I didn't because it was still far away from my profit target. I thought I was "disciplined" by holding on to my position.

Come to think about it; there were many signs that showed that the market was reversing south. Prices were starting to form lower lows, but I kept telling myself that the price would break above the downtrend line. I could have exited my position with minimal losses, but I didn't.

So from a marginally profitable trade, I ended up losing heavily from that one trading idea. It was a pretty devastating experience for me.

Philip: So you busted your account for the second time because you weren't aware of the important best practices of trading? Or was it due to you not being disciplined enough to follow those best practices?

Gary: I already knew the best practices, as these were already taught to me. These were like all the fundamental trading best practices that people take for granted. Although my trading mentor already taught me that 70% of the success comes from money management, most newbies, including myself, still insist that trading strategy is the ultimate reason why traders succeed or fail.

Gradually, I learned that those trading mentors were right and I was wrong. It was merely a lack of control. I couldn't objectively make decisions. The part of me not wanting to lose because of the significant position that I was stuck with forced me to self-filter out the trading knowledge that I knew and was supposed to follow.

After I blew up my account for the second time in a month plus, I had a wake-up call. This was one of the lowest points in the history of my trading journey.

Philip: How did you recover from it then? Were there some things that you did differently? Was there an "aha" moment that you figured that you wanted a third try?

Gary: I'm quite a stubborn person, and it may also be because I am a Christian. As Christians, we do quiet time at night. Quiet time means we reflect on the day and appreciate what we have. This is a habit that has been with me for tens of years already, so I tend to reflect on things.

After I blew my account for the second time, I stopped trading for two to three months. I was emotionally very down, but subconsciously I reflected a lot during those months. I concluded that the reason for my failure was entirely my own problem.

I knew that the issue was not really about the strategy. We all know strategies work and fail all the time because market conditions change. Through certain experiences, you will be able to tell if your strategy is working or not during a particular market condition.

But the biggest problem for me was that regardless the market going higher or going lower, I continued to hold on to my trades for the wrong reasons. At the end of the day, it was really about self-discipline. I needed to control my emotions and not allow myself to distort reality.

That period was the turning point in my trading career. I really reflected and studied what I could have done better.

And the most important person who helped me the most during that turning point was not any trading teacher, trading guru, or even my trading friend. That person was a non-trader. That person was my wife.

Philip: Wow, okay. So what happened?

Find A Risk-Averse Person to Be Your Accountability Partner

Gary: She was actually quite supportive of what I was doing. Although she didn't know how to trade, she was very risk-averse, which placed her in a perfect position to help me overcome my issues.

When I was working as a full-time employee, I had to report to a boss. Bosses make us accountable for the projects and the deadlines, including your actions and your results. When I started trading, I was very much by myself, and there was no one whom I was accountable to.

So I guess that's where my wife came into the picture. Because she was very risk-averse, it became beneficial for me. She doesn't understand the trading strategy. Basically, she just looked at the various email statements from my broker regularly. She would just roughly calculate the stop-loss size and the lot size to see if I was over-risking.

This new arrangement created a fear in me about over-risking because I now had my wife to answer to for any trade that I took.

This accountability process helped me much. The other key turning point was based on my reflection about myself. I realized that while I am usually comfortable with my strategy, but sometimes I kind of get into a panic mode when things start to shake up.

I came to realize that in most cases it was because I didn't have full confidence in the strategy that I was using. This was also the reason why in the earlier part of my trading journey I kept jumping from strategy to strategy, from guru to guru, like what most newbie traders do.

Build Confidence in Your Trading Strategy Through BackTesting

So I added in another process to my trading workflow, which was to backtest the strategy that I planned to use. Because I didn't know how to programme, that's why I had to do manual backtesting. It was very tedious, as I literally printed out the charts to do manual backtesting on them.

As I backtested manually on those printed charts, I could see when my strategy was profitable, when my strategy was losing money. It kind of showed me some stats that my strategy worked for the last three years on an annual basis.

There may be losing months and losing days, but if I controlled my risk on a twelve-month basis, I was actually in the green.

All these stats gave me the confidence to trade on a strategy, to know when to cut and when to hold. So this backtesting process, together with the part that I need to be accountable to somebody, turned out to be the turning point.

From this process of paper trading, I learned to analyze the charts. Doing this trained my eyes to look out for patterns and it also led me to discover other things in the process. On the other hand, when I moved on to the actual trading, my wife became that "fear factor" for me, as I needed to account to her and make sure that I didn't over-risk.

Philip: So after you busted your account for the second time, you decided to continue for the third time with the help of your wife. So, what were the other actions that you took that slowly brought you back on the right path again? Were there some other actions that you did differently in terms of your analysis or execution?

Gary: One that was mentioned was the backtesting. That helped me refine some of my strategies. It helped me find something I'm more comfortable with because my original strategy had a larger stop. So I reduced the distance between my stop-loss price and entry price while reducing my position size at the same time.

I realized that the size was also affecting me. Most greedy retail traders hope to get 10% returns a day. In the long run, whatever gains you make so fast, you will probably lose just as quickly. So I fine-tuned my risk until it dropped down to just 1% per trade. Based on this risk parameter, I can lose five times in a roll, and it still doesn't really hurt me.

Philip: So how long did that phase last when you were onto your third account and what was the evolution for you after that?

Gary: For about six months, I was on a demo account, and I managed to double my demo account during that period because there were some strong trends. I was basically in the right place and at the right time. Unfortunately, those gains were made in the demo account, so I didn't recover the losses from my two busted accounts.

The good thing that came out from this demo trading period was that I recovered my confidence. I realized that if I continued trading in this manner and manage my downside, I would just have to wait for the trend to happen. The market truly humbled me then.

The market taught me that I am not a rainmaker. I can't order the weather to rain, so I needed to go where the rain is pouring and maybe collect the rain as much as I can with the use of a small bucket. Following these six months of transition, I became a very different person. During my first year of trading,

I was relatively successful and became very cocky and thought I knew the market very well.

Nowadays, I'm hardly over-confident even when I am on a winning streak. I don't know when the market could just whipsaw, and I could get hurt. Of course being human, this part about being over-confident still comes back once in a while, but when it hurts me, it's usually not as bad as before. The memories and the scars are always there to remind me to be careful.

Philip: So from then on, I supposed you finally become more proficient and profitable. How long did that phase take you before you come to a point where you started to think about becoming a full-time trader?

Gary: I started trading Forex around 2008, and by 2010 I was already a more consistent trader. It took me another two years before I decided to turn full time in July 2012. By December 2011, I was already registering almost two years of positive record and relative consistency.

That was when I told my wife that I might just be able to make it as a full-time trader. At that point, my mom happened to be pretty sick as well, and I often had to take leave from my job to bring her for her medical appointments.

Due to a combination of these push-and-pull factors, I was convinced that I wanted to become a full-time trader. As a full-time trader, you have all this freedom. You trade for yourself. But that isn't what a lot of people imagine.

Many people think you can just trade whenever you like because the Forex market is open 24/7. But that isn't true because generally certain parts of the trading hours have more trading opportunities and lesser in other parts.

So in a way, I still have a working routine hour around the best trading hours of the day, and that is very satisfying. I can schedule my daily commitments around my work, and because of this I could bring my mom around for her medical appointments without delaying projects and taking leave, which I think sometimes frustrated my colleagues.

Philip: Was it generally a hard decision for you to make as well as for your wife to accept you becoming a full-time trader?

Gary: I've been very fortunate. In a way, the decision was built up over time. My wife had been with me on my trading journey for more than two years when I was a part-time trader.

For two years, she was actively monitoring my trading statements every week. Through the process of tracking my statements, she saw the improvement and the consistencies in my trading. Subconsciously, I believed that I had already received approval from her.

Besides that, my wife was still working full time. So in a way, our risk was mitigated with one of us working for cash and the other person trading for profits. In the worst-case scenario that I failed as a full-time trader within the one year I gave myself, I guessed I could just contact my former boss and go back to work for him. This was the backup plan for me.

Over two years of part-time trading, I managed to build up a substantial capital base of about mid-five figures. It was a much bigger capital base compared to what I had in the past, which was just five to 10 thousand dollars.

My wife had been very supportive, so I did not actually receive many objections. The person who turned out to be more worried was my mum. She was more traditional and believed that I should be working for somebody, for a company with medical leave and all the benefits.

Three Things to Think About Before You Dive into Full-time Trading

Philip: I believe there are many retail traders with the ambition and desire to become full-time traders. But many of them don't really put into thoughts the minimum amount of capital base they need to generate a viable amount of profits to sustain their lifestyle. Do you have any advice based on this?

Gary: First, I want to state an important point here. If they already have a family, they need to speak with their spouse.

I came across some retail traders who quit their job and become full-time traders after a few months of initial success, and they didn't even bother to tell their spouse before making this decision. That creates a lot of tension within the family, and this will become pressure for the trader as his emotions and psychology will be affected.

Next, let's talk about the amount of starting capital a trader needs to start full-time trading. It's really about doing some basic reverse financial engineering.

Let's assume that you need $5,000 a month to sustain your entire family's lifestyle and your average monthly trading return on capital is 2%. This means you need a starting capital base of at least $250,000. In the scenario where your spouse is also working and can share half of the family burden and expenses with you, then $125,000 might be a viable starting capital amount for you.

Ideally, you should also have another set of savings that should be enough to pay for your family's daily necessities for one year assuming that you're unprofitable for that entire year. After a while, you'll realize that trading is really about survival. When you place survival as a priority, your returns will generally tend to be lower as you emphasize adopting lower risks.

Aiming for very high returns is attractive, but when you're going through a losing streak, it can be very stressful if you have no other source of income.

So to summarize on the point about the starting capital amount, you just need to do basic math, track how much you're spending now and reverse-engineer to find out how much you need for the capital. If there's any shortfall, see if your spouse can and is willing to help to cover it from her income, if any.

Ideally, you should continue working in your day job until you have this minimum amount of starting capital base plus the additional savings for emergencies. Only then, can you start thinking about becoming a full-time independent trader.

I would also like to share another point with new retail traders who are just starting out. If I could go back to my past in 2008, I wouldn't have put the full $10,000 into the first trading account that I busted. I would have put that $10,000 into three or four accounts instead.

Based on the traders that I've met, chances are, most of them bust at least once or twice. So if I had apportioned that $10,000 into three accounts, I would not have lost $30,000 in total for the two accounts that I busted.

Essentially, whatever amount you plan to put into your first trading account, divide it further into more portions. If you can survive your first year without busting your account, maybe you have earned your right to increase your capital base progressively.

Philip: That's an excellent point. So during the transition from a part-time trader to a full-time trader, did your psychology and emotion see a huge change?

Gary: I initially thought that I wouldn't have much of an issue because I had already been trading profitably as a part-time trader for a pretty long time and things were slowly building up. But when I finally went full time, that transition affected me negatively because I started to have too much time on my hands, which caused me to overtrade.

At that point, I was also very active in a Forex Facebook group. Because I was bored, I started to share my trade calls in the group. Over time, I began to build up a small group of followers who were often eagerly waiting for me to share my trade calls with them.

This became additional stress for me because now I felt the extra pressure to be right with my calls. In summary, because I had too much time on my hands, I started dabbling in activities that added pressure to me in my trading.

Philip: That's an interesting and candid sharing from you. I suppose this is also one of the reasons why I noticed many highly profitable traders tend to keep a low profile. They understand that if they start to become more high profile, people start following them. This puts additional pressure on them to keep on being right. Was that what you experienced?

Gary: You are correct. On some days there were no good setups to find and no good trades to take. But that subconscious part of me wanted to post something because people were asking me for trading ideas. They just wanted to make money and were not there to learn. Because of this, I started to overtrade in sub-optimal trading setups as well.

I know of a few traders who are doing pretty well trading for a living, and they're generally pretty low profile. Like me, they just trade for a living. They're not teaching, they're not doing marketing, and they're not selling anything.

Philip: Exactly. One of the reasons why I wanted to interview you and get insights from your perspectives was because you're just trading for a living and you're not out there selling anything. I figured that your profile might be more relatable to many of the retail traders out there.

So you mentioned that you started trading full time from 2012 until today. That is about six years in total. What do you think are the most significant growth or obstacles you've encountered during these past six years?

Gary: I think having too much time on hand became an unexpected obstacle for me. Many people think about becoming full-time traders because they want freedom. But when you suddenly have so much freedom, you don't know what to do with it.

For those intensive intraday traders, this might not be a problem because they're sitting at their trading desk the whole day looking for trading ideas and trading them. But personally for me, my trading strategy generates me just one to three trades a day, so most of the time I was just sitting there waiting.

It became very boring for me over time. Fortunately, this issue of having too much time didn't bother me for too long. I used to pay people to do programming for me, but now that I have free time on my hand, I decided to teach myself programming instead.

I'm not really at an advanced stage, but I can do some editing and initiate trade automation using the programming skills I learned. Usually, when I identify a trade setup that I would like to take, I will enter the trade into my Expert Advisor (EA) to let it manage my position from there. After that, I will go walk my dog or do something else.

Philip: Wouldn't that mean you have even more time on your hands now which makes life boring for you?

Gary: When I was still a full-time employee, I put in around nine to 12 hours of hard work every day out of responsibility. After I became a full-time trader, I was spending about three to six hours a day sitting at my desk waiting for trade setups and managing my trades. It was tedious because it was boring.

Because of the need for me to sit at my desk to wait for trade setups and manage my trades periodically, I ended up watching a lot of movies and became an active gamer. It was not a very productive outcome. I decided that I needed to get away from my desk to avoid depending on films and games to fill my time.

Currently, I'm almost entirely automated. Because of automation, it frees up my time and allows me to move away from my desk without missing trade setups, entries or trade management exits. Nowadays, it is a lot cheaper and economical to get a VPS. Such technology is now much more accessible to traders to help handle their trade automation.

So in a sense, I have more free time away from my desk and can afford to take my wife out for lunch. Every Monday, I get to bring my dog out for dog therapy sessions to help patients recovering and recuperating in the community hospital.

This is my sixth year being a full-time trader. But interestingly, I think I only began to enjoy full-time trading since last year after

I could finally move away from my desk and let my EA take care of my trades for me.

Unlike most EAs out there, which are black box strategies designed by other people, my EA is based on my personal strategy that I have confidence in. So I have no problem trusting my EA to handle my trades for me under most circumstances.

Philip: That's an excellent insight because like what you said, full-time traders in the past usually needed to be in front of their screen constantly to wait for trade setups or wait for the right time to exit their trades.

Sometimes, when you have itchy fingers, you start to execute some trades that are not optimal. Sometimes, the waiting becomes so dull that you feel like you're wasting your time although you might be making money from trading itself.

Managing Your Trading Workflow and Risks Using Algorithmic Trading

Now let's go a bit deeper into understanding more about your daily trading workflow. Maybe that can provide some insights on how to become an efficient and effective full-time independent trader who gets to enjoy the lifestyle that he wants. Can you tell us more about your daily routine?

Gary: I usually wake up around 7:00 am. I will look at the daily chart and write in my journal the kind of trade I am looking for.

For example, if the euro-USD is down on the daily chart, I will be looking to sell. By 12:00 pm, I'm usually ready to head to my desk with my early lunch taken. Between 12:00 pm to 1:00 pm, I should be at my desk and scanning for intraday setups.

Usually around 1:00 to 2:00 p.m. Singapore time is when I start my real trading.

Philip: Is that the European market?

Gary: Yes, it is the European market. I mainly trade the euro-USD currency pair after going full time. Personally, I feel that the European market works better for me. If I do get a trade and it turns out to be profitable, mostly I can just call it a day in two to three hours. That's the rough workflow for me.

Usually, I try not to plan any other activities between 12:00 pm to 6:00 pm daily. I just sit there and focus on my trading. Over time, that three to six hours of sitting at the desk can be quite tedious for me. My trading desk is just by my window and sometimes the afternoon sun can get pretty hot as well.

Today, my daily routine has changed so much. Instead of sitting at my desk to check my trades, I'm more actively checking on my phone instead because I'm alerted to whatever my EA does.

Essentially, my daily routine is still the same. In the morning, I will usually look at the daily chart and decide on the trading plan for the day. My EA will still initiate the buy and sell orders, but I might interfere in the rules of my EA based on the market situation for the day. Sometimes, I ask my EA to just trade on the long and sometimes to just trade on the short.

At the moment, there's still a limitation to my programming. My EA is not yet able to operate like an AI that can analyze the bigger timeframe market condition to decide whether to just focus on buying or selling for the day.

My EA has now become my personal trader, and my routine has become quite easy. I'll usually turn off my EA by midnight

Singapore time. I do that just in case there might be a bug that I didn't realize or if my server goes down while I'm asleep.

Philip: Does that mean that generally, your workflow hasn't changed much since you started full-time trading compared to now? Is it just a matter of using technology to help you become more efficient with your typical workflow?

Gary: Yes. Technology has helped me become way more efficient. I spend less time at the desk, and my EA can follow strictly the rules that I set. If I were to execute the trades myself, emotions and discretion might kick in and result in me not following my rules.

So yes, my workflow is pretty much similar compared to before. It's just that I no longer need to sit at my desk, as my EA is monitoring the market and executing the trades for me between 1:00 pm to 6:00 pm. Meanwhile, I could be doing other things while checking my phone on and off to see if my EA is behaving correctly.

Philip: Were there any occasions when your EA caused you to lose a significant amount of money? And under what kind of circumstances did that happen?

Gary: The thing about EA is that it requires a lot of testing. For example, one version of my EAs is up to version 44. Somewhere between version 39 and 40, I did some minor editing to one part of the EA, but it ended up affecting some other parts of the EA. In this case, a bug was created in my risk management parameters.

Instead of my usual 2% risk exposure per trade, my faulty EA initiated a trade with a trade size that had a 10% risk exposure. The signal came, but I didn't hear the alert. I could have done something to rectify the order if I was aware of that trade.

Somehow, I just missed that alert, and the trade moved against me very quickly that day. It was a huge spike down, and I was not able to get out in time.

Philip: So this is one aspect that a trader needs to know about EA if he decides to use it to automate his trades. Are there any other potential downsides that a trader needs to think about when deciding to automate his entire trading workflow from analysis to execution entirely?

Gary: I will say that bugs are still the biggest potential issues that could arise in the use of EA for your trading workflow. Your EA might be at version 44 and is running perfectly from all the previous testing you have done. But when you introduce a new change or edit, you never know if that could affect some other features of your EA due to conflicts or hidden bugs.

My suggestion is that when you introduce anything new to your EA, whether it's a new feature or edits, always test to ensure it works in a compatible manner with the features from your previous versions. In short, whenever you update a new feature, check to make sure that the old features still work as intended.

How You Can Use Algorithmic Trading to Manage a Portfolio of Trading Strategies

Philip: Do you currently have a portfolio of strategies or rules that you get your EA to trade for you? If you do, how do you go about distributing the amount of risk among the different strategies? Is it based on a portfolio perspective or based on a per-trade kind of risk management?

Gary: I'm slowly moving toward a portfolio perspective in terms of risk allocation between my different strategies. At the moment, the risk is still evenly spread out among my strategies, but I'm trying to move toward a methodology that will tell me to allocate more risk to a performing strategy and reduce my trade size in another strategy that is undergoing a losing streak.

Right now I'm risking about 0.5% of my equity on each trade from each strategy. Should things go wrong, I'm usually down a maximum of around 3%. I haven't encountered a situation where all my strategies fail at the same time. In a way, the strategies are hedging one another as they are based on different timeframes.

Philip: So you're using the different EAs as a means of diversification so that you're less likely to be hit with consecutive losses or a losing streak across your entire portfolio of trades?

Gary: That's right.

Philip: While you're using your EA to manage your trades, are you notified whenever any of your EAs executes a trade? Or do you just let your EA do its job, and you only come back to check your trades at the end of the day?

Gary: I have a total of about five to six EAs running at the same time. Whenever any EA executes a trade, I will be notified. Because I'm not a high-frequency trader, each of my EAs generate at most one to three trades a day, and I receive a notification for each of the trades that my EAs execute.

I check the alerts just to make sure the EAs are functioning as intended, but there are occasions that the alerts get delayed. That's why I try to log in to my EA every hour on my mobile regardless if any alerts were triggered. I just want to check and ensure that nothing is breaking.

Philip: So do you activate your EA manually on every single trading day? Is there an occasion that you might totally switch off your EA, for example when you go on a holiday?

Gary: During some major events or news driven occasions, I will turn my EA off because my strategies are meant for regular pullback trades and not meant to trade sudden movements during news and events.

When I go on holidays, I will turn off those EAs that trade intraday strategies because I don't want to keep checking my phone for alerts and executions. However, I will usually leave my EAs running for those longer timeframe swing-trading strategies because those trades don't have much impact on my trading portfolio on a day to day basis.

Philip: Let's talk about risk management and money management perspective. What are the general principles or rules that you use to manage your risks and size your trades?

Gary: In the past, I tended to over-risk. At that point, I didn't see myself as over-risking even when my risk per trade was 5% because I thought I had a high chance of winning. I didn't think that there was a chance that I could have losing trades ten times in a row. I don't risk that much nowadays in any individual trade.

Over time, as my accounts grew, the actual dollar value risked in each trade has a psychological impact on me even if it is just 1% or 2% risk per trade.

The main reason is that I could still remember that terrible experience of me busting my two accounts one after another. As such, I made a conscious effort to take a small risk in each of my trades.

Based on the current four to six strategies that I am using, my rule of thumb is that 3% is the maximum total risk that I'm willing to be exposed on any day. It is unlikely that I'll lose the entire 3% in a single day because my strategies are diversified.

Philip: So if you already have a certain number of open positions that expose you to a total of 3% risk, does that mean you won't take any more trades?

Gary: That's right. At any one time, each EA will only have a single open trade. That automatically limits my maximum potential loss to 3% if I risk just 0.5% per trade on each of my four to six trading strategies. These days, I don't pyramid into my winning trades anymore. That's why I won't have more than one open trade in each trading strategy at any point in time.

I find that this methodology works better for me and my mindset. I know of traders who pyramid into their trades aggressively, and they trade during the news. They could be pyramiding into their winning trade every minute.

If the trade goes their way, they could very quickly make a 10% profit on their capital. But it could also swing the other direction very quickly and cause the trader to lose 10% in one day.

I don't think that's the right way to take the risk especially if you're not that experienced yet. For new traders, I'll suggest that whenever you have a losing trade, reduce your trade size by half because you never know when you will get into a losing streak. When you start to see more winning trades, you can increase your size again.

Try not to have this urgency of wanting to recover your losses quickly. Try to focus more on a survival mindset.

Philip: Are your strategies mainly intraday strategies? Do you have like one or two strategies that tend to carry your open trades over to the next day?

Gary: Yes, I have. My swing-trading strategy carries the open trade overnight, but it's pretty short term as well. The holding period of my swing-trading strategy is usually about two to three days. If you look at the daily candles, you don't often see more than three or four candles in the same color in the same direction even during a trending period.

So if you use the first candle as a guide to initiate an entry, which is then followed by another two to three candles movement in the same direction, you've pretty much captured the bulk of that move before the retracement happens. Trades like this might not give you a 1:3 risk to reward ratio but the reliability is pretty high.

Philip: Because of the nature of your short-term swing-trading strategy, your position size is likely to be bigger compared to that of a position trader, whose trade is expected to run for weeks and months on ends. Does holding short-term swing trades overnight cause you to lose sleep? Or do you believe that your EA will be able to get you out in time regardless what happens overnight?

Gary: The EA will get me out if my stops are hit overnight. As long as the position size is not too large, I should still be able to sleep.

So essentially, it goes back to my confidence in my strategy and more importantly, the size of my trade. In the worst-case scenario, I lose both my swing trades of around a 100 pips stop-loss each. But generally, it isn't common to see a 100-pips swing on most days unless something major happens.

Philip: There is often this argument saying that it's quite unlikely anyone can consistently generate 30% per annum regardless whether he is a long-term position trader or whether he is an intraday trader.

Let's say that hypothetically, a long-term position trader generates on average of 12% per annum based on 12 trades done over the year. This means that on average, he generates a 1% return and executes one trade per month.

Let's assume you're an intraday trader and your system expectancy is similar to this long-term position trader. But instead of generating one trade a month on average with a 1% return per trade, you are now able to generate one trade per day because you're now trading intraday.

If you're able to maintain a similar expectancy as a position trader, this means that you could potentially generate 1% a day and profit more than 100% return in a year. Do you think that's realistic?

Gary: It is realistic. It's definitely possible to generate a few percents of returns on average every month. I've done it. I have friends who have done it.

Philip: As an intraday trader yourself, do you think it's possible to see an equity curve that just trends higher and higher on a month-to-month basis without seeing any monthly drawdowns? Theoretically, if you have a trading system with positive expectancy and over a total of 50 to 100 trades a month, you should not see any losing months, right?

Gary: That depends on the strategy. From an intraday trading perspective, most traders tend to use a negative risk-to-reward ratio. This means that for a 100-pip stop-loss, for example, they're willing to take a profit of fewer than 100 pips. For example, there's this famous trader call Boris Schlossberg whose trades I used to follow for a while when I first started.

Generally, he would have 30 pips of stop-loss for 10 pips of profit. I think he generates about ten trades a day. His equity curve is quite smooth, but when there's a dip, he tends to see a larger drawdown than others because of that negative risk to reward ratio strategy that he uses.

On the other side, when you study the Turtle traders, you'll notice that they tend to have many losses, but once a trend starts, their equity curve will swing up significantly.

So while it's possible for an intraday trader to have a smooth month-on-month uptrending equity curve, the dip during drawdowns can be larger than usual. So as long as you can manage the periods of drawdown well, it should still be manageable.

On some months, Boris could have a 100% win rate because those months were very suitable for his strategy. But on those occasions that he lost, each losing trade probably amounted to three of his winning trades.

So if you have proper backtesting and stats to back your strategy, knowing that over a 12-month period that your strategy is going to turn out fine, then it's not a problem using such a strategy. Of course, you will also have to apply proper risk management to protect the extent of your downside during a losing streak.

Some traders who followed Boris saw his 100% win rate and thought it would be safe to risk more to take advantage of the occasional winning streak. But when the losing streak came, their excessive risk caused them to lose so much that they could not recover from it.

Meanwhile, Boris was still able to end up being profitable for that month because of the more conservative amount of risk that he takes during the losing streak.

This is how drastically different the outcome can be between two traders who are using the same strategies but with varying parameters of risk.

Philip: I see. So the critical difference here is probably about position sizing and money management. Hey Gary, thank you for sharing so much about your experience transitioning from a part-time trader into a proficient and profitable full-time trader. I believe that your experience will inspire many part-time traders out there who are looking to trade full-time.

One final question before we end this interview. What will be three main pieces of advice for all the part-time traders out there who are working toward becoming full-time traders?

Gary: Whether it's part-time or full-time trading, the foundations are still the same. First, I think it is essential that you find someone to be that accountability partner you will answer to. Generally, for most independent traders (including myself), we tend to focus on our winning trades and would like to think that we're good traders.

As such, we tend to forget about those losing trades and how things can deteriorate quickly if we risk too much. That accountability partner is like your boss or a reporting officer; someone who is there to make sure that you're managing your risk correctly, following your rules and not over-trading.

Second, I think it is important to find a strategy that is suitable for yourself. The conventional wisdom is that a trader should merely find a profitable strategy and just be disciplined enough to stick to it and follow it.

But the problem is that the strategy may not be suitable for that individual. It's not just about time constraint or about your working habit. It's also important to consider whether the strategy is a good fit for your personality.

I don't believe that one strategy can fit everybody. If you've studied the stories behind the Turtle traders, we learned that eventually only a few of them made it. What if those Turtle traders wannabes who failed were given another set of profitable trading strategies and rules that fit their individual personalities? I think that might have worked for some of them.

You have to find something that you're comfortable with. This is actually a chicken-and-egg problem. Many traders, including myself, have probably jumped from one system to another in the past. Without doing that, you wouldn't know which systems you're comfortable with.

But at the same time, if you keep jumping from system to system without deciding on one, you'll never settle down to master that one strategy that will help you become a proficient and profitable trader. Ultimately, you need to understand and reflect a lot to conclude within a limited time, what is suitable for you.

In my case, for example, all my trading strategies across the different timeframes have something in common. My strategies tend not to generate many trades even on an intraday level. Many people's perception is that an intraday trader usually produces about 10–20 trades per day, but my intraday strategy generates just one to three trades per day.

Essentially, I prefer a slow and steady style of intraday trading, and I'm glad I found a trading methodology that I'm comfortable with.

Finally, there's one thing that I find common among 80% of the full-time traders that I know, including myself. We do manual backtesting on our trading strategies because we understand the benefits of manual backtesting.

It's a very tedious process, but if you train your eyes to do that over a prolonged period of time, you'll be able to get a very good idea on whether or not your strategy has an edge and, if it does, to build up your confidence in your strategy.

You'll be able to see what the worst drawdown looks like for your strategy. With such backtesting insights, you will be less likely to jump from one system to another when an expected drawdown comes. You'll know from your manual backtesting that the drawdown is temporary and expected, so you'll have the confidence to continue applying your strategy as planned.

Backtesting your strategy is the only way for you to build confidence when that strategy is still untested in your live account.

These days, the backtesting process is becoming easier because you can use a software program with a 99% high-quality tick data to backtest your strategy. I know it's not going to be 100% accurate, but at least it provides me the necessary confidence to follow through with it even during drawdowns.

If market conditions change for good and that strategy no longer works in the way it should, I can always analyze to see what else I need to change to flow with the new market condition.

I attended Andrea Unger's trading course before. I got started with algorithms when I took his trading course.

He provided an example in which he backtested his strategy for ten years and marked the point where the worse drawdown occurred. He applied a standard deviation of two to that worst drawdown and used that point as a reference to inform him whether that strategy needed to be scrapped or not.

As long as the drawdown of this strategy remains within the two standard deviation value, he will continue to implement the strategy as planned. This is how you can become absolutely objective when trying to decide if your trading strategy is simply in a regular losing streak or is genuinely losing its trading edge.

So regardless of which trading rules you were taught or which book you read, I think you ought to test it for yourself. Don't take anyone's word for it. After learning about a strategy from someone you trust, do what is needed and test it yourself.

If you can backtest and prove that the strategy is profitable over a one-year period with, say, eight out of 12 months being profitable months, then go ahead and ask yourself whether that is a strategy you're comfortable implementing. If your answer is still yes, then why not just try it?

I know a lot of people like to use this statement, that what worked in the past doesn't guarantee that it will continue to work in the future. But the question to ask here is this. If you can't even prove that it has worked in the past, how are you going to have any idea at all if it will work in the future?

It doesn't make sense to discard anything that you've learned about the past just because there's no guarantee that it will continue to work in the future. Everything that happened in the past forms the basis that allows you to develop some objectivity.

Over time, maybe your gut feeling will tell you otherwise about sticking with what worked in the past; that's fine. Yes, markets do change, but until you sense that change coming, your biggest chance still lies with you objectively using the past to make your future decision.

Yes, I agree that what has happened in the past doesn't necessarily mean it will happen exactly the same way in the future. But how is anyone able to confidently jump into a trading strategy if he doesn't even know if it has worked in the past?

I know that most part-time retail traders don't test their trading strategies. They import their trading strategies wholesale from their trading guru simply because the guru tells them that the strategy worked for him.

Now, this is where the problem arises. When you don't test the strategy that you use and when the strategy that you import seems to go temporarily out of sync, you lose confidence in it and just write it off as a strategy that doesn't work.

This is the main reason why people jump from one system to another. And the most ironic thing is that after you jumped, that trading strategy starts working again, without you on board of course.

That's it. I hope the above points will be able to help any trader become more consistent in their trading as they continue to work towards becoming a full-time trader like myself.

Philip: Hey Gary, that was really a fantastic session. Thank you so much for being so open and transparent about sharing your experiences. I'm sure any trader who has the opportunity to check out your interview will benefit greatly from your insights. I wish you the very best in your trading!

Gary: Thank you!

CLOSING THOUGHTS

If you've made it this far in the book, I congratulate you for having displayed the persistence to learn and absorb the trading wisdom as shared by the trading mentors interviewed in the book.

I hope that by now, you've established a good understanding of the typical trading principles and best practices that every trader should adhere to. They include things like trading psychology, risk management, positions sizing, etc.

In addition, you have now understood that some aspects of trading allow more room for creativity, particularly in areas where you attempt to find a trading edge that fits your worldview and is something that you can execute with confidence. They include elements like trading styles, trading horizons, trading setups, and specific trading strategies.

While knowledge is the first step toward trading mastery, taking actions to apply what you've learned is the most crucial step towards becoming a proficient and profitable trader in the long run.

Ultimately, there are multiple paths to trading mastery. You'll have to find that path that is suitable for you and which you are willing to embark on with discipline and consistency.

My biggest hope for you is that you can persist through the trading rites of passage and emerge at the other end of the tunnel as a winner.

Let me know when that day comes. I'll be happy to share your story with other aspiring traders out there, and inspire them to trade their way to financial freedom as you did.

To put it simply, I look forward to welcoming you into our league of "Trading Mentors".

Finally, before I leave you to continue on your trading journey, I'd like to share with you the closing thoughts from Jeremy Ocumen, a new and aspiring trader from the Philippines who has been kind enough to help me review the book manuscript before the official publication.

If you are a relatively new and inexperienced trader, I believe that Jeremy's insights from reading this book will offer you a fresh perspective, regarding what you can and should do next, to upgrade your trading competency.

I hope you can get inspiration from Jeremy and continue to work your way towards trading mastery.

Yours Sincerely,
Philip Teo

Closing Thoughts from Jeremy Ocumen

To the reader: I am glad that you have reached the end of this book. If you are an experienced trader, I hope the book has boosted your confidence in what you have been doing right and also pointed out some mistakes that you may have to correct.

If you are generally new to trading, I believe you will benefit exponentially from this book because this book will probably save you much time, effort and frustration in learning how to trade.

I am a new trader as well. As of this writing, I have been trading for about three months; but my journey into the financial markets started before that. Previously, I couldn't even differentiate investing from trading. I was averaging down on stocks and index funds, I was paying to get stock recommendations, and I was halfway into a stock market "investing" book that I've since abandoned.

Fortunately, after watching countless YouTube videos, I started to understand the difference between investing and trading. Once I realized that I wanted to trade and not invest, I searched for more trading knowledge online, more trading books to read and more trading seminars to attend. I visited many different trading websites, watched numerous YouTube trading videos and joined different trading Facebook groups.

Because of my intensive learning over the past few months, my general trading knowledge built up quickly. Still, although I was learning and growing every day, I felt lost at the same time because I didn't know who I could trust and truly look up to for mentorship.

Trading Mentors was a timely appearance for me because the book introduced me to ten different proven trading mentors at the same time. The presentations and interviews by the mentors profiled in this book provided me insights to who I can continue to learn from in the months and years ahead.

Finishing the book is just the beginning for me, and probably for you as well. Going back to each mentor and expanding your understanding of their trading styles and methodologies is the next step you can consider taking.

Below are some of my humble suggestions on how you can use what you learned in this book as the stepping stones to further your learning. I hope it will be helpful for you.

TAKE THE FREE COURSES – Adam Grimes, Adam Khoo, Rayner Teo have free training materials on their websites and YouTube channels. Most of their content is arranged logically, so it is easy for a newbie to learn. Go through their free materials, learn as much as you can, and practice as often as possible. This step will save you a lot of time and money.

FOLLOW THE MENTORS – You now have ten mentors at your disposal. You have read about them and got to know them. They are no longer strangers and you know they are genuine.

Follow them on social media and YouTube. Save their blogs and websites as bookmarks in your internet browser. Look for their books and training materials and decide if they are the right ones for you. You now have a broader perspective, so use that to focus on what you want to study.

CREATE YOUR SYLLABUS – Plan to read the book again, but in a sequence that you think is appropriate based on your learning stage. List the topics covered by the mentors and arrange them according to how you would like to relearn them. The goal is not to finish the book again but to expand on the concepts that you think you have a shallow understanding in. Try to expand your knowledge by researching the different topics that the trading mentors have discussed in the book.

BACKTEST THE SETUPS AND CREATE YOUR SYSTEM – You now have different setups suggested by the different mentors. Select at least one set-up and backtest it manually in your market. Or better still, if you know how to program, test it using backtesting software.

Practice and use that one setup that makes sense to you. Do not follow any set-up blindly. Use Andrea Unger's A.T.T.E.M.P.T model to create your manual or automated system. You may take some points from Jet Mojica for exploring variables you can use to rank your watchlist and prioritize the stocks to put in your portfolio, which is different from your entry and exit rules.

GET TO KNOW THE MENTORS OF YOUR MENTORS – Look for the authors and people who have influenced the trading mentors in this book. Learn from them as well.

That's it from me. I hope I was able to multiply the return on investment of this book to you by several times.

I trust that you will come back to this book again in the future, as you continue to improve your trading skills, psychology, and character.

I hope that not too far in the future, we can both look back at this book and think about how far we have come.

Good luck in your trading journey.

With The Best Wishes,
Jeremy Ocumen

WE NEED YOUR HELP!

ENJOYED THE BOOK?
HELP US WRITE A BOOK REVIEW

Steps:
1. Visit TradingMentorsBook.com/Review
2. Click "Write a customer review" in the Customer Reviews section.
3. Submit

Write A Book Review For Us Here!
www.tradingmentorsbook.com/review

DON'T FORGET YOUR FREE BOOK BONUSES

Claim Your FREE Book Bonuses Here!
www.tradingmentorsbook.com/bonus

ABOUT THE AUTHOR

" *Trading is like sailing a yacht. Sometimes, the wind blows in your favour, sometimes the waves can be unpredictable. The question is... Are you adaptable enough to navigate through what the ocean may bring?*

PHILIP TEO is the founder of Traderwave, a Singapore-based trading education, and software company. He is also a trading coach partner with SGX Academy, where he regularly conducts free trading seminars to the public.

Previously, Philip served as the Chief Technical Analyst for OCBC Investment Research for seven years, where he offered his trading advisory service to the bank's trading, premium, and private clients.

Philip is a strong advocate of personal financial literacy and firmly believes that financial freedom is a realistic goal for anyone provided they learn and apply the right tools and know-how to their trading decisions.

Through the many seminars he has conducted for tens of thousands of retail traders, and with more to come in the years ahead, Philip aims to educate as many people as he can about trading methodologies and best practices to help them become the most proficient and profitable traders that they can be.

Learn more about Philip at his LinkedIn profile (https://www.linkedin.com/in/philipteo/), and please feel free to contact him with any comments, questions, or concerns at philip@traderwave.com.

GET IN TOUCH WITH THE MENTORS

Adam Khoo
https://piranhaprofits.com/

Nishant Arora
http://traderwave.com/tfs/

Edmund Lee
https://www.cayluminstitute.com/

Bramesh Bhandari
http://www.brameshtechanalysis.com/

Louise Bedford
https://www.tradinggame.com.au/

Adam Grimes
https://adamhgrimes.com/

Rayner Teo
https://www.tradingwithrayner.com/

Jet Mojica
https://www.bohsociety.com/

Andrea Unger
https://ungeracademy.com/

Gary Yeo
https://www.linkedin.com/in/myfxplaybook/

www.ingramcontent.com/pod-product-compliance
Lightning Source LLC
Chambersburg PA
CBHW051305220526
45468CB00004B/1209